EDUCATION and COLONIALISM

Educational Policy, Planning, and Theory
Series Editor: Don Adams, University of Pittsburgh

Marc Belth
The Process of Thinking

Martin Carnoy
Education as Cultural Imperialism
Schooling in a Corporate Society: The Political Economy of Education in America

Martin Carnoy and Henry M. Levin
The Limits of Educational Reform

Hector Correa
Analytical Models in Educational Planning and Administration

Seymour W. Itzkoff
A New Public Education

Philip G. Altbach and Gail P. Kelly
Education and Colonialism

Donna H. Kerr
Educational Policy: Analysis, Structure, and Justification

Robert E. Mason
Contemporary Educational Theory

Henry J. Perkinson
The Possibilities of Error: An Approach to Education
Two Hundred Years of American Educational Thought

Richard Pratte
Ideology and Education
The Public School Movement: A Critical Study

Joan I. Roberts and Sherrie K. Akinsanya
Educational Patterns and Cultural Configurations: The Anthropology of Education
Schooling in the Cultural Context: Anthropological Studies of Education

Nobuo Kenneth Shimahara and Adam Scrupski
Social Forces and Schooling: An Anthropological and Sociological Perspective

Joel Spring
The Sorting Machine: National Educational Policy Since 1945

Norman C. Thomas
Education in National Politics

EDUCATION and COLONIALISM

Philip G. Altbach
Gail P. Kelly

State University of New York at Buffalo

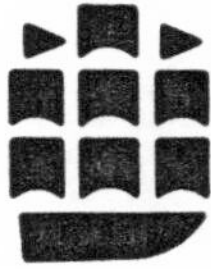

Longman
New York and London

Education and Colonialism

Longman Inc., New York

Associated companies, branches, and representatives throughout the world.

Design: Pencils Portfolio, Inc.
Manufacturing and Production Supervisor: Louis Gaber
Composition: Fuller Typesetting of Lancaster
Printing and Binding: Book Press, Inc.

Library of Congress Cataloging in Publication Data

Main entry under title:
Education and colonialism.

(Educational policy, planning, and theory)
Bibliography: p.
Includes index.
1. Minorities—Education—United States—History.
2. Education of women—United States—History.
3. Underdeveloped areas—Education.
I. Altbach, Philip G. II. Kelly, Gail Paradise. III. Title.
LC3719.E36 371.9′7 77-22777
ISBN 0-582-28003-6

Manufactured in the United States of America

Contents

Neocolonialism

Preface

The purpose of this volume is to extend the idea of colonialism and its relationship to education to a contemporary setting. We have long been convinced that it is useful to look through the lens of colonialism to understand key elements of contemporary educational reality. This volume is intended to provide a series of carefully researched studies written from an interdisciplinary perspective. While the contributors take particular methodological approaches in their analyses, it is clear that elements of psychology, political economy, sociology, history, and perhaps even philosophy pervade most discussions of colonialism and education. The strength of this interdisciplinary approach is that we can view our topic in the broadest possible context.

We view this volume as exploratory. We posit no "iron" theory, although we do, in our introductory essay, attempt to bring together many of the perceptions of our contributors as well as our own perspectives. We hope that this book will stimulate further research and analysis. We are entirely convinced that the framework of colonialism is a useful one with which to examine not only the educational experiences of the formerly colonial areas but also to look at the realities of contemporary education. If we have stimulated thought, research, and careful analysis, then our purposes will have been served. We would, finally, like to thank our contributors. They tried to frame their own original research in the context of the editors' theoretical schemes. They have succeeded in producing original essays of high scholarly quality while at the same time placing their analysis, at least to some extent, in a common frame.

This volume stems from some of the concerns of the program of comparative studies in education in the Faculty of Educational

Studies, State University of New York at Buffalo. Graduate students in our seminar on education and colonialism helped to sharpen the focus of some of our arguments. We are grateful to Robert Arnove, Thomas Eisemon, Sheila McVey, Irving Spitzberg, and Lois Weis for their comments on the introductory essay.

PHILIP G. ALTBACH
GAIL P. KELLY

EDUCATION and COLONIALISM

Introduction

Gail P. Kelly and Philip G. Altbach

This symposium on colonialism and education investigates how nation-to-nation domination (classical colonialism) affected educational development. Additionally, it examines colonialism's continuing impact on those parts of Europe's overseas empires that are now independent nation states (neocolonialism) as well as on populations still dominated by foreign nations existing within the same national boundaries (internal colonialism).

We have divided this volume into two parts. The first is an introductory essay in which colonialism in its three manifestations is analyzed in terms of its relationship to education. The differences and similarities between classical, internal, and neocolonialism are explored. This essay is speculative in nature and is meant to stimulate thinking about the various elements of colonialism. The second part of the book, which consists of eleven data-based case studies, provides documentary evidence for many of the points made in the introductory essay. These essays, most of which were written especially for this volume, are studies of colonialism's impact on educational institutions, policies, and outcomes.

CLASSICAL COLONIALISM: ITS EDUCATIONAL MANIFESTATIONS

Colonial educational systems have certain characteristics that distinguish them from noncolonial educational systems. This section defines these characteristics in the hopes that by so doing we will clarify the phenomenon called "colonial" education and contribute toward understanding the similarities and differences between education under traditional, internal, and neocolonialism. In this essay we do not deal with the root causes of colonialism or the motivations underlying the colonial enterprise. Others have done this in detail, pointing out that the colonial enterprise encompasses the political, social, and economic life of those countries involved in a situation in which the colonizer rather than the colonized holds power for purposes the colonizer defines.[1]

Schools which emerge in colonies reflect the power and the educational needs of the colonizers. While the educational systems that were established served some of the needs of the indigenous population simply as a result of the interaction between those making policy, the colonizers, and the colonized, schools were primarily designed to serve the needs of the colonizers. The aspirations of the colonized were for the most part ignored. Colonial administrators, when they took interest in education at all, were concerned with training literate clerks who could staff the lower ranks of the civil service.[2] The colonial administrators exhibited substantial confusion about education policy.[3] Some felt that offering any education was a mistake, while others felt that schooling would promote colonial policies. Missionary groups often had substantial control over educational policy. For them, religious motivations were the key element in establishing schools.[4]

Missionaries and administrators, both part of the colonial effort, did not always agree on the lines along which education should develop. Missionaries did not necessarily emphasize the vocational training that government administrators urged them to. They preferred, instead, to stress moral education. What vocational training the churches sponsored centered on developing catechists, clergy, and auxiliaries in the missionary effort. Government preoccupation with specific employment needs was not of central importance to the missionaries but despite differences concerning educational policy and curriculum, there were many points of agreement between missionaries and administrators. Both saw education as a means for accomplishing their own ends. Neither consulted with the colonized in determining the scope and content of schooling. The thread that ran through all colonial education was the fact that it was offered by the colonizer without the input or consent of the colonized.

While the control of education and the role of the colonized in the school are important when thinking about colonial education, there are other aspects of education under colonialism that clearly set these schools apart from schools within the homeland of the colonizer. Among these are school/society relations, organization and structure of educational systems, educational content, and the uses to which education could be put by those who went to school.

School/Society Relationships

In any society, schooling never has been an organic outgrowth of the entire community. Rather, except in small-scale preindustrial societies devoid of social stratification, schooling has grown out of the interests of one or several parts of that society. In preindustrial Britain, for example, the aristocracy educated its sons for roles in the state or as gentlemen scholars who could make use of their leisure time. Change came about in part as ascending classes could exert enough pressure to have schools serve their own interests. In short, in noncolonial situations schools historically have not been representative of the entire society; rather they have been connected to dominant modes in that society, serving the needs of a class within the society, and tied ultimately to social and economic place, which underclasses could aspire to if not achieve.

The relation of colonial schools to the social fabric contrasts with that of noncolonial schools, for in the colonial situation the school was detached from indigenous cultures in the languages and in the social values they taught. Colonial schools were set up as alternatives rather than as complements to the colonized's educational practices. Colonial schools never held out the prospects of integration into indigenous culture to those who attended them; neither did they prepare the colonized for leadership in their own society. This kind of school/society relationship is a phenomenon peculiar to colonial schools, especially to the schools of preindependent Africa, Asia, and Latin America.[5]

Why schools had little relation to the colonized society should be clear from our preceding remarks about who controlled the schools. The colonizer established the schools to fit people into a world different from the one in which they were born and in which their parents lived and worked. This was the case whether these schools taught in indigenous or Western languages, were "adapted" to the preconceived "mentalities" of the colonized, or appeared to be reproductions of metropolitan institutions. Many schools were boarding institutions separated physically from the communities from which students came. They were often located either in compounds apart from indigenous society or in the colonizer's administrative centers. Even the "adapted" schools of the interwar years in Britain's East African colonies shared this trait. While they stressed what British schoolmen thought was Bantu culture, the schools were located away from Bantu villages and students, and parents had no role at all in determining educational content, even that part of the curriculum that emphasized indigenous culture.[6]

The colonial school was an alien institution, alien in the sense that whatever it taught had little to do with the society and culture of the colonized, either purposely or unwittingly, and served as a mechanism whereby the schooled would gain a new social place and a new culture rather than be prepared to work within the context of indigenous culture. This was quite different from schools in Europe, where the school reinforced the cultural and social context of the students it served, giving the elite the baggage to remain elite, grounding it in its own culture and norms while trying to maintain the social place of working-class children who entered charity and state schools.

While colonial schools were disjointed from the society and culture of the colonized, they were not necessarily an integral part of the society and culture of the colonizer, even though the colonizer controlled the schools. Most Europeans, especially colonial administrators, questioned the educability of those they ruled, particularly if education involved teaching European culture and norms. Colonial governments put their efforts into supporting schools "adapted" to their conceptions of the colonized's mentalities and needs and disapproved, in many instances, of any attempts to give the colonized the best of European education. Missionaries, while they did not always share in their compatriots' prejudices, opened schools in the British colonies that were modeled on their own proselytizing endeavors at home, such as charity schools. The clientele of the charity schools was the poor of Britain's slums who were offered an education distinct from the classical education of the upper class public schools.

French and British educational planning bodies devoted themselves to developing a school curriculum for the colonies that would differ from metropolitan counterparts. France strove for such a policy in all her colonies and implemented it in the interwar years in Indochina.[7] Britain developed similar policies and by the 1920s put her efforts into developing "adapted" schools like the Malangali schools and Jeanes schools of East Africa, whose curriculum bore no resemblance to that of *any* European schools. These schools did not teach vocational or industrial skills as did many European schools designed for the lower classes. Instead, some taught spear-throwing, herding, and basket-making. Those that were less skill-oriented, such as the Franco-Vietnamese schools, described in one of the articles in this book, taught Vietnamese children about their own culture as the French perceived it. That many of these "adapted" curricula ended up as cruel parodies of the colonized's culture is irrelevant to our discussion here. The point is that colonial schools, while they were detached from the colonized's societies and cultures, were similarly detached from the societies and cultures of the colonizers. This aspect of colonial education, often overlooked in the literature, accounts for the resulting "marginality" of those educated in colonial institutions where a new culture was created among the few who went to school.[8]

Organization of the Schools

In general, the European pattern of schooling during the eighteenth and nineteenth centuries, the height of the colonializing era, was age-specific and hierarchical. Metropolitan schools were characterized by a bottom level (primary education) that usually had some kind of competitive examination that eliminated a large segment of the age group from upper levels of the educational system. This primary level often was not "common" schooling; the rich went to schools offering education of higher quality and of different substance than the poor. In France, for example, the poor, if they went to school at all, started in a five-year primary school supported by public funds; the rich, on the other hand, sent their children to tuition-charging *lycées* or *collèges* where they could receive classical primary and secondary education.

In most colonizing countries, postprimary education was differentiated. Children could, on completion of the primary examination, depending on talent and/or money, opt for either vocational training (in France given in primary-superior schools) or academic training, which after the 1920s gave the student a choice between the sciences or humanities. Those who were successful in academic training—and they were few—could go on to universities. In short, schooling in the nineteenth century in European countries contained primary, secondary, and tertiary education, each of which was built on its preceding levels. Beyond the primary level, metropolitan schools provided education by social class, thereby giving students the credentials to fit into the class structure of the society. For the poor, the system did hold the promise that, if one were talented enough, one could cross over into elite education and eventually become a member of the elite.

The organization of schools in the colonies superficially resembled that of the metropole. In fact, in most colonies metropolitan schools existed, at least at the primary level, and in most French colonies at the secondary level as well. These metropolitan institutions, as in Kenya, Vietnam, Indonesia, and Algeria, were designed to serve the children of the colonizer. They offered only one form of education—metropolitan elite education—and usually channeled their students to Europe for secondary and higher education. Many were given scholarships by colonial governments for this purpose.

European schools were not usually accessible to the colonized, however. Some colonized did attend them, but by the turn of the century these schools adopted segregationist policies and thereafter no more than a handful of the colonized went to them.[9] Selective admissions practices were one barrier to the colonized attending European schools; cost was another. Metropolitan schools charged tuition that was beyond the means of most Africans and Asians, even those who held relatively high-paying jobs. In Indochina their fees were the equivalent of the yearly wage of a Vietnamese school principal.[10]

Metropolitan schools existed in most colonies, but they by no means constituted colonial education, serving as they did the European community. Their existence was important in that they served as a constant reminder for the colonized of educational possibilities. Dualism, then, was a hallmark of colonial schools. By dualism we mean the existence of two distinct school systems in the colonies that were controlled by the colonizer—that for the colonizer himself and that for the colonized. In most colonial territories there was also a third school system—indigenous education—that lay outside government control but was watched closely by governmental authorities who feared "subversive" influences.

Schools for the colonized superficially resembled those in Europe, except for a few glaring omissions. Until the 1930s, except in India and Indochina, no higher education and, in most of Africa, no secondary education existed. Colonial school systems tended to be systems of primary education. These systems of primary education were marked by a structural differentiation that characterized postprimary education in the metropole. That is, there was a variety of educational routes on the primary rather than the secondary level—and these routes were designed for distinct populations. Differentiation at the primary level becomes evident on examining the types of schools found in the colonies. By far the most widespread institutions were three- to five-year schools, most of which gave elementary rather than primary education (elementary education being three years of schooling). These were the missionary schools in British colonies, the schools in the bush that emphasized moral training, some "practical" skills like agriculture, animal husbandry, or manual trades for boys and child-rearing and "domestic" skills for girls. The rural three-year school was not solely a missionary preserve. The British colonial government set up such schools in East Africa; the French colonial government did the same in Indochina and in Africa. These three- to five-year schools were disconnected from the rest of the school system—primary and postprimary—in the sense that they provided all the education deemed necessary and desirable for the youth they served. This meant that many gave education peculiar to the individual school and not particularly of value in passing other school exams.

The rural school was not the only institution offering primary education in the colonies. Within urban and administrative centers five- to nine-year primary schools existed, serving the children of the rich who could afford to pay boarding fees and often tuition and/or children from the local area who could live at home while attending school. These schools were the ones that taught in European languages and followed a curriculum agreed on by the government. They were also the only schools that led to the little postprimary education that was available. Within these primary institutions, there was "specialization" in many colonies. Some primary-level schools offered academic preparation; others had a purely vocational bias, teaching students woodworking, mechanics, or crafts. In French colonies some primary schools offered teacher-training courses. In the metropole, such diversification existed only at the postprimary level.

To call colonial education systems of primary education, as we have done, implies a lack of postprimary education—but, as we will see, this is only a half truth. By the twentieth century most colonies had postprimary education of some sort, although that education was confined to an extremely small number of individuals and was not exactly secondary education as it was known in Europe.[11] The French called the postprimary education they offered in Dakar, St. Louis, Abijan, and Saigon "complementary" education, meaning "higher" primary education. It consisted of teacher training, secretarial and business education, and some medical/midwifery preparation as well as instruction in the French language and mathematics. It led sometimes, if there were four years of training, to a higher primary degree examination. This "complementary" education became prerequisite to entering secondary schooling.

In British colonies in Africa and most of Asia, postprimary schooling was also not necessarily secondary education as the British knew it but rather an extension of primary schooling and was offered to a very small number of people. Like its French colonial equivalents, it tended to be vocationally oriented; in the case of Fourah Bay College it entailed preparation for the African clergy, which by the turn of the century had become subordinate to European-trained clergy.[12]

Postprimary education, especially in Africa, developed only in the twentieth century, usually because of the pressures of the colonized in urban areas. It received its real impetus after World War I when European manpower became scarce (due to depletion in the war) and the Depression made greater use of local people (and the lower wages they were paid) mandatory. Yet, even during these years in which secondary education gained a foothold there was greater development and diversification of primary schooling and a concomitant detachment of many of these schools from any system of education. It was during the 1920s and 1930s that the rural schools, Jeanes schools, Malangali schools—all dead-end institutions—flourished. The secondary sector, compared to this scattered differentiation, appears a sound educational system.

Many colonial postprimary schools were multinational institutions. They were, like primary schools, controlled by foreigners. However, unlike most primary-level schools, they served the colonized from many distinct cultural and social groups, for they were few in number and set up to serve colonial territories rather than one colonized nation. Sultan Idris Training College in Malaysia, for example, recruited its students from all the Malay states as well as from the Straits Settlements; Makerere College students came from the African nations of Kenya, Uganda, and Tanganyika; in Algeria the postprimary schools were attended by not only peoples from Algeria but also Vietnam; the Ecole William Ponty drew its students from the many nations that were called "French West Africa."[13] The polyglot population of the postprimary schools made it more difficult to "adjust" school curriculum to the locality, as most primary schools did. It was on this level that the schools, despite their doubtful status as secondary-education institutions, tended to look more like European schools in terms of dress, school life, and curricular content. While the diversity of the student population forced these schools to resemble their European counterparts, at the same time it tended to disconnect them further from the primary education that had "adapted" to the nationalities it served.

Higher education was very limited in most colonies until World War II. India was the exception to this, with higher education developing in the nineteenth century, largely through Indian private effort and in the face of an ambivalence that manifested itself in many reports criticizing a "lack of standards" in the colleges.[14] Except for India, French Indochina was the first colony to develop higher education. In 1906 the Indochinese University began its tenuous existence. Higher education in Indochina, like most colonial secondary education, was not really integrated into the rest of the colony's primary and secondary education. The university did not necessarily require either completed higher primary or secondary education—or their degrees—for admission. When stating their admissions requirements, university officials preferred individuals with French metropolitan rather than local degrees.[15]

In short, the structure of colonial education, as we have pointed out, was distinct from noncolonial education. First and foremost, it lacked the organizational coherence of metropolitan education. This meant that the ability of an individual to obtain educational parity with the colonizer was severely constricted, for one had seemingly to start from scratch at each level if one were to "make it" through all these levels. This "starting from scratch" entailed changes in language medium and curricular offerings as well as a change in environment and culture. Going from one level to the next meant leaving successive cultures behind. A child from a rural area might begin education in his native tongue and learn the rudiments of what the colonizer thought was the child's way of life. If the student were talented and/or his family wealthy, he could perhaps finish primary education in the city, the European's domain, learning the European's tongue and something about the culture of the "African" or the "Indochinese." If he fared well on exams, he could travel still farther to postprimary schools, where students were given something approximating European education and where indigenous culture simply did not exist, either within the school's curriculum or perhaps even the school's student subculture.

Advanced schooling almost inevitably resulted in increased alienation from indigenous society, since schools were organized on a Western model. After graduation, as we will discuss later, the schooled usually became government employees in jobs not necessarily suited to their education or aspirations. They became part of an urban scene which as yet lacked real definition but which was one that placed them in an uneasy world apart from both indigenous traditions and from the colonizer's society. Their speech, dress, and pretensions were often objects for mockery by the colonizer.

School Curriculum

Throughout the preceding discussion we indicated that schools for the colonized were organized quite differently from the colonizer's schools. We implied at the same time that the curricular offerings differed as well as the structure and content of education. In this section we will substantiate this allegation. Before so doing it is necessary to make some cautionary remarks. We pointed out earlier that colonial schools were marked by diversity. This diversity extended beyond structure to what schools taught and the degree to which colonial governments standardized what was taught in missionary, private, and government schools. The degree of this standardization varied by colonial government. France, for example, had a long tradition of state-controlled schooling, albeit until 1903, only in secondary and higher education. After 1903 all education in France was centralized under government control. Text selection, teacher training and certification, degree granting, examinations, and the like were government functions. French colonies closely followed this pattern. In Indochina and Algeria, for example, an Office of Public Instruction supervised teacher hiring and performance, commissioned textbooks and drew up lists of those texts permissible for use in the classroom, published curriculum guides, inspected public and private schools, and set degree examinations and appointed grading committees. In British colonies centralization on such a scale never occurred. Most schools were missionary enterprises, and the missionaries sometimes were not English, such as the Swiss Basel missionaries who operated a series of schools in the interior of what is now Ghana. What these schools taught was up to the societies running them as long as they did not threaten the colonial order. Missionaries could teach what they wanted as long as their activities were confined to geographical boundaries acceptable to the colonial government.[16]

The fact that missionaries were free to teach what they wanted to teach did not mean that they operated without government supervision or minimal control. By the 1920s most missionary societies could no longer support their numerous schools and solicited grants-in-aid from colonial governments. With the financial support of the state, missionaries found themselves tied to minimal standards, which involved curriculum set by the state.[17]

The varied patterns of educational control and standardization that existed make it somewhat difficult to discuss colonial curriculum in a manner that accurately describes the particulars of educational content in each and every colony and in each school serving the colonized. However, we believe that there are certain curricular characteristics that can be found in all schools for the colonized that distinguish that curriculum from that of metropolitan schools. Among these are languages taught in the school and curricular emphases—particularly in the type of knowledge imparted in these schools.

Most colonial schools, regardless of whether they were urban or rural, government or missionary, emphasized two things—language instruction and moral education. Kelly's article on Vietnamese interwar schools documents this. The schools also taught "practical" subjects—namely, Western hygiene (often called general sciences), computational skills, and agriculture or some kind of craft or manual labor. French government colonial schools also taught history, geography, and drawing. On the surface, this appears the same as the metropolitan school curriculum; in practice it was not.

The languages taught in the schools were seldom the languages spoken by the students who attended them. In British colonies urban schools invariably were English-language medium schools. In French colonies urban schools sometimes instructed in indigenous languages in the first three years. Most urban schools in France's African colonies taught only French. Rural schools in British colonies sometimes were indigenous language medium institutions.

The degree to which the language of the colonized was taught in the schools varied. Regardless of whether individual schools used indigenous languages, the educational system as a whole devaluated these languages.[18] If taught at all, the school system instructed in them only at the most rudimentary levels of education and considered them transitional to learning European languages. When indigenous languages were taught, they were taught in schools serving populations who, it was assumed would go to school for only two or three years. European languages, on the other hand, became the educational medium of all those presumed destined either for urban living or leadership roles either in indigenous society or in the colonial order. Students who went to urban schools and/or beyond three years of education invariably were taught the language of the colonizer and were instructed in that language.

Because most colonial schools taught in the colonizer's language does not mean that in so doing the schools exposed the colonized to the colonizer's culture and thereby prepared students to take a place in that society. There is ample evidence to suggest that colonial schools taught a version of European language and culture "adapted" to the colonized. In Vietnam, for example, French language instruction, as Kelly points out in this volume, was specifically devised for Vietnam and taught the students about Vietnam rather than about France. Such a policy was outlined for schools in French West Africa by French administrator Georges Hardy in 1917.[19] There is no clear analysis as to the content of the school curricula in most colonies, although available research in southern and eastern Africa indicates that curriculum was different from that taught in the metropole, even when European languages were used.[20]

Language was not the only subject of instruction in the schools, despite the fact that language took up more time than any other single subject. School curriculum varied greatly. Some colonial schools taught no history or geography, or taught them only at the postprimary levels. Missionary schools taught Christian religion; state-run schools in French colonies instructed children in moral behavior without specific religious references. Some schools provided instruction in agriculture using a school garden or farm attached to the school; others had woodworking shops, while still others taught sewing, découpage, basketry, or constructing objects from paper under the general rubric of manual labor.

While it is not possible to describe in detail here the content of each subject taught in colonial schools, several points can be made about the curriculum that are important to our overall aim in this essay—to discover the peculiar characteristics of colonial schools versus noncolonial schools. The curricular emphases of colonial schools were distinct from those of European schools in more than language. In most European schools students were required to know the history of their own country, even at the primary levels. The schools devoted at least three hours a week to these subjects in France.[21]

In colonial schools history was rarely taught at the primary level. When it was taught, as in Indochina and Algeria, only a half hour a week was devoted to it, and it was never included within the degree or school entry examinations. What history that was taught revealed a devaluation of indigenous cultures. History in the main, if it touched on the colonized's past, was only the history of the colonized since they were ruled by Europeans. If precolonial history was touched on, it usually emphasized, through chronology, civil wars, tribal conflicts, famines, and barbarism in order to contrast them with the peace and orderly progress under colonial domination.[22]

Science instruction also is a good example of the differences between the colonial and the metropolitan curriculum. Colonial schools taught less science than metropolitan schools, and the science taught was substantially different from that taught in the metropole. It was adapted to the colonized's needs as the colonizer perceived them. Thus science became instruction in domestics and personal hygiene at the primary level and practical and applied sciences—biology, botany, plant raising, zoology (emphasizing care of domestic animals), and some chemistry—at the postprimary level. Agricultural work was often considered a part of science instruction and was offered in postprimary teacher-training schools as well as in rural elementary schools.[23]

Colonial school curriculum is distinguishable from metropolitan school curriculum in both substance and its relationship to its students and the culture in which they were born and bred.

On the substantive side, colonial schools emphasized language teaching more than did metropolitan schools—and because teaching language involves teaching culture, they inevitably emphasized this beyond what a school run by Europeans for Europeans might have done. Such an emphasis was an implicit recognition that the culture being taught by the school was different, if not at odds with, the culture of the children the school taught.

The school's curriculum, while not an outgrowth of the society from which the child came, was not an outgrowth of the colonizer's society either. It was not merely a diluted version of metropolitan education; it was something else. It represented a basic denial of the colonized's past and withheld from them the tools to regain the future. The schools omitted the child's past, as in history instruction (something that was not done in the colonizer's school), and at the same time denied him skills for anything other than what he had traditionally done—farming and engaging in crafts—except in the area of hygiene. The implications of this are enormous, for what occurred in colonial education was a simultaneous obliteration of roots and the denial of the wherewithal to change, except on limited terms. With this education, one might become a secretary or interpreter; one could not become a doctor or a scientist or develop indigenous cultures on their own terms.

Colonial Schools and the Colonized

Colonial schooling was to a large extent tied to employment outside indigenous occupational structures like farming, handicrafts, and fishing. Some who went to school learned to read and write the colonizer's language and became qualified to work in jobs subordinate to the colonized in government, private industry or trade, or in missionary or government schools. Their salaries were, for the most part, a third that of Europeans doing similar work. While education qualified the colonized for limited roles in colonial institutions, it did not necessarily lead to such employment, for the number of educated exceeded the number of jobs open to the colonized by the turn of the twentieth century.[24] Furthermore, colonial governments often preferred to rule through indigenous bureaucratic structures and leadership, regardless of whether that leadership had received colonial education. In northern Nigeria, for example, the British ruled through the Hausa chiefs; in central Vietnam, the French administration worked with the Vietnamese monarchy and its traditionally educated bureaucrats.

The employment possibilities schooling opened are important in discussing colonial education for many reasons. We have mentioned them because they explain much about the contradictions inherent in colonial education and the conflicts to which they gave rise.

The respective goals of the colonized and the colonizers for education differed in many ways. Western education was seen for the most part as a means of social mobility. Families, even whole villages and kinship networks, would help to support the brightest boy through school in the hope that he would be able to get a relatively well-paying job with the colonial administration. The colonized did not send their children to schools that were so foreign and often so much at odds with their society unless there was a payoff. African families—as Foster has so well documented in the case of Ghana and as is spelled out in many novels written by the colonized—sent their children to schools for economic betterment and with the expectation of a good job, regardless of what government authorities might say about the desirability or probability of this. The children of indigenous elites went to school in the hope of maintaining their status in a world in which entry into relatively elite positions began to depend on education.[25]

The expectations of the schooled and the positions actually available to them were not the same, either for reasons of caste or economy. While colonial bureaucracies were indeed large and employed more of the colonized than the colonizers—in India, for example, there were at least ten Indians employed for every European in government; in Indochina, over 9,000 Vietnamese in 1938 served as schoolteachers—the number of positions available was still smaller than the number of educated who applied for them. This was the case despite the fact that in most colonies less than 10 percent of all school-age children entered school and about 95 percent of those who did enter dropped out before completing primary education.[26]

The government was not able to absorb all educated manpower. Neither was private industry. Most colonies had little industrial production; rather, colonial economies centered on cash-crop agriculture (tea, coffee, cotton, and other plantation crops) and raw-materials extraction. These enterprises required field labor and were not appropriate for schooled persons seeking white-collar employment and relatively high wages.

Under colonialism, the relationship between education and wealth and social mobility is a complex one. While schooling often removed those who acquired it at least in part from traditional norms and instilled a desire for upward social mobility and participation in the small "modern" sector of the economy, in many colonies only a minority of educated individuals achieved success in these ambitions. Control of the upper levels of colonial society was in the hands of Europeans, and in most colonies the modern sector simply did not provide sufficient openings for even the modest output of the educational system. Thus, while it is true that most, if not all, of those indigenous individuals who successfully participated in the modern economy and who gained wealth as a result of colonialism were educated, the exact relationship between education and success in the modern sector is unclear.

While economic self-betterment was the major motif in the colonized's acceptance of colonial schools, it was not the only reason why, by the end of the nineteenth century, the colonized flocked to the schools and demanded the expansion of the schools. In colonies where nation-states had preceded foreign domination, nationalism figured prominently in many parents' decisions to send their children to colonial schools. The fact of foreign rule and its seeming permanence shook the faith of many of the indigenous people in the viability of their culture and institutions as they were. Learning Western technology and science seemed the key to revitalization of their own societies and their return to autonomy. In other colonies where nation-states had not developed coinciding with European-defined borders, education became a route for developing incipient nationalism. Many among the colonized saw education as a way of learning new ways and developing new states free from colonial control.

Indigenous elites sometimes welcomed colonialism and its institutions for their own reasons. Hausa chiefs, Vietnamese monarchs, and Indian rajas, for example, found themselves dependent on colonialism. Traditional elites faced with internal challenges found colonial power a means of preserving their status, albeit under the overall domination of the colonial powers. Furthermore, their children, if properly "trained," took their parents' place in society.

Others in colonized society saw the schools as an opportunity for social advancement. Individuals without much status in indigenous society could gain status through colonial institutions. Former slaves in African societies often welcomed an order in which they were no longer slaves and could become "respectable" as clerks and relatively well-paid workers through the schools. Women could gain some independence through missionary schools, particularly in China, that redefined authority. Further, converts could find more of a place in urban colonial society than in indigenous society and use education to gain it.

While some colonized reacted favorably to colonial schools, others did not. Apathy was probably a more pervasive response than anything else; for many the schools were simply irrelevant and out of the range of possibility for their children, either because there were no schools available near home or the family lacked resources for school fees or to cover the lost labor of school-age children.

Outright hostility to colonial schools also existed. Parents often opposed their children attending school. In Vietnam, for example, schools were considered "forced labor" and the education given in them a fundamental threat to the society's continuance. The Muslim elite in India had a similar reaction in the early period of British domination.

In short, the colonized made a multifaceted response to colonial schools that reflected new and old divisions among the colonized. The various responses indicated that the colonized were not free to determine the direction of education along their own lines and had only the choice of rejecting or accepting what the colonizer offered and making the best of it.

Colonial Schools—A Distinct Set of Relations

We have in this essay attempted only to describe the education of persons under colonial domination and to distinguish it from education of persons not under colonial domination. We have pointed to several distinctive characteristics of colonial education—first, that education under colonialism lay beyond the control of persons or groups being educated. The content, medium, format, and uses of education were determined by the colonizer, not the colonized. The schools, regardless of the motive force behind their establishment—bureaucratic manpower needs, the missionary desire to do good works and save souls, exploitation of the resources of the colony, or a simple desire to bring progress to so-called backward areas—were set up by the colonizer on his own terms to meet needs the colonizer, not the colonized, perceived.

While one can argue that schools in any society are removed from some communities, classes, or subcultures within that society, education under colonialism differs because it is separate from practically all elements of its own social system. Not only are colonial schools separate from all elements within the social system, they also are not equal to the colonizer's education. The nature of this inequality is best illustrated in organizational terms. In our discussion of school organization it was clear that inequality was not only system-to-system inequality. That is, schools for the colonized were not working-class versions of the colonizer's education, which might have led us to postulate that elite education for the colonized is the same as education for the colonizer's working class. Rather, what we found was that elite education for the colonized was in fact only similar to the colonizer's working-class education. Colonial education's model, as we pointed out, was the British charity school, the French lower-class primary and higher primary schools, and the schools for ex-slaves in the United States. The systems of education that evolved used these metropolitan working-class precedents as the models for schooling the elite of the colonized.

Despite the fact that schools for the metropole's working classes served as models for the colonized elite's training, these models were very freely "adapted." Those adaptations insured a measure of educational inferiority that could be seen both in the structure of the system as well as in the content that was taught.

We have posited a class relation between the education of the colonizer and that of the colonized. Colonial education itself was also stratified. As we have tried to point out, colonial schools developed a distinct class bias, paralleling to some extent the class biases of metropolitan education. The differentiation within colonial education, unlike metropolitan education, occurred at the rudimentary levels of education within the first three or four years of schooling rather than at the end of primary education. Economic distinctions in many colonized societies were minimal; differentiation was not solely on economic grounds but rather on ascriptive and geographic (and therefore ethnic) bases. It reflected as well the degree of cooperation with the colonizer and the amount of economic wealth derived therefrom. If one were born in the interior, the likelihood of attending anything but schools teaching the rudiments of farming and moral behavior, unless one were a member of the cooperative indigenous elite, was low. If one were the son of a government bureaucrat or the son of a chief, the likelihood was that one would attend a different institution preparing students for such leadership as was available to the colonized.

This part of the essay has defined the peculiar characteristics of education under classical colonialism, an education that developed under conditions of foreign domination. We will now explore the education of groups within nation-states which have been absorbed into those states in the past or which have attained colonial status in recent years—that is, education associated with internal colonialism. We will explore the similarity between education for those under classical colonialism and those under internal colonialism rather than the similarities and differences between colonial and noncolonial education explored thus far.

INTERNAL COLONIALISM

Internal colonialism is the domination of a "nation" (defined geographically, linguistically, or culturally) within the national borders of another nation-state by another group or groups. Some of these dominated "nations" may at one time have been independent, such as American Indian tribes, but they are not at this time independent. Part of the problem of clearly defining internal colonialism is the fact that there is much disagreement concerning the definition of "nation" and of the role of such elements as class in the equation of domination. Despite these definitional problems, we feel that it is useful to attempt to develop a conceptual framework for internal colonialism.

For some of these nations within nations the fact of colonialism—indistinguishable from classical colonialism—has not been disputed. Native American nations, for example, are generally considered colonized. They existed as independent political entities prior to the white man's conquest of what is now the United States, maintaining treaty relations with the United States and, until the late nineteenth century, often at war with the United States. Even in defeat the U.S. government considered Indians subjugated nations, granting them territoriality and a degree of self-government (similar to that accorded cooperative Hausa chiefs by the British in northern Nigeria) within those territories. Similar to Native American nations are the Indian nations within most Latin American countries, the aborigines of Australia, and the Basques of Spain. The rationale for their conquest was the same as that used in classical colonialism, with some notable distinctions.

Under classical colonialism, colonies were established for exploitation and trade rather than for settlement. In most instances, the colonizer merely ruled and exploited; he did not seek to replace the colonized. Internal colonialism, historically, has entailed usurpation and replacement. America's thrust westward and its concomitant warfare against the Indians was to take land and resources from these nations.

The development of education for Native American peoples, discussed in Katherine Iverson's essay in this book, parallels the educational development under classical colonialism. Initially, Americans sought to educate the indigenous elite at places like Harvard, while missionaries strove to convert whole tribes through education and preaching. Education given by Americans had little to do with Indian nations' culture and society but rather was directed toward remaking Indian children in the white man's image. It was an education imposed on Indians without their consent. Most nineteenth and early twentieth-century schooling took place in boarding institutions where children were taken from what was considered to be the unfortunate influence of their parents and put under the twenty-four-hour-a-day supervision of Americans, taught Christian morality in a foreign language (English), and trades consonant with the "American" way of life.[27]

The boarding schools openly ignored the cultures from which Native American children came. They could not do otherwise. The schools rarely contained children of one nation; rather, their student bodies came from many different nations, like the student bodies of Fourah Bay College or Ecole William Ponty in West Africa. The schools lumped these cultures together as "Indian" and were oblivious to distinctions between sedentary agriculture, herding, and/or hunter-gathering cultures and proceeded to ignore not only the differences among Native Americans but also that such a thing as Native American culture existed.

Education for Native Americans, Havighurst and Fuchs have pointed out, has traditionally been an avenue for leaving the Indian community, just as colonial education was for Africans and Asians.[28] The schools not only taught behavioral norms inappropriate to living in Native American societies, they also taught narrow vocational skills that could not be practiced anywhere but in the colonizer's domain. Indian schools were for the most part concerned with assimilation into the mainstream of American society. But due to overt discrimination against Indians and the second-rate nature of the education that was provided, very little success or mobility was achieved.[29]

While internal colonialism has common roots with classical colonialism and shares educational characteristics, there are some differences between the two, which we have implied in our brief discussion. Under classical colonialism, integration of the colonized into the colonizers' culture was not a major goal for practical or ideological reasons. France, for example, rejected all ideological pretense to assimilation when it became clear that assimilation might ultimately lead to the colonized exerting power over the colonizer. If one allowed all Senegalese to vote and have proportional representation in the French National Assembly as the Four Communes of Senegal had, would they not take over the Assembly? This realization made naturalization laws in other French colonies so rigid as to prevent Vietnamese, Algerians, and other colonized from acquiring citizenship. As the colonized they could be ruled; as citizens they would rule.

Internal colonialism implies the absorption of the colony into one nation-state, controlled by the colonizer. As the colonizer expropriates more and more, the issue becomes eradication by the colonizer. In the modern world eradication may not entail genocide but rather obliteration of nationhood through assimilation. The peoples of internal colonies have become termed "minorities," "ethnics," or "lower classes" rather than peoples, nations, or cultures. This, Van den Berghe in his essay in this book points out, has happened to Peruvian Indians. Iverson underscores this vis-à-vis Native Americans. Education for them is no longer a problem beyond the problem contingent on being "poor" or culturally deprived. It is a class rather than a colonial problem within the Peruvian as well as American context, at least according to American and Peruvian government authorities.[30] The colonizer, often called the dominant power in the case of internal colonialism, proceeded in many cases to redefine the nature of the colonized group, calling them "culturally disadvantaged" or an "underclass." No longer are Incas Incas or Sioux Sioux; rather they become an amorphous mass called "Indians" or "Native Americans" whose distinctiveness resides in having ridden ponies (which most did not), lived in tepees, and beat on drums—their quaint ways become a single, undifferentiated way of the past; their needs become those of being brought into the mainstream while keeping an "Indian" heritage. Further, the heritage becomes "domesticated" in white terms, for in schools, the media, and elsewhere we find the "Indian" being removed from his own context and taking on the cultural features and behavior of whites. Our point is that in assimilation, the cultural/national past becomes rewritten to show similarities rather than differences, almost beckoning the colonized to become assimilated because it is *his* rather than the colonizer's way.

Internal colonialism and the schooling it gives rise to, while being more assimilationist than classical colonialism and its schools, does not necessarily lead to integration any more than the classical colonial schools did. Once designated as the lower classes, the internally colonized have to deal with inequalities in schooling that keep lower classes within the society lower classes. Integration or assimilation through education becomes impossible except in urban situations. That is, access to education is inequitable in both Peru and the United States if one wishes to live in Indian society. If one lives on an Indian reservation or in rural Peru, education beyond the primary level is usually inaccessible simply due to demographic factors.

Women, Blacks, and the Working Class in America

Nations within the geographical confines of another nation, conquered and dominated by that nation, aspiring toward autonomy, certainly are part and parcel of what we know as colonialism. But can minorities or classes within nations be considered colonized as some analysts of colonialism and members of those groups claim they are? Women, blacks, and the working class have at various times been called or call themselves "colonized," and it has been asserted that schools and the education given in them is one of the major instruments of colonization. Colonial status in these cases is delimited by sex, race, or economic relations under capitalism and is simply reducible to oppression of a definable section of a population by another. In the case of the working class and women, unlike internal colonization of nations, this definition entails oppression of majority by minority and implies that colonialism is not a nation-to-nation phenomenon, in the sense of linguistic/cultural, geographically defined nations, but rather a set of relationships that evolves from the peculiar development of capitalism. When applied to the working class, it is simply a question of class relationships to the means of production that cut across national lines; in the case of women and blacks, oppression (or colonialism) operates on a gender or race basis, across both national and class lines. The case for considering women's oppression and the plight of the working class as colonialism is discussed by Bonnie Freeman and Gene Grabiner in their respective essays in this book. It is questionable whether women, blacks, and the working class can be considered "colonized" in the same ways that national minorities are. These groups clearly have been exploited in the historical and contemporary context in America and have on many occasions defined their oppression in "colonial" terms. For these reasons we have chosen to consider them in this volume. However, to include them in this book does not necessarily imply that their oppression derives from colonialism. Let us first examine the case for considering these groups colonized. Once we have done so, we will outline our reasons for not equating their status with colonialism.

The arguments for considering women, blacks, and the working class colonized are based on metaphor and analogy—how these groups are like the colonized: how black Americans are like colonized Africans, women like blacks, working class like blacks on a set of variables, particularly that of cultural oppression. Lyons, in his article in this book, draws such an argument, showing how similar the views of the educability of the black in America were to views of the educability of Africans by Britons. Both are similar to views held about women's mental capacities. Those who consider these groups colonized have yet to base their arguments on clear-cut analyses of relationships between classes and castes in comparison with those found under classical conditions of nation-to-nation dominance.

Several arguments have been drawn for considering women, blacks, and the working class colonized. First, much of the literature considers these groups colonized because they are poor, on the economic underside of the country, and consequently have little or no power, economic or otherwise. The case is made on the basis of income differentials—blacks because they are black earn less than whites as a whole—and because of their blackness remain in lower-income brackets. Women because they are women earn less than men, and, regardless of whether they are born wealthy or poor, black or white, they still remain, relative to men, poorer and less powerful. Income also is used to document the colonized status of the working class, be it male, female, black, or white. And, across generations, those born in the working class remain in the working class, especially in Western capitalist societies.[31]

Another analogy that has been used to bolster the conception of women, blacks, and the working class as colonized is that of similarities in institutional experience. We will focus on the analogy as it relates to educational institutions. Martin Carnoy's *Education as Cultural Imperialism* considers that blacks and the working class in America have basically the same relationship to schools as Africans and Asians under classical colonialism. Carnoy argues that blacks and the working class do not control schools, either their uses or their content, just as the colonized had little control. Second, he maintains schooling has but one function, which the capitalist class controls—socioeconomic allocation in the interests of producing surplus. Thus, the educational history of blacks and white working classes follows the lines of the educational history of Africans. Schools were set up in both instances to teach them proper behavior relating both to the work place and the state, the need to consume goods produced by capitalists, and occupational skills necessary for working in the capitalist economy at the level they would participate in it (crafts, farming, trades, vocational skills). Such education led to emotional and economic dependency, keeping those born black, working class, African, Native American, or Asian in their respective places. Schooling as social control and economic allocation is synonymous with colonialism.

While Carnoy did not deal with women in his volume, others have seen women's education working similarly, as does Freeman in her essay in this book. The schools basically reinforce sex-role stereotyping in behavioral, emotional, and occupational terms. Girls are taught that they are inferior to boys; they are taught that they should be mommies and wives (or work in occupations approximating these roles), that they are dependent and are nurturers of others, that they need to consume what is made by men.

The educational similarities that emerge are mostly drawn from the stated or real goals of those who are said to control schools, from content analyses of curricular offerings, and from analyses of the work force by class and racial origins, sex, and educational background. This material clearly documents what some people—educators, government officials, and some businessmen—think the goals of education should be, the social messages of texts and curricular offerings, and the glaring inequalities in income and educational levels between classes, races, and sexes. Are such inequalities substantively the same as inequalities born out of colonialism? And, if they are, can we reduce colonialism to inequality? To our knowledge those who have argued, like Carnoy, that inequality is in fact colonialism have not dealt with this issue; and before one can argue cogently that this is the case, one needs to examine whether in fact inequality constitutes colonialism and whether inequalities born out of nation-to-nation colonialism are in fact the same as those that arise out of race, sex, and class oppression. We believe that colonialism and the inequalities that are born out of nation-to-nation dominance are substantially different from those that arise from inequalities related to sex, race, and class.

We argued earlier in this essay that under classical colonialism schools were substantively different from metropolitan schools, including metropolitan working-class institutions. We pointed out that in fact the relation of colonial schools to those working-class institutions appeared to be in terms of comparable class status, not in that they were equivalent institutions. Second, we argued that education under colonialism lacked ties to any existing society, either that of the colonized or the colonizer. Language, the culture conveyed in the schools, etc., was essentially foreign to the student, was not his own, and ill-equipped him to live or work in any society. However, within a given country the schools allocate people into the class structure of that society; schools put people into a place, constricted or oppressive as that place may be, within the existing social fabric. Colonial schools do no such thing.

The existence of differences between the education of the colonized under classical colonialism and education for blacks, women, and the working class should not obscure the similarities in education and status. Schools for blacks in the American South became the model for colonial schools in Britain's African colonies; European conceptions of the African's mentality shaped Americans' views of blacks. Educational goals also were similar—to counteract the perceived unfortunate nature of the child's family, genes, and/or culture. In England, missionaries who trained the working class designed their education to counter the weaknesses and evils of the child's heritage just as they designed education for Africans in their country's colonies to overcome the invidious effects of indigenous cultures and genetic makeup. Women have been treated by schoolmen similarly. They saw education as a means of overcoming female libidos and a natural tendency toward lasciviousness, as Lyons' essay in this book documents.

Not only are the predispositions and life-role adjustment needs conceptions of the colonized and women, blacks, and working class seen as similar; there are also similarities in the ways school curriculum treats these peoples. One has only to turn to American textbooks in use in the schools to find out that women, blacks, and workers are noticeably absent, in much the same way that British and French texts denied the existence of those they colonized. American history texts until recently were histories of great white men, rich ones at that. These great white men built the country, made people safe. To be like them was the only way that one could be good. George Washington, Ben Franklin, Abraham Lincoln, and John F. Kennedy are the stuff of American history, not Mother Jones, Lucy Stone, W. E. B. DuBois, Nat Turner, or Eugene Victor Debs. In recent textbook revisions we find some women and some blacks (but not workers), either as background to the great white men or in the roles of great white men working to build the great white society. Martin Luther King, Jr., a favorite for inclusion in these texts, is helping make America strong. His appearance in these texts is quite similar to the appearance in Vietnamese colonial texts of the precolonial Emperor Gia Long, depicted as making Vietnamese society strong by inviting Frenchmen to his court.

Whether one can consider the working class, women, and/or blacks colonized as one considers Native Americans or Africans and Asians in the British and French empires of the nineteenth and twentieth centuries is an issue that warrants careful analysis. It is, as we have pointed out, contingent on the definition one gives to colonialism. Definitions that allow only nation-to-nation interrelationships would preclude consideration of blacks, women, or the working class among the colonized. Those whose units of analysis are the relationships that arise out of colonialism perhaps allow us to include them.

Internal colonialism when applied to nations within nations is quite similar to classical colonialism in that it shares common roots and has common manifestations, particularly in education. The differences between the two reside, in the main, in the fact that internal colonialism's goal is the eradication of the nation (or nations) within the nation, either through assimilation and integration or through expropriation. This is possible because internal colonialism exists under conditions where the colonizer can absorb rather than be absorbed by the colonized. Our discussion of internal colonialism has raised the issue of whether categories of persons delimited by race, sex, or economic relations, regardless of nationality, can be considered colonized. Our discussion here explored whether colonialism is reducible to oppression and whether educational institutions tend in any society to oppress underclasses, be they nations, different races, women, or proletarians in the same way. We have tended to distinguish between colonialism and this type of oppression but we believe that a more careful analysis than is possible here is necessary.

In our introduction to this essay we noted that colonialism does not necessarily entail direct political governance of one nation over another. Rather, we pointed out, it implies domination, control of one nation over another. Contemporary African and Asian leaders have asserted that colonialism still has a stranglehold on their nations, regardless of whether British, French, or American flags wave in their lands. They have called this *neocolonialism* and have defined it as the persistence of foreign control despite seeming national independence.

NEOCOLONIALISM: THE HIGHEST STAGE OF COLONIALISM

It is our contention that, in some ways, the colonial era has not ended and that the domination of the industrialized nations over the Third World continues in different forms. Most parts of the globe have achieved formal political independence, membership in the United Nations, and the other accouterments of sovereignty. Yet, the Third World is inextricably bound in a network of relationships with the West. Some of these relationships are related to the colonial past, to the sheer economic and technological advantages of the industrialized nations and to other "natural" elements in an unequal world. These elements constitute a part of the Third World's dependency on the industrialized nations. Such dependency, in many areas at least, is probably inevitable under present conditions. Neocolonialism constitutes the deliberate policies of the industrialized nations to maintain their domination. It may function through foreign-aid programs, technical advisers, publishing firms, or other means. Dependency and neocolonialism are linked, but our concern in this essay is with how the policies of the industrialized nations work to maintain their position of domination.

Neocolonialism is both complicated and controversial.[32] It is somewhat heretical to argue that Third World nations are not fully independent and that, in fact, the West holds a powerful position in the affairs of the Third World. The illusion of independence is an important one for both sides of the equation. The industrialized nations, and especially the former colonial powers, are formally committed to the independence of Third World countries and have attempted to appear as friends of these nations by providing foreign assistance and aiding in the "development" of these nations. For the governments of Third World countries, an admission that the often hard-fought struggle for freedom resulted in part in a different kind of domination would be a bitter pill to swallow and would weaken their legitimacy at home. Further, the ruling groups within the Third World are closely linked with the economy and culture of neocolonialism, and it is not in their interest to change the status quo or to recognize any need to change it.

Neocolonialism is linked with the colonial past in that quite important elements of the structures built up under colonialism continue to operate in the Third World, and these have a continuing impact. The essential structure of the educational system is perhaps the most dramatic example of the continuing impact of colonialism from the viewpoint of this volume. Along with school structures come curricular orientations and often the language of instruction and of intellectual discourse and books and journals. Third World nations that were under the control of specific European countries generally retain elements of the specific colonial heritage of that country.[33]

This nexus of postcolonial relationships is in part a result of "natural" forces—trade relationships, the domination of the industrialized nations because of superior military and technological development, substantial differences in standards of living, the location of major universities, publishing houses, and the other accouterments of modern society in the industrialized nations. The industrialized nations have a need to maintain their domination over the Third World for reasons of power politics, access to raw materials, markets for their goods, and other reasons. Neocolonialism has become part of a policy aimed at maintaining global inequality.

We have argued that the forces impelling industrialized nations to maintain controls over the nominally independent states of the Third World are similar to those that led to classical and internal colonialism. Yet, clearly there are differences between neocolonialism and classical and internal colonialism, particularly in the mechanisms by which control is exercised and influence attained. While education is but a small arena of the struggle for supremacy in the world, it does play a role. As former United States Under Secretary of State Philip Coombs has stated, education and culture are a "fourth dimension" of foreign policy.[34]

There are also less direct reasons for neocolonialism. One of these is the fact that the industrialized nations, by virtue of their wealth, technological development, and well-established educational and research institutions, constitute "centers" of international educational and intellectual life. Third World countries are at the "periphery" and are dependent on many of the products of education and modern technology. The world's leading universities, journals, publishing houses, research institutions, and the other elements of a modern technological society are centered in the industrialized nations—and particularly the former colonial powers plus the United States and the Soviet Union and Japan. For these reasons we call the "northern" industrialized nations the "center" of the international intellectual and educational system and the rest of the world the "periphery."[35] It is not surprising that Third World nations should turn to these centers for technological expertise, publications, and guidance since the bulk of the world's research is done in these countries.

It might be argued that it is natural for Third World nations to turn to industrialized nations for assistance in the process of modernization. Modernization is generally defined as industrialization, and it is often assumed that as a nation modernizes it becomes more like the industrialized West in terms of its social structure and culture as well as in purely economic terms. A few Third World nations, such as Tanzania, are attempting to raise living standards and provide the structures of a modern state without adopting all of the baggage of Westernization. But Tanzania is an exceptional case. Given the usual definitions and aspirations of the elites of the Third World, it is probably true that some element of neocolonialism is a more or less integral part of the process. If nations seek to become like the West, it is natural that they should use the available Western models for development. And if the technologies, models, and techniques are Western, strong elements of neocolonialism enter into the equation. Neocolonialism need not be the result of overt policies of domination by the industrialized countries, but it can come as a by-product of policies pursued by the Third World nations themselves. The result is the same—Western influence and perhaps control of elements of the Third World.

The Workings of Neocolonialism

The motivations of the various parties involved in the relationship may differ, and the results may be beneficial to the Third World or to groups within the Third World, but our point is that neocolonialism—the continuing impact of the industrialized nations on the Third World—is a reality and that it must be understood on many levels in order to understand fully the current status and future possibilities of the Third World.

One of the key elements of the neocolonial relationship is the difficulty of breaking with past patterns of behavior and established institutions. As has been pointed out, colonial powers established infrastructures of government, education, industry, and culture that were often the first outposts of "modern" society in their colonies. No doubt had the colonizers not been present, elements of Western technologies and institutions would have been adopted in any case, as they were in Japan, Thailand, and other Third World nations without a history of foreign rule. The impact of colonialism was different, however, in that the colonies had virtually no authority to prevent or endorse new institutions established in their country. Further, the purpose of these new institutions that colonial powers brought was not as it had been in Japan, to strengthen the country, but rather to make the colonial system operate efficiently. This is a crucial distinction. There is no question but that many of the colonial institutions, such as the schools, had both positive and negative results for countries colonized and their long-term modernization. For the purposes of this discussion it must be remembered that European institutions were established without the consent of the colonized.

Once established, it is very difficult for the governments of Third World nations to break with preindependence institutions. Inertia is a strong force in that functioning institutions, even if they are not ideal, are often seen as sufficient. There are often no readily available models to take the place of the colonial structures. Universities, for example, are Western institutions that have been transplanted throughout the world.[36] They have to some extent been adapted by individual nations, but they remain essentially Western in orientation, background, and ethos. The point is that there are no other usable models of higher education to follow readily.

Not only is there a lack of readily available models, but the cost of changing structures is often quite high. This cost is perhaps magnified in societies that are, for the most part, poor and have many competing demands for scarce resources. Some small examples will indicate the scope of the problem. The development of new textbooks for all levels of the educational system to take the place of old colonial books is an expensive and time-consuming proposition. There is no backlog of information to aid in writing textbooks. There are few curriculum experts who can provide guidance. The market is in many cases not assured, and if the nation is small, the market may be too small to provide profitable distribution. Printing and publishing facilities may not be available. The cost of textbook development is high in any country, but in the countries that can least afford such expenses, the costs tend to be highest because of small markets, developmental expenses, and the like. In response to these obstacles, many Third World nations continue to use colonial textbooks, or use foreign publishers to produce textbooks for them, sometimes improving the situation but retaining external influence in the textbook field.

The costs of significantly changing teacher-education programs, of decentralizing school systems, of moving major educational institutions out of the capital cities, of expanding education to the rural areas, and other commonly suggested reforms are even higher. And the ramifications of such changes are often considerable in terms of unforeseen expenses.

The constraints against radical departures from preindependence educational patterns and from dependency on the industrialized world at all levels of education are both internal and external to Third World countries. Most Third World countries are poor; they are neither industrialized, particularly rich agriculturally, nor do they control whatever mineral or fuel wealth they have. Their financial problems are indeed enormous, and some nations are kept from default by foreign loans or outright gifts. For most Third World countries, people's expectations exceed what in fact the government can afford and the economy can bear. Through years of foreign rule it was clear that getting education meant getting jobs with high pay and entering urban life and its material, cultural, and social trappings. The demand for education, thus, is such that not to spend money on expanding educational opportunities, both horizontally and vertically, is politically risky for the government in power. This has been aptly demonstrated in the case of Nigeria, where leaders who tried to put a brake on educational expenditures have been removed from office. This political pressure explains why many African governments spend upward of 15 percent of their national budgets on education (much higher than is common in Western countries) and divert funds that might otherwise go into manufacturing to developing schools, whose relation to economic growth is, in the long run, dubious.

Many Third World nations have accepted foreign aid to assist them in meeting the massive demands for expanded education programs. This aid, from both foreign governments and private foundations, has financed projects ranging from creating universities and educational research institutes to providing scholarships to Third World students for university education abroad and money to buy texts and other books published in America or Europe. Such aid is generally welcomed by Third World nations and given willingly by industrialized nations eager to strengthen their influence in countries whose raw materials they use or where goods (like books) produced in their country can find a ready market. Objectively, such assistance often increases dependency.

The colonial past and contemporary dependency on industrialized nations by Third World nations results in their status at the periphery of the modern world. The equation is further complicated, as Johann Galtung points out, by the fact that within Third World countries there is a "center" that is closely linked with the center in the industrialized nations.[37] The Third World center consists of segments of the indigenous elite that control the educational and cultural apparatus and which, by virtue of its mastery of the techniques of Western education, and often Western languages, holds considerable power. This center has a vested interest in the maintenance of the Western-oriented educational system, since this system helps to maintain its monopoly over credentials and thereby over prestigious positions in government and the private sector.

The policies of the industrialized nations themselves are central to the neocolonial framework. These nations have in general tried to maintain their influence over the Third World through policies at several levels. We are concerned in this volume with the educational and intellectual ramifications of colonialism and its offshoots and so will limit our discussion here to that element. The industrialized nations operate at a number of levels in the Third World. They seek to foster broad policies that are favorable to their own interests and ideologies through foreign-aid programs, informational efforts, and similar activities. Private business firms, such as publishers and film companies, function in the Third World, and while they are mainly concerned with their own commercial activities, they assist in furthering the goals of the industrialized nations both by distributing materials reflecting the orientations of these nations and by helping to maintain dependence on educational and cultural products from the industrialized countries. Foundations and universities also have a role in the neocolonial equation. They are directly involved with research programs concerning the Third World, advisory work with governments and other institutions, and with aid projects of various kinds. Government policies and the activities of private commercial interests are often coordinated to provide maximum impact in the Third World.

Foreign-aid programs of various kinds are seen as a means of maintaining influence in the Third World, of advancing the interests of the "donor" countries, and of creating political and economic conditions that will create conditions in the Third World favorable to the interests of the industrialized countries. There is adequate evidence in the stated rationales of the industrialized nations to support these generalizations as well as the logic of the situation. It is not insignificant that the aid of the former colonial powers tends to be concentrated in their former colonies, and in many cases, particularly in the former French colonies in Africa, ties between the metropole and the ex-colony remain very strong. American educational assistance has generally been targeted in countries that are important to American foreign-policy interests or related to Cold War politics. The nature of scholarship programs, which bring students from the Third World to study in industrialized countries, of book subsidy projects, of assistance to specific educational institutions, and other kinds of foreign aid are linked to foreign policy objectives.

It is clear that neocolonialism is caused by a complicated nexus of relationships. Some of these are the result of "natural" forces in a world of inequalities in which the Third World is dependent on the industrialized countries for many products, intellectual and educational as well as technological and industrial. The Third World also finds itself with limited power to act on an international stage, giving the industrialized nations considerable advantages. Some neocolonial relationships are determined by the interests of groups within the Third World itself, which depend for their continued power and influence on their links with the industrialized nations and the intellectual culture of the West.

Some elements of neocolonialism are related to the colonial past and to the institutions and structures that colonialism built in the former colonies. And finally, the policies and programs of the industrialized nations have a direct bearing on the neocolonial reality. Foreign-aid programs and technical-assistance efforts are almost axiomatically linked to the foreign policy and economic interests of the donor countries and tend to contribute to continuing dependence.

The Manifestations of Neocolonialism

The question of language is a key element of the neocolonial relationship. As has been pointed out earlier in this essay, the colonizers often imposed their language on their colonies and used this language for important societal functions. Typically, the legal system, most of the educational system, most governmental functions, and the commercial spheres tied to the colonial power were conducted in a European language. Over time the European language became *the* language for "modern" communication, with the bulk of newspapers, journals, books, and serious discussion taking place in this language. With very few exceptions, such as Indonesia, newly independent Third World nations made few efforts to supplant the European language. Some, with serious internal language problems, have quite consciously continued to use the European language for virtually all key purposes. Other countries have made some efforts, usually not especially effective, to replace European languages with indigenous media of communication. In India, after thirty years of independence and more than a decade of trying to diminish the importance of English, more than half of the books are published in English and almost half of the newspapers are printed in this language.[38] This is dramatic when one recalls that only 2 percent of the Indian population is literate in English, as compared to approximately 35 percent literate in all Indian languages.

The continued use of European languages has many implications. Of course, given linguistic diversity and the political problems of language selection, a European language may be a necessary compromise for some Third World nations. European languages essentially guarantee that the former colonial power will have some impact on the intellectual development of the Third World nation. The key journals in professional and scholarly areas are invariably published in the industrialized nations and books are exported from them. Often authors in the Third World will send their manuscripts to the West to be published not only because of the prestige of Western publishers but because facilities for publishing often do not exist in many Third World nations. The Western books that are imported, particularly for use in the schools, may not be relevant to the needs or desires for cultural independence of the Third World. The use of a European language in the educational system almost immediately creates a kind of caste system of those who know that language and can thereby qualify for prestigious and remunerative positions. Upward social mobility is effectively limited to the minority speaking the metropolitan language. While the continued use of European languages has some advantages for Third World nations, there are clear disadvantages as well in terms of orientating the intellectual life of the nation toward the metropole and in skewing patterns of social mobility and structures of prestige toward those conversant with the metropolitan language.

Language is by no means the only important manifestation of neocolonialism. There are numerous other aspects of modern intellectual and educational reality that exhibit elements of neocolonialism and dependency. One of these is the international balance of research productivity and expenditure. The industrial countries expend the large share of the world's funds for basic research. This figure is probably in excess of 90 percent, and this means that most scientific advances are not taking place in the Third World. The problems to which research funds are devoted are not necessarily relevant to the Third World and may, in fact, be detrimental to at least their short-term interests. Third World nations may have to import technological information, make use of experts from industrialized nations, and/or expend funds to purchase licenses to use new technological innovations. All of these relationships are those of dependence, which place the Third World at a considerable disadvantage. The bulk of the world's universities and scholars are located in the industrialized nations. These institutions are, in many cases, well funded and able to carry on high-level research and training.

It would seem that there are very few ways in which this balance of power might be rectified. The industrialized nations, by virtue of their control over the centers of intellectual production, are simply dominant in this area. It is not surprising that these nations exercise their power in their own interests and in order to maintain their dominance. They consciously seek to extend the influence of their languages throughout the world by means of educational programs and foreign aid. The French, British, and Americans are especially active in this area, and the Germans and Russians are also involved. Experts from the industrialized nations on various matters related to education are often provided, and their advice generally involves ever deeper involvement with the "donor" nations. Sponsorship of students from Third World nations to study in the industrialized nations fits well into this pattern, as these students often return home imbued with the norms and values of their host nation. There is, additionally, the problem of the "brain drain," a complicated process by which some highly trained individuals from Third World nations migrate to industrialized nations, taking with them valuable skills. The immigration regulations and scholarship policies of some industrialized nations make this brain drain easier in some cases.

Educational neocolonialism is not a neat concept that can be convincingly argued in all situations in all Third World countries. As indicated here, it is a combination of historical forces, the perhaps inevitable results of international inequality, and the interests of classes within the Third World. The concept is further complicated by the fact that neocolonialism is for the most part voluntary; no gunboats are ready to sail to defend the right of a Western nation to distribute college textbooks in the Third World. The basic thrust of our argument is that most Third World nations are in fact dependent on industrialized countries for many aspects of their educational and intellectual existence, and we have called this dependency neocolonialism because we see it as an integral part of the broad thrust of colonial relations stemming from the historical past and because we see the industrialized nations attempting to maintain this status quo at the expense of independent development in the Third World.

Some Western social scientists have implicitly argued that at least some element of neocolonialism and dependency is inevitable as part of the struggle for "modernization" and "development."[39] This line of argument sees modernization as a unidimensional process toward an industrialized society. It is assumed that as a part of the modernization process there will be the growth of Western-style institutions such as schools, research institutes, and parliamentary democratic institutions as part of the "infrastructures" that are needed for a modern industrial state. It is also assumed that the economy will be organized on a capitalist basis, although with more state participation than is customary in the West. Finally, it is assumed that both the class divisions and the attitudinal constellations common in Western capitalist societies will be reproduced in the Third World.

Our concept of neocolonialism in education is an effort to link the enforced dependency and subjugation of the past with the more complicated reality of the postindependence world. From our perspective, postindependence dependency—neocolonialism—is just as real as its historical antecedents. In some respects it is even more difficult to understand and deal with, since it is part of a complicated set of relationships each of which is seemingly under the control of independent nations. The unidimensional bogeyman of the colonial era—the colonizing power—no longer exists as a clear goal to fight. Rather, reality is complicated and involves not only foreign influences but entrenched elements within the Third World nations themselves.

CONCLUSION

In this essay we have compared classical, internal, and neocolonial education, charting the similarities and differences between them to see if colonialism in education was, in fact, distinguishable from noncolonial education and, if it was, what was the significance of such differences. We embarked on such an enterprise because current thought on colonialism in education has not addressed these issues in a methodical fashion.

Education under classical, internal, and neocolonialism has certain common characteristics that we have identified. In all cases it represents education planned and largely controlled by foreigners for less powerful and/or wealthy nations. Under classical and internal colonialism the rulers are the ones who make educational decisions—who shall go to school, how long they shall go to school, what shall be learned in school, what language it shall be learned in, and the parameters of the use to which education can be put. Education clearly serves the needs of the colonizer, not the colonized. In classical colonialism those needs did not permit educational parity between colonized and colonizer. Under internal colonialism, schooling, while it could hardly be considered equal to that of the colonizer in terms of quality and access (and until recently in some cases in content as well), was nonetheless directed at the assimilation or eradication of the colonized as a nation, to insure their incorporation into the colonizer's culture. Under neocolonialism foreign control of education is far more subtle. It is not exerted through direct political occupation of a country but rather through international inequalities in wealth and power and the legacy of classical colonialism that contributed to the development of not only inequalities but expectations of the uses to which education could be put. Because former colonies are poor and because during direct foreign occupation demand for a certain type of education was stimulated, most Third World countries find that they cannot, without major social revolution, depart from education structures of the past. While they cannot depart from them, they also find that, as they expand and develop their educational systems, they become as dependent as they were during the time of direct foreign rule on the educational goods and services of foreigners. Money determines the path of educational development, and that money comes in part from outside the nation. This has meant that school texts, books, curriculum, language of instruction, and even schoolteachers are imported from abroad and are accountable not primarily to the parents of students or to Third World nations but in part to either the United States, French, Soviet, Dutch, or British governments or the Ford, Rockefeller, or Carnegie foundations.

A result of the nexus of foreign control of colonial education was that schools were detached from the communities they served. Education and schools often siphon off talent and skills from Third World countries. In classical colonialism, those who were successful in schools joined the European enclaves in the colonies and worked for the Europeans implementing their policies. In internal colonialism, the schools become the means by which the colonized are "assimilated" into the colonizer's society and work. In neocolonialism, schooling integrates those who go to school into the culture and economy of the former colonizer and becomes the means by which the most skilled and talented individuals leave their countries. The "brain drain" is nothing less than the educated of former colonies settling abroad to practice the skills in which they have been trained in schools supported both by their nation's tax dollars and the foreign assistance usually of the country in which they settle. It represents a phenomenon no different from what we witnessed under classical colonialism, the use of the colonized by the colonizer.

Colonial education, as we have pointed out in the preceding pages, is a logical extension of class relationships within a colonizing country but differs in several important ways, for it involves class relations between nations. We argued initially in this essay that education under classical colonialism was modeled on the working-class variants of metropolitan education. But while it was modeled on working-class metropolitan education, colonial education was not the same as class education in the colonizing nation. Rather, the education destined for the colonized elite was in almost the same relationship to the metropolitan working-class education as that working-class education was to elite education within the metropole. The relationship varies in that, within the colonizing nation, it is theoretically possible for an individual to transfer between working class and elite schools; in colonial education, transferral between colonial and even metropolitan working-class education becomes less and less possible.

Schooling in internal colonies historically has had the same relationship to education in the colonizing nation as classical colonialism has. In most recent times, education for internal colonies has pointed more to integrating the colonized into the working class of the colonizer.

While one can point to a theory of colonialism in education based on class relations along national lines for classical and internal colonialism, it is more difficult to make such a case concerning neocolonialism. With titular independence came the real development of European education, the greater usage of texts published in the metropole in the Third World's schools, and the greater diffusion of non-Third World languages (English and French). Yet, despite great changes in education in the 1960s, one can still argue that in fact most Third World school systems do not represent the "quality" scientific and technical training of the industrialized world. For training of this nature, or, in fact, for any advance in education, Third World students must go abroad and assimilate into the educational system of foreign countries. As one becomes "assimilated" in neocolonial education, one acts quite the same as those who are successful in education in internal colonies.

Basic to our argument about the nature of colonialism in education are inequalities. We have argued that inequalities between nations are in some ways different from inequalities born out of class or sex distinctions within a country. Theorists of colonialism have included the working class, racial minorities, and women among the colonized, seeing oppression as synonymous with colonialism. While we believe there is heuristic value in looking at forms of oppression as colonialism, we have, in this essay, raised questions about so doing simply because it obscures real differences by class, sex (e.g., women workers versus bourgeois women), or among nations (e.g., Native American women versus white American women versus African women in South Africa).

In summary, we conceive of colonialism in education as a class relationship among *national* school systems that bears some resemblance to educational class relationships within a colonizing nation (indeed, which grows out of those relationships). Colonialism in education entails inequalities in education on a national basis and, at its highest level, neocolonialism, entails the assimilation of an elite of the colonized into the nation of the colonizer. Colonialism in education involves education controlled from without for the aims and profit of a foreigner rather than for the nation.

We have tried to set the stage for the data-based chapters that follow. We have attempted to describe colonialism as it relates to education in its three important manifestations: "traditional" colonialism, "internal" colonialism, and "neocolonialism." This, then, is an exploratory volume that seeks to relate theory in the broadest sense to reality, both historical and contemporary. It is hoped that the reader will approach it in the spirit of exploration and will, in the last analysis, contribute to our common search for understanding. For it is only through careful analysis and understanding that inequalities can be diminished.

Notes

1. See, for example, Martin Carnoy, *Education as Cultural Imperialism* (New York: David McKay, 1974); Raoul Girardet, *L'Idée Coloniale en France, 1871–1962* (Paris: La Table Ronde, 1972); Henri Brunschwig, *French Colonialism, 1871–1914: Myths and Realities* (New York: Praeger, 1966); Ronald Robinson, John Gallagher, and Alice Denny, *Africa and the Victorians: The Climax of Imperialism* (New York: St. Martin's, 1961).
2. This argument was made in 1923 by Albert Sarraut, Minister of Colonies of France and former Governor General of Indochina, in his book *La Mise-en-Valeur des Colonies Françaises* (Paris: Payot, 1923). The British also argued this. See, for example, Basil A. Fletcher, *Education and Colonial Development* (London: Methuen, 1936). See also Abdou Moumouni, *L'Education en Afrique* (Paris: Maspero, 1964).
3. Councils planning education rarely included the colonized. See Eric Ashby and Mary Anderson, *Universities: British, Indian, African* (Cambridge, Mass.: Harvard University Press, 1962); F. C. Clatworthy, *The Formulation of British Colonial Education Policy, 1923–1948* (Ann Arbor, Michigan: University of Michigan Comparative Education Dissertation Series, no. 3, 1971); Thomas Jesse Jones, *Education in East Africa* (New York: Phelps Stokes Fund, 1922).
4. A. Victor Murray, *School in the Bush* (New York: Longmans, Green, 1929); Clatworthy, *Formulation of British Colonial Education Policy.*
5. This criticism of colonial schools was made by both colonizer and colonized. See particularly O. Mannoni, *Prospero and Caliban: The Psychology of Colonization* (New York: Praeger, 1964); A. Memmi, *The Colonizer and the Colonized* (Boston: Beacon Press, 1967).

6. These schools are described in detail in W. Bryant Mumford, "Malangali Schools," in *Africa* 3 (July 1930): 265–90; W. B. Mumford, "Native Schools in Central Africa," in *Journal of the African Society* (26 April 1927): 237–44. For a discussion of Sultan Idris Training College, see William R. Roff, *The Origins of Malay Nationalism* (New Haven: Yale University Press, 1967).
7. This is clear in Georges Hardy's *Une Conquête Morale: L'Enseignement en AOF* (Paris: Libraire Armand Colin, 1917). Hardy later became Director of the Ecole Coloniale in Paris.
8. See A. Memmi, *The Dominated Man* (Boston: Beacon Press, 1968).
9. Ernest Stabler, *Education since Uhuru* (Middletown, Conn.: Wesleyan University Press, 1969); Gail P. Kelly, *Franco-Vietnamese Schools, 1918 to 1938* (unpublished Ph.D. dissertation, University of Wisconsin, 1975).
10. Kelly, *Franco-Vietnamese Schools,* chaps. 2 and 6.
11. This is clear in descriptions of the schools. See, for example, Jean Capelle, "Education in French West Africa," in *Overseas Education* 21 (October 1949): 956–72; Henri Labouret, L'education des indigènes: méthods britanniques et françaises," *L'Afrique Françaises* 38 (October 1928): 404–11; Colin G. Wise, *A History of Education in British West Africa* (London: Longmans, Green, 1956); Eleanor G. Knight, "Education in French North Africa," in *The Islamic Quarterly* 2 (December 1955): 294–308.
12. E. A. Ayandele, *The Missionary Impact on Modern Nigeria: 1842–1914: A Political and Social Analysis* (New York: Humanities Press, 1967).
13. For a description of the student body at Sultan Idris Training College, see Roff, *The Origins of Malay Nationalism;* at Makerere College in Uganda, see J. E. Goldthorpe, *An African Elite: Makerere College Students 1922–1960* (Nairobi: Oxford University Press, 1965); Peggy Sabatier, "African Culture in French Colonial Education: The William Ponty School Cahiers and Theater" (paper presented at the 18th Annual Meeting of the African Studies Association, San Francisco, California, October 29–November 1, 1975).

14. Ashby and Anderson, *Universities.*
15. Kelly, *Franco-Vietnamese Schools,* chaps. 2 and 6; Joanne Marie Coyle, *Indochinese Administration and Education: French Policy and Practice, 1917 to 1945* (unpublished Ph.D. dissertation, Fletcher School of Law and Diplomacy, 1963).
16. David Abernathy, *The Political Dilemma of Popular Education* (Stanford: Stanford University Press, 1969).
17. Clatworthy, *British Colonial Education Policy.*
18. Daniel P. Kunene, "African Vernacular Writing: An Essay on Self-Devaluation," in *African Social Research* 9 (June 1970): 639–59; Thomas Jesse Jones, *Education in East Africa;* Hardy, *Une Conquête Morale.*
19. Expurgation of the French language, when taught to the colonized, was first proposed by Georges Hardy when he was Governor-General of French West Africa. See Hardy, *Une Conquête Morale.*
20. Murray, *School in the Bush;* Mumford, "Malangali Schools"; Mumford, "Native Schools in Central Africa."
21. Kelly, *Franco-Vietnamese Schools,* chaps. 3 and 4.
22. Kelly, *Franco-Vietnamese Schools,* chap. 4; V. Jones, "The Content of History Syllabuses in Northern Nigeria in the Early Colonial Period," *West African Journal of Education* 9 (October 1965): 145–48.
23. Jones, *Education in East Africa;* Hardy, *Une Conquête Morale;* Clatworthy, *British Colonial Education Policy;* Albert Charton, "The Social Function of Education in French West Africa," in W. Bryant Mumford and G. St. George Orde-Brown, *Africans Learn to Be French* (New York: Negro Universities Press, 1970; originally published in 1935); T. G. Benson, "The Jeanes School and the Education of the East African Native," in *Journal of the Royal African Society* 34 (October 1936): 418–31. A detailed description of science curriculum in Indochina can be found in Kelly, *Franco-Vietnamese Schools,* chap. 4.
24. Klobukowski is quoted in "Indochine—le congrès de perfectionnement de l'enseignement indigène," in *L'Asie Française* 10 (October 1910): 435.
25. See, for example, Philip Foster, *Education and Social Change in Ghana* (Chicago: University of Chicago Press,

1965); Claude Tardits, *Porto-Novo: Les Nouvelles Générations Africaines entre leurs Traditions et L'Occident* (Paris: Mouton, 1958); Remi Clignet and Philip Foster, *The Fortunate Few: A Study of Secondary School Students in the Ivory Coast* (Evanston, Ill.: Northwestern University Press, 1966).

26. These figures vary by colony. See Capelle, *Education in French West Africa.* In the Ivory Coast only 5.10 percent of school-age children entered school; in Guinea, 3.47 percent; in Senegal, 10 percent; in Dahomey, 12.4 percent; in Sudan, 3.79 percent. (Capelle, p. 965.)
27. Margaret Szaz, *Education and the American Indian: The Road to Self-Determination, 1928–1973* (Albuquerque: University of New Mexico Press, 1974).
28. Estelle Fuchs and Robert J. Havighurst, *To Live on This Earth: American Indian Education* (Garden City, New York: Doubleday, 1973).
29. Szaz, *Education and the American Indian.*
30. Fuchs and Havighurst, *To Live on This Earth.*
31. Samuel Bowles and Herbert Gintis, *Schooling in Capitalist America* (New York: Basic Books, 1975).
32. An increasing number of analysts have recognized neocolonialism as a viable concept in recent years. See, for example, Tibor Mende, *From Aid to Recolonization: Lessons of a Failure* (New York: Pantheon, 1973).
33. For further discussion of this topic, see Philip G. Altbach, "Education and Neocolonialism," in *Teachers College Record* 72 (May 1971): 543–58. See also Chinweizu, *The West and the Rest of Us* (New York: Random House, 1975).
34. Philip Coombs, *The Fourth Dimension of Foreign Policy: Education and Cultural Affairs* (New York: Harper & Row, 1964).
35. The center-periphery idea is further developed in Johann Galtung, "A Structural Theory of Imperialism," in *African Review* 1 (April 1972): 93–138; and in Edward Shils, *The Intellectuals and the Powers and Other Essays* (Chicago: University of Chicago Press, 1972); and Edward Shils, *Center and Periphery: Essays in Macrosociology* (Chicago: University of Chicago Press, 1975).

36. See Ashby and Anderson, *Universities*, on this point.
37. Galtung, "Structural Theory of Imperialism."
38. For further discussion, see Philip G. Altbach, *Publishing in India: An Analysis* (Delhi and New York: Oxford University Press, 1975).
39. See, for example, Marion J. Levy, Jr., *Modernization: Latecomers and Survivors* (New York: Basic Books, 1972); C. E. Black, *The Dynamics of Modernization* (New York: Harper & Row, 1966); and I. R. Sinai, *The Challenge of Modernisation: The West's Impact on the Non-Western World* (New York: Norton, 1964).

"Classical" Colonialism

Policy and Conflict in India: The Reality and Perception of Education

Aparna Basu

Education is one instrument by which colonial powers sought to maintain and strengthen their domination over dependent areas. In the history of colonial policy, education therefore is a subject of crucial importance. The Indian experience is significant because in India one finds colonialism displayed more openly and dominant over a larger mass of humanity than in any other part of the world. The British stayed longer in India and exercised greater influence here than any other European power did in its colonial territory. India was of first-rate importance to the British Empire on economic grounds. She was also a source of military and political strength. There were other less easily quantifiable reasons for British concern for India: pride in possession of the second largest oriental civilization, stimulated by the romantic title "Empress of India," which Disraeli contrived for Queen Victoria in 1876; institutional traditions and personal associations established by civil servants, soldiers, planters, and merchants. Such factors combined with economic advantages to make India an integral part of Britain's view of world affairs and one of her greatest national interests.

It was in India that the British first tried the unique experiment of educating an elite through a foreign tongue. There were certain inherent contradictions in this experiment that had not been quite foreseen. British education policy in Africa and Southeast Asia was derived from the Indian experience and tried to avoid the mistakes committed on the subcontinent.[1]

It was not part of the East India Company's original policy to impose a Westernized system of education on its Indian subjects. This is not surprising, since it was a commercial corporation and its primary motive was trade and profit. From 1757 onward, however, as the British acquired their empire in India, they were faced with determining their stance vis-à-vis indigenous Indian institutions. The East India Company's officers, both in London and Calcutta, were determined to interfere as little as possible and to support indigenous education. The British had no bonds of race, religion, culture, or color between them and those they ruled and therefore were eager to conciliate the traditional elites. Patronizing oriental learning seemed one way of doing so. Warren Hastings founded the Calcutta Madrassa in 1781, and in 1792 Jonathan Duncan established the Banares Sanskrit College. The Company's policy was based on political expediency as well as on administrative requirements, since the Company needed a class of judicial officers well versed in Sanskrit, Arabic, or Persian. Among some of the British officials there was also a genuine appreciation of India's cultural heritage.

BRITISH REACTION AGAINST TRADITIONAL EDUCATION

The encouragement of indigenous education was soon questioned in England by the Evangelicals, the Liberals, and the Utilitarians. As it happened, those of their numbers who were concerned with India included the foremost exponents of the day of each of these three points of view. While there were numerous differences between these groups, they were all agreed that Indian society needed to be transformed radically. The prime Evangelical figure was Charles Grant, who had been associated for nearly forty years with the East India Company's administration in Calcutta and London. "The people of Hindustan are a race of men lamentably degenerate and base," he wrote in an influential pamphlet first published in 1792. Hinduism was "a fabric of error" and the Hindus erred because they were ignorant, and this darkness could be dispelled by the introduction of Protestant Christianity and the arts and sciences of Europe.[2]

In England, Charles Grant was a member of the influential Clapham Sect that included, among others, William Wilberforce.

The Evangelicals were convinced of the superiority of European laws and institutions and even more so of British institutions over those of India. They succeeded in 1813 in securing an entry for Christian missionaries into India and made the East India Company set aside "a sum of not less than one lakh of rupees in each year for the revival and improvement of literature and the encouragement of the learned natives of India" and "the introduction and promotion of a knowledge of the sciences among the inhabitants." [3] Grant believed that the spread of Christianity and English education would reconcile Indians to British rule.

These views were shared by the Liberals, who were equally sure of the superiority of Western learning. They attributed England's economic and commercial prominence to the superior education of her people. The most important figure here was the historian and politician Thomas Babington Macaulay. Macaulay wrote that "a single shelf of good European Library was worth the whole native literature of India and Arabia." [4]

The Utilitarian connection with India was through James Mill and his more famous son, John Stuart Mill, both of whom served at India House. James Mill shared Grant's views on the "hideous state" of Indian society. In his *History of British India,* published in 1817, Mill made a scathing condemnation of Indian religion and culture. The Utilitarians did not, however, think that education alone would bring about the desired transformation. They placed greater reliance on legislative and administrative reforms. But Mill agreed with Grant and Macaulay that the plan to support oriental institutions was "originally and fundamentally erroneous." In a dispatch of the Court of Directors in 1824 he asserted that "the great need should not have been to teach Hindu learning but useful learning." The former he dismissed as "obscure and worthless knowledge." [5]

The enthusiasm for introducing Western education to India was not confined to these groups in England only. In India the missionaries as well as individual officers of the Company were working for it. By the 1820s there had also emerged an Indian demand for Western education, initially in Calcutta and associated with Raja Ram Mohun Roy. In 1823, in a letter to Lord Amherst, the acting governor-general, Ram Mohun Roy vigorously protested against the establishment of the Sanskrit College in Calcutta, which would only "load the minds of youth with grammatical niceties and metaphysical distinctions of little or no practical use to the possessors or to society." [6] The success of the British armies had convinced these Indians that their country could improve only through a study of Western science and literature. Raja Ram Mohun Roy believed that India must assimilate Western knowledge for her own regeneration. But there were others who wanted to learn English because it was useful for worldly success. It was necessary for those who had commercial or administrative contacts with the rulers. The rich and leading families in Calcutta and Bombay owed their success to the rise of British power. They had become prosperous as trading middlemen, moneylenders, and landlords under British protection and in the Company's service. There was a fair amount of social intercourse between this class of Indians and Europeans. Knowledge of the English language thus possessed both cultural and utilitarian value for the Indians.

The impulse behind the forthcoming educational changes did not flow from the calculations of British policymakers alone. English education was not forced on the Indians. Rich citizens of Calcutta and Bombay had come forward to set up English schools and had been active in the good work done by organizations such as the Calcutta and Bombay School Societies. Their ideals of education were evident in the setting up of the Hindu College in 1817 and of the Elphinstone Institution ten years later. Adopting the language and culture of the metropolitan power seemed to them to be the only way by which they could modernize their society.

The East India Company's government in India was not, however, easily convinced. There were oriental scholars like H. H. Wilson and H. T. Princep who were influential and ardent supporters of the study of Indian classical languages. They maintained that there was public demand for indigenous learning and that the Charter Act of 1813 bound the Company to encourage it. Within the General Committee of Public Instruction, which had been constituted in 1823 for formulating an education policy, there appeared in the 1830s a younger element that thought Sanskrit and Arabic studies to be a waste of money and time. The General Committee of Public Instruction was evenly divided between the orientalists and anglicists, and both sides appealed to the governor-general in January 1835. Lord William Bentinck asked Macaulay, in his dual capacity as law member and president of the General Committee of Public Instruction, to give his views. The result was his famous Minute of February 2, 1835, which was a sweeping condemnation of the entire orientalist policy. He maintained that government funds should be utilized for teaching English not only because of its inherent superiority to the classical languages but because of the preference expressed for it by enlightened Indians. The vernaculars were dismissed as "poor and rude" and devoid of any literary or scientific knowledge. The choice therefore lay between English and the classical languages, and Macaulay unhesitatingly decided in favor of the former.

Bentinck was a Liberal influenced by Benthamite and Utilitarian ideas. He saw "limitless possibilities of mankind as 'civilised Europe' with its factories and its two-chamber Parliaments, its newspapers and its scientific academies. . . ."[7] When confronted with the educational controversy, his impulse was to support Macaulay, whose persuasive rhetoric undoubtedly moved him. But the governor-general must also have been influenced by the views of his officials like Trevelyan and Metcalfe, as well as by the Scottish missionary Alexander Duff, who shared Macaulay's supreme contempt for India's cultural heritage. Barely a month after Macaulay had written his Minute, Bentinck put an end to the protracted controversy by ruling that "the great object of the British Government in India was henceforth to be the promotion of European literature and science among the natives of India" and that "all funds appropriated for the purpose of education would be best employed on English education alone."[8]

The anglicists wanted the moral and social regeneration of India through the assimilation of European ideas and knowledge. This process was to be primarily originated in, and subsequently guided and controlled through, a system of Western education. Spreading English education was not an act of disinterested magnanimity. It was to provide a positive bond between the rulers and the ruled. "The spirit of English literature cannot be but favourable to the English connection," wrote Trevelyan. English education would stop the Indians from regarding their rulers as foreigners and in fact make them "intelligent and zealous co-operators."[9] It would lead to the permanence and stability of the British raj. The political benefits of the diffusion of European ideas and knowledge were clearly perceived.

In framing his education policy Bentinck was also guided by practical administrative considerations. In 1833, when the Charter Act was passed, the East India Company was once again in financial difficulty. One of Bentinck's principal tasks was to economize, and one of the main items of expenditure was the high pay of English officers. He therefore considered employing Indian subordinates in the judicial and revenue branches. It was necessary that these Indians know English. The Charter Act of 1833 paved the way by opening the civil service to Indians. It was also argued by Holt Mackenzie, among others, that employment of Indians under European control would strengthen their attachment to British rule.[10]

In the estimate of foreign rulers, the admission of an Indian to Western learning reflected his potentiality as a consumer of British imports. They expected English-educated Indians to develop a taste for the products of Lancashire and Sheffield. As Macaulay said, he would prefer that Indians were ruled by their own kings "but wearing our broadcloth, and working with our cutlery," that they should not be "too ignorant or too poor to value and buy English manufactures."[11]

Thus the decision to introduce English education in 1835 was the result of a combination of complex religious, moral, political, administrative, and economic motives.

The popularity of English increased when it replaced Persian as the official and court language in 1837 and even more so in 1844 when Lord Hardinge announced that Indians who had English education would receive preference in all government appointments. Education in the new schools thus became a passport for entrance to government service.

The policy laid down in 1835 and reaffirmed in Wood's Despatch of 1854 was with minor modifications adhered to till 1947. The content of education was to be Western science and literature, and the medium of education in the high schools and colleges was to be English. The government decided, however, to concentrate on the higher education of the upper classes. In

England in the 1830s there was no notion that it was the government's duty to promote education of the people. Besides, limited funds and inadequate staff made it difficult for the Company in India to embark on any program of mass education. For political, economic, administrative, and cultural reasons, what the British wanted was a small class of English-educated Indians to act, in Macaulay's words, as "interpreters between us and the millions whom we govern; a class of persons Indian in blood and colour but English in taste, in opinions, in morals and in intellect."[12] It was hoped that knowledge would filter down from this class to the masses.

This "filtration theory" was not successful because of the highly stratified nature of Indian society. The professional classes, who belonged to certain higher castes among the Hindus, were more than eager to get English education for themselves to enable them to get comfortable jobs, but showed little enthusiasm for spreading education among the masses.

Concentration, since 1835, on the urbanized upper and middle classes led to the neglect of mass education. The education system became top-heavy and lopsided. While India was covered with a network of colleges and high schools, primary education lagged behind. At the turn of the century three out of four villages were without a school, and less than one-fifth of the boys of schoolgoing age were in schools.[13] Despite pious exhortations from many sides from 1854 onward, elementary education was left very much out in the cold. The percentage of enrolled to educable population at the primary stage was 31 percent in India on the eve of World War II as against 100 percent in most advanced countries.[14] Of the total government expenditure on education, only about 30 percent was spent on primary education.[15] Like all countries under colonial rule, India suffered from educational underdevelopment. Hardly 16 percent of her population was literate at the time of independence. This low rate of literacy was one of the most serious handicaps in India's economic development and growth of political democracy.

Education in the colonial era was not only quantitatively inadequate but also qualitatively deficient. Indian education had a predominantly literary bias. In schools there was little provision for vocational training, and at the tertiary level the number of students in arts colleges was far greater than in professional colleges. In 1916–17, for instance, while there were 4,468 BAs and 1,228 LL.Bs, there were only 74 engineering graduates and 219 Bachelors of Medicine.[16]

The exclusion of commercial and technological courses in the curriculum and the small number of institutions offering such courses was closely tied to the employment policy of the colonial government. All higher appointments in the engineering service, railway service, irrigation department, ordnance factories, posts and telegraphs—and in fact in all superior services—were reserved for Europeans. In the private sector, except in Bombay, modern methods of manufacture were confined to Europeans (in the pre-1918 period), and when these industries required men with technical knowledge, they always preferred Europeans. Thus the opportunities for qualified and trained Indians were limited.

The government had itself no policy of industrialization, nor did it encourage private Indian enterprise. If a provincial government made some effort—as Madras did in 1906—to start a Department of Industries, the European business community reacted sharply. Lord Morley, the Secretary of State, asked Madras to withdraw its proposed plan.[17] Given the low rate of industrialization and the official economic and employment policy, there was not much point in encouraging the growth of technical education.

As regards content, there was an overemphasis on the study of languages and humanities. The syllabi of the older universities had a strong linguistic and classical bias. The curriculum for first-year class in Hindu College, Calcutta, in 1832, for instance, consisted of English literature, which included Shakespeare, Milton, Pope's Homer and Dryden's Vergil; history, mainly of Greece, Rome, England, and modern Europe; mathematics and geography. The Indian classical languages and vernaculars were completely neglected.

The secondary-school curriculum was determined by the matriculation or school-leaving examination, which, till 1937, was conducted in English. English was exclusively employed at the university stage; and familiarity with English as a spoken and written language was indispensable to success in official and professional life. Therefore, the Indian schoolboy's mind was saturated with English. So much time was spent in mastering a foreign language that often the main purpose of education was missed. Despite all this effort, what most students picked up was a smattering of indifferent English and a tendency toward mechanical repetition of half-understood sentences. This encouraged memorizing and an incapability of thinking for oneself. A high premium was placed on memory work, on accumulation of data rather than on development of judgment and capacity for sustained argument. Lessons were imparted in a mechanical way, learned by heart and reproduced by students. Growth of inquisitiveness and an experimental bent of mind, so necessary for economic development, were not cultivated. An excessive emphasis on examinations dominated high schools and universities.

The quality of teaching also suffered from a lack of trained teachers. The training of schoolteachers was neglected both at the primary and secondary level. In 1936–37 the percentage of trained male teachers in government primary schools was 57.0 and trained secondary schoolteachers 57.2. Only 23.1 percent of them possessed any university degree.[18] In private aided and unaided schools, the position was much worse. Even the trained teachers were not of a particularly high caliber, and their salaries were low. Usually only those who could not join government service or practice law became schoolteachers.

The Indian Education Service did not attract the best Englishmen. The experience of recruitment for government colleges revealed that the bulk of the teachers recruited from Britain were ideally suited to be sixth-form masters in British public schools or junior tutors in colleges.[19] Indians were discouraged from joining the service, and even men of the caliber of Prafulla Chandra Roy, Jagdish Chandra Bose, and R. G. Bhandarkar were relegated to the Provincial Education Service. Since 1881 the salary of Indians in the graded education service was two-thirds that of Europeans. After 1896 the creation of the Imperial Service and the Provincial Service and the *de facto* exclusion of Indians from the former further diminished the attraction of the teaching profession for the brightest Indian graduates.

The colonial education systems usually represented an uncritical transfer of the educational philosophy and structure of the metropolitan countries to their colonies. The Indian universities founded in 1857 were modeled on London University. Later, when residential and teaching universities were started, it was the Oxbridge pattern that was followed. Directors of education in the provinces tried to introduce methods and ideals they had seen used in their youth in England and advocated systems that had been tried and discarded in their own country. Wood's Despatch in 1854 suggested giving grants-in-aid to schools, a system introduced in England in 1839. Payment by results was another English practice that was introduced in India. The policy of state withdrawal from higher education advocated in 1854 and more emphatically reiterated in the Hunter Commission in 1882 was based on the English practice of leaving education in private hands.

INDIAN REACTIONS

Not only did the British have faith and confidence in their own educational system; so did the early generations of educated Indians. When nationalist leaders like Surendra Nath Banerjea and Gopal Krishna Gokhale opposed Curzon's university reforms, what they were asking for was not a different kind of education but expansion of the prevailing system. The national schools that were started during the Swadeshi movement also did not really evolve a different pattern of education. In fact even after independence, while the Radhakrishnan Commission acknowledged that the universities of modern India owed very little to our ancient or medieval centers of learning and that "a radical change of spirit was essential," it recommended little that was new. It merely stressed the need to broaden and equalize opportunity for higher education. The commission in its questionnaire asked, "In what way would you suggest a reorientation of the present system of education at the universities and colleges so as to achieve the best results? Please suggest concrete steps of reform." The evidence of witnesses reveals that no really new suggestions came forward. Many felt that no special reorientation was even necessary. The improvements suggested were mainly in the nature of expansion of facilities and improvement in quality.[20]

There was, however, some dissatisfaction with the use of

English as the medium of instruction. It was with this in view that the Arya Samajists started Gurukuls, where Hindi was used as a medium and emphasis was laid on the study of Sanskrit. At Shantiniketan, Rabindranath Tagore established a school with Bengali as the language of instruction. The Vidyapiths founded by Mahatma Gandhi during the First Non-cooperation Movement gave instruction through the mother tongue.

Since the 1880s, educated Indians demanded more government expenditure and facilities for technical education. In 1887 the Victoria Jubilee Technical School had been established in Bombay through private effort. In 1904 an association was started in Calcutta for the advancement of scientific and industrial education of Indians, with the object of sending students to Japan, the United States, and Europe. Jamshedji Tata had a scheme for starting a research institute for training Indians in the advanced sciences that ultimately resulted in the Indian Institute of Science at Bangalore. The leaders of the Swadeshi movement in Bengal started a college of engineering at Jadavpur in Calcutta in 1907.

The educated elite, which had in the nineteenth century been mainly interested in funds and facilities for higher education, began to take some interest in the education of the masses. In 1911 Gokhale introduced a bill in the Central Legislature for the permissive and gradual introduction of free compulsory primary education through the local bodies. The bill did not receive official support on the ground that it was premature and financially unsound.

Gandhi also condemned the literary and academic bias of the educational system and its divorce from manual work. He launched the Basic or Wardha Education Scheme, which envisaged free compulsory education in the mother tongue for eight years, with the curriculum organized around manual work.

The initial access to English education was seized by the urban upper classes—traders, moneylenders, banians, and absentee landlords. The first groups to respond to it were the traditionally literate castes, such as the Brahmins and the Kayasthas. The professions open to the new educated class in India were civil service, law, journalism, teaching, and medicine. The occupational structure the intelligentsia entered was notably different from that of industrialized countries. Under colonial conditions India lacked the effective demand that would permit a modern intellectual class, in its full variety, to come into existence. Poverty and the absence of a significant development of industry prevented the emergence of a demand for technically trained people. Illiteracy prevented the emergence of a market for literary products, and India lacked a stratum of authors who could live from the sale of their literary works. The economic policies of the colonial government denied the educated class a role in advancing the production economy. English education became the most important avenue of mobility in colonial society.

The educated middle class in the pre-Mutiny era had expected a dependent but nevertheless substantial development of Indian capitalism in collaboration with free traders and bankers. Ram Mohun Roy and the leaders of the Bengal Renaissance believed in the do-gooding mission of British capitalism in India. In the meantime the process of colonialization was gradually but ruthlessly changing the structure of the Indian economy. All entrepreneurial activities were being subordinated to the import-export bias of the economy and strengthened the colonial aspect of the relationship between the economies of Britain and India. This calamity was not apparent to Ram Mohun Roy and his generation, and they genuinely believed that under British rule the country was proceeding on the path of economic development.

There was a change in the attitude of educated Indians to the economic consequences of British rule in the last quarter of the nineteenth century. The lead in this direction was given by Dadabhai Naoroji, who spoke of the economic drain from India and of how India had become poorer under British rule.[21] The theme was taken up by many distinguished nationalists, including Ranade, Joshi, Wacha, R. C. Dutt, and Gokhale.

In the 1850s and 1860s numerous journals and newspapers were started that opened their columns for ventilating the grievances of the urban middle class. A number of political associations were established, to begin with in Calcutta and Bombay, and many of them were farsighted enough to comprehend the problems of India as a whole. These endeavors culminated in the establishment of the Indian National Congress in 1885. One main purpose of these associations was to press for constitutional reforms leading to increasing participation of Indians in framing government policies and implementing them. The masses were not interested in programs of constitutional advance that had no relevance for them in terms of representative institutions and Indianization of services. Appeals in economic terms were more likely to touch them. This was perhaps one of the reasons why the political leadership turned its attention to economic problems and the "masses of India who do not get enough to provide the basic necessities of life." [22] From the time of Lord Dufferin's Viceroyalty higher education came to be regarded as the root cause of political unrest in the country. The report of the committee appointed to investigate revolutionary conspiracies in India in 1918 revealed that most of the conspirators were educated young men.[23] As the educated class became more vocal in its criticism, earlier doubts about the wisdom of launching English education were reinforced. While Macaulay's decision was lamented it seemed too late to reverse it. However, in their other colonies the British were careful to avoid the growth of political consciousness and national sentiments, which in India appeared to be the result of university education.

The Indians who opted for the path of nationalism still continued to be influenced by Western methods and ideology. They appealed to Englishmen in England and placed their reliance on English history and English political ideals. The nationalists accused British rule in India of being un-British and wanted the Westminster model introduced into India.

After the 1920s the Congress program made a wider appeal than merely to the educated middle class. When Gandhi took over the leadership of the nationalist movement he found an elite out of touch with its indigenous culture, unable, in the most literal sense, to speak to the people in their own language. He proclaimed that India could not be free till she had freed herself from the bondage of the English language. "Among the many evils of foreign rule this blighting imposition of a foreign medium upon the youth of the country will be counted by history as one of the greatest. It has sapped the energy of the nation. . . . It has estranged them from the masses. . . ." [24] Gandhi's crusade against Western technology and cultural symbols was born out of his desire to free Indians from the cultural domination of the West. He wanted to establish in the economic, political, and educational fields a genuinely Indian base or countercenter.

CONCLUSION

The prolonged period of colonial rule, however, produced a dependent and servile attitude that educated Indians even after independence find difficult to shake off. Models derived from the West continue to dominate the thinking of the Indian intellectuals today. Political freedom has not meant the disappearance of the colonial frame of mind, which regards everything indigenous as inferior and everything foreign as inherently superior. Academic colonialism is reflected in the desire to publish in foreign journals, attend conferences abroad, deliver learned lectures to foreign audiences, and to look for approval and inspiration to London, New York, and Moscow. The modern culture of the educated Indian is still very largely derived from a metropolitan culture. The textbooks he studies at the university are from the metropolis. Some of the teachers are educated there in fact or in spirit. The language in which he is educated is not of his own people but of the metropolis. All this is a colonial legacy.

British education created an urban elite that was alienated from its own people. The creation of this class was in a sense a positive achievement, since it was this group that provided the administrators, the professionals, the social reformers, and the political leaders of modern India. But their role as modernizers was strictly limited under conditions of colonial rule where the economy was not being modernized except in a very small sector. The new intelligentsia were stirred by various elements of Western thought—the ideas of freedom, rationalism, humanism, and scientific and industrial advance. But their goals and aspirations could not be achieved under colonial conditions. The role of Western education as an agent of modernization in a colonial context was beset with curious contradictions.

Notes

1. Lord Lugard, Ormsby-Gore, Oldham were all anxious to avoid the growth of political consciousness which in India appeared to be a result of higher education. Cmd 2374, "Educational Policy in British Tropical Africa."
2. Charles Grant, "Observation on the State of Society Among the Asiatic Subjects of Great Britain . . ." written in 1792, published in 1813. It appears in the *Report from the Select Committee of the House of Commons on the Affairs of the East India Company*, 1832, appendix 1, pp. 82–87.
3. H. Sharp, ed., *Selections from Educational Records, pt. 1 1781–1839* (Calcutta: Government Printing Press, 1920), p. 22.
4. Ibid., pp. 92–98. Macaulay's Minute of February 2, 1835.
5. Ibid., p. 92. Despatch to Bengal, February 18, 1824.
6. Ibid., pp. 99–101.
7. John Rosselli, *Lord William Bentinck–The Making of a Liberal Imperialist, 1774–1839* (Delhi: Thomson Press (India) Ltd., 1974), p. 292.
8. H. Sharp, p. 130.
9. Charles E. Trevelyan, *On the Education of the People of India* (London: Longman, Orme, Brown, Green and Longman, 1838), pp. 189–90.
10. Parliamentary Papers (H. L.), no. 445 (111), 1833, p. 142.
11. G. M. Young, ed., *Speeches by Lord Macaulay* (London: Oxford University Press, 1935), p. 153.
12. H. Sharp, p. 116.
13. Indian Education Policy Resolution of the Government of India, 1904.
14. *Year Book of Education* (London: Evans Brothers, 1938), pp. 37–131.
15. A. Misra, *Educational Finance in India* (Calcutta: Government Printing Press, 1918), p. 540.

16. *Progress of Education in India, 1912–17*, vol. 2 (Bombay: Asia Publishing House, 1962), p. 111.
17. *Report of the Indian Industrial Commission, 1916–18* (Calcutta: Government Printing Press, 1918), vol. 1, p. 70.
18. *Progress of Education in India, 1932–37*, vol. 1 (Simla: Government of India Press, n.d.).
19. *The Royal Commission on Public Services in India* (1886–87), *Education Appendix* (London: H.M.S.O., 1888) and *Royal Commission on Public Services in India* (1913), *Education Appendix* (London: H.M.S.O., 1916).
20. *The Report of the University Education Commission, December 1948–August 1949* (Simla: Government of India Press, 1951), vol. 2, pt. 1.
21. Dadabhai Naoroji, *Poverty and Un-British Rule in India* (London: Swan Sounen Schein & Co., 1901).
22. Ibid., p. 31.
23. *Report of the Committee Appointed to Investigate Revolutionary Conspiracies in India*, Sedition Committee Report (London: H.M.S.O., 1918), pp. 13, 15.
24. M. K. Gandhi, *True Education* (Ahmedabad: Navjivan Publishing House, 1962).

Colonialism and Schooling in the Philippines from 1898 to 1970

Douglas Foley

Philippine educational development has been generally characterized as a progressive policy that promoted political democracy and social equality. This study argues that the policy of developing an educational system is so intimately related to the larger historical pattern of Western economic and cultural imperialism that mass education is ultimately and essentially a part of that exploitation. The colonial records suggest how the American colonials, collaborating with the Filipino ruling class, conceived of education as a "human resource development" plan for a dependent agricultural colony. Ultimately, these early leaders created a politically dominated, highly centralized public educational system run by a Western-oriented, relatively powerless professional group to serve this end. This interpretation of twentieth-century Philippine educational development will first describe the sociopolitical context of educational policy—i.e., the general American colonial policy and collaboration with the emerging Filipino ruling class. The second section will describe the major ideological and policy orientations of Philippine education during the Colonial Period from 1898–1946. The third section will describe how many of the earlier educational policies continued after independence and how new foreign-aid programs for public education have continued to promote economic, political, and cultural dependency in the Philippines and Southeast Asia.

AMERICAN COLONIAL POLICY AND AN EMERGING FILIPINO ELITE

Under Spanish rule the Philippine colony had developed an extensive national legal-bureaucratic system and had the beginnings of a commercial agricultural export economy.[1] Indeed, nineteenth-century Philippine economic history was dominated by the emergence of an urban and provincial Chinese *mestizo* (mixed-blood) class of commercial entrepreneurs.[2] This relatively small group (150,000 and 300,000, or 6 percent of the population) gradually infused or "modernized" the existing provincial landed gentry of Spanish and "Indio" (Malay) chieftains. The gradual development of a cash-crop agricultural economy (sugar, tobacco, abaca) created major changes in land holding, utilization, and settlement patterns familiar to most students of colonialism. A more Western-oriented, capitalist entrepreneurial class evolved that dominated the cultural, political, and economic life of the provinces and Manila. The old feudalistic relationships of the *barangy* (villages) evolved into much more efficient, extensive forms of agricultural production that generated greater surplus for fewer people. By 1900 the American colonial government inherited a nascent capitalist political economy with a growing set of class contradictions and a well-entrenched indigenous ruling class.

The American colonial regime generally promoted the emergence of this class structure through their policies of political and economic development. Perhaps the policy of suffrage best exemplifies American rule. Only males over twenty-three, with a real property worth $250, who spoke Spanish or English were allowed to vote. In effect this meant that only the landed gentry and commercial class participated in the elections. Although this was somewhat more democratic than the Spanish colonial policy of local elections by a committee of ex-village/town headmen, the common *tao* (people) were generally distrusted. The Americans developed this policy of "regulated liberty" to avoid anarchy.[3] By 1902 the Americans had largely abandoned any plan to shift power to local governments. Virtually all the important government functions—taxation, public works, health, education, constabulary, and exploitation of lands, forests, and mines—were under colonial supervision.[4]

Yet, the more the colonial government centralized its powers and control, the more it had to contend with the ambitions of the emerging Filipino ruling class. Rather than quickly create autonomous local governments with high levels of mass participation, the Americans followed a policy of political collaboration with and manipulation of the power-seeking Filipino elite. They did this initially through a relatively powerless parliamentary forum and through an American-oriented, loyalist political party. These American loyalists, the Federalist Party, which contained a number of the more conservative factions that "sold out" the Filipino resistance movement against the Americans, received many appointments in the early colonial government. From 1900 to 1905 they assisted the Americans in pacifying the countryside and establishing a new government.[5] By 1907 an advisory national assembly to the colonial government was filled with the young, aristocratic, educated elite who had made up the original Philippine government in revolt against the Spaniards.

By 1907, however, the Federalist Party, then renamed the Partido Nacional Progresista, lost badly in national elections to the Partido Nacionalista.[6] The Nacionalistas, led by Serigo Osmena and Manuel Quezon, were generally a younger, more nationalistic intelligentsia, and they sought immediate independence. They captured control of the new national assembly and continually harassed the conservative colonial governors (generally Republicans) to speed up the Filipinization of government agencies and to give the Filipinos political independence. From this power struggle between the American colonial rulers and the new Filipino ruling class, Manuel Quezon emerged as the single most important and interesting figure. He best exemplifies the type of international and national power broker that necessarily developed to articulate interests between the rising provincial Filipino elite and their impoverished peasantry and the new colonial rulers. Quezon was a master at using the Anti-Imperialist League, the American and Filipino media, the American Congress, and particularly his friendship with Governor-General Harrison.[7]

By 1917 the more liberal American colonial leaders (generally

Democrats) had worked out a system of collaborative governance. This system avoided the earlier confrontations that conservative Republican governors had with the rising young independence-minded Nacionalista leaders. This national-level decision-making body, called the Council of State, although denounced by minority parties as undemocratic and oligarchic, accumulated a wide range of powers. The Council issued bonds for public works, made a budget, named all committee chairmen and department heads, released emergency funds, controlled administrative officials, judges and treasurers, and, most importantly, distributed public-works patronage, among which were school buildings, teaching positions, and promotions.[8] In short, the Council became a weekly meeting where the Nacionalista leaders and the American governor-general sat down and distributed the government patronage to solidify their political faction of provincial entrepreneurial elite and their following of tenants and wage laborers.

Given this collaboration between American colonials and the emerging Filipino elite, other American policies intended to "develop" the Philippines actually helped further subordinate and impoverish the Filipino peasantry and urban working class. Their general view of and policies toward labor dramatically illustrate this point. American colonials and businessmen consistently viewed Filipino labor as indolent and in need of heavy doses of vocational and character education, or replacement with Chinese labor. Further, the Americans consistently restricted the Filipino labor movement.[9] Taft and the Commission outlawed strikes, and the Director of Labor frequently intervened to "protect laborers from unscrupulous labor leaders." By 1927 a strong labor act existed to fine and imprison laborers who failed to live up to the terms of their contract. Yellow-dog contracts and company unions were also common in the sugar and coconut industries. With such weak workmen's compensation laws and the general indifference and hostility of the colonial government, Filipino laborers remained disorganized and largely non-unionized.

There were also a number of colonial policies concerning public lands that were intended to aid the increasingly impoverished rural peasantry but did not.[10] Generally, the American colonial leaders viewed large friar estates, untitled small homesteads, and increasing tenancy as obstacles to creating a class of independent small farmers. To achieve this end the colonial government initially attempted to break up the vast friar estates and to restrict the rise of large plantation agriculture. Taft and the Commission did redistribute 202,167 hectares of friar lands, but the Catholic Church remained a large landlord. Corporations and associations were limited to 1,024 hectares and individuals to 16 hectares under the Homestead Laws of 1902, but anomalies and some plantation agriculture still developed.

Other public land policies were even more spectacularly unsuccessful. The Americans used a Torrens classification system of lands wherein only properly surveyed, classified "agricultural land" could be homesteaded. Each homesteader of 16 hectares had to clear and cultivate at least 20 percent of his land and survey and register it with the Bureau of Lands. However, under this "modern" system of land titling, the time and expense of surveying, verifying the title, and registering land worked against the small, poor landholder. The proposed free government cadastral surveys of public lands actually covered only 3.5 million of the proposed 29.5 million hectares, and only 35,000 applicants and 350,000 hectares were actually patented and approved from 1904 to 1935. Consequently, much of the newly declared homestead land quietly went over to local landed gentry, merchants, moneylenders, lawyers, and those who had money, legal knowledge, and bureaucratic connections. The colonial records often express a concern over these problems, but there appeared to be no massive effort to correct such inadequacies. Nor were there very adequate programs proposed for providing agricultural infrastructures such as credit, technology, irrigation, and better marketing systems.

Finally, one cannot understand the increasing impoverishment of the peasantry without some reference to the American colonial tariff and tax policies. The Payne Bill (1909) and the Underwood Bill (1913) eventually created a free trade relationship between the Philippines and the United States. Such an arrangement greatly stimulated several major cash crops, notably sugar and, to a lesser extent, coconut oil, cordage, and tobacco. By the mid-1930s 77 percent of the total Philippine trade, 65 percent of the Philippine imports, and 87 percent of the Philippine exports, were with the United States.[11] This emphasis on exportable cash crops strengthened the new entrepreneurial class by infusing it with more capital. Other related fiscal policies also enhanced the position of this entrepreneurial class.[12] For example, preferences were given to them through very low land and produce taxes, no corporate tax, and no inheritance tax. Conversely, however, the *Cedula* (a direct poll tax), the excise taxes on alcohol, tobacco, and cockfighting were very regressive taxes levied on the poor. Taken together, the colonial tariff and tax policies clearly benefited the landed and commercial entrepreneurs, particularly the sugar barons. How, then, did educational policy fit into this general colonial "development" policy?

COLONIAL EDUCATIONAL POLICY FOR NATIONAL DEVELOPMENT

The American colonial educators and key members of the Filipino intelligentsia held very similar political and educational philosophies.[13] Early Filipino intellectuals such as Rizal, Mabini and Jacinto derived their ideas from the eighteenth-century Enlightenment. Rizal speaks of man's natural goodness and perfectable intellect. Man is a moral being, and society is a system of moral relations. He and the others also emphasized the tyranny of Spanish rule that denied Filipinos this right to develop, and that belittled their race and culture. This government had to be replaced by a more representative body that assists man in his moral and intellectual development.

None of these intelligentsia wrote extensively on the organization of universal public education, but their great faith in the educational process is clear. The common man is educable, and once all men develop their intellectual and moral powers, their combined morality will add up to a more moral social order. Further, they stressed that the state must take responsibility for a free universal elementary system and that the church should be strictly separated from the government and the public educational system. Rizal emphasized how the Spanish deprived Filipinos of education. His own experimental school in Dapitan and his plan for a liberal arts *colegio* indicate how important more education was to the Filipino elite. When the Americans promised a universal public education system, Filipino leaders from this intelligentsia down to the provincial landed gentry were highly receptive.

Given, then, such shared views, the American colonials and a collaborating Filipino elite set in motion a general policy of massive educational expansion. A familiar dialectic between the masses and elites recorded in other cases of educational expansion was also present in the Philippine case.[14] The educational system was propelled toward overproduction as the political elite sought mass support through distributing education and as the impoverished masses sought mobility through the promise of educational credentials. In this case, the general philosophy of American colonial educators and a series of commission reports and aid programs have historically stimulated this educational overexpansion. There are numerous other factors in the dynamics of this expansion, but the important role of the foreign and indigenous elite of the central government cannot be underestimated. What, then, were the specific policy directions initiated in developing a mass educational system?

David Barrows, the first director of schools, sums up the American theory of education and social progress quite succinctly:

> Public instruction in the Philippines was organized with the conscious purpose of transforming the condition and position of the *gente baja* (the lower class). Our aim is to destroy *caciquismo* and to replace the dependent class with a body of independent peasantry, owning their own homes, able to read and write, and thereby gain access to independent sources of information, and to perform simple calculations, keep their own accounts, and consequently to rise out of their condition of indebtedness, and inspired, if possible, with a new spirit of self-respect, a new consciousness of personal dignity and civil rights.[15]

Education is central to a gradualist theory of breaking down social classes. The independent peasantry "owning their own homes" and "keeping their own accounts" lift themselves out of indebtedness. An educated man becomes a moral man, a self-driven yeoman farmer-entrepreneur who makes his own success and happiness, irrespective of the social order. Related to this emphasis is the theme expressed by Governor-General Forbes:

> Disaster inevitably follows placing powers in the hands of an illiterate, uneducated, or oppressed peasantry. . . . The efforts on the part of China and Russia to establish democracies without the background of an intelligent and informed public opinion have resulted in disorders and disasters. . . .
>
> The essence of America's promise to the Filipinos is that they be assured a stable government. Stability depends on the width of its base. The width of the base can easily be measured by the portion of people who have the right to vote. With this in view, it is clear that the quickest way of providing this element of stability is the extension of primary schools.[16]

Mass education, guided by the elite, is the means for taming the irrational passions of the ignorant masses. There is no way to build a political democracy without the literacy and citizenship training of the primary schools. The colonial records are full of such rationales linking education to the building of a political democracy.

It should be noted that not all the Philippines agreed with the American colonial educators' "progressive" policy of free universal education. The first director, David Barrows, discussed the strong opposition from influential American businessmen in the American-sponsored colonial newspapers. But the shortsighted demand for cheap, uneducated labor was replaced by a policy of developing and improving the working classes through education.

The major rationale for using mass education to create a stable political democracy is intimately related to an educational policy that would *also* develop the Filipino working class as a human resource. Once developed, this improved labor force would fit into a variety of commercial, agricultural and handicraft export industries. Initially, the Schurman Report (1901) emphasized that Filipinos had considerable contempt for the dignity of labor and that many educated people preferred a life of ease. Commissioner Dean Worcester stated that:

> It was apparent from the outset that any educational system adhering closely to academic studies would simply serve to perpetuate this [i.e., the low regard for labor] condition.[17]

The goal of the Americans was to resocialize Filipinos to have the same respect for an honest day's work that the industrious American had. This attitude was apparently reinforced by considerable pressure from the American community for a more practical education. Director of Schools David Barrows stated in the 1907 annual report:

> There has long been prevalent in the Philippines the impression among influential men, particularly among Americans, that the schools are not sufficiently practical. . . . The cry is the common one that the public schools interfere with the availability of labor, train boys away from the fields, and expend large sums of money.[18]

Later reports stress their efforts to satisfy the pressures from "influential Americans and Filipinos" to turn out a better student for commercial needs. Several references were also made to American and European progressive educators who made public education more practical. Most colonial educators appear to have borrowed their educational philosophies from the more industrially oriented progressive educators.[19] Consequently, the combination of ethnocentrism toward the "lazy Filipino," pressures from the commercial community, and their own crude progressivism moved the colonial educators to create a highly practical vocational elementary and intermediate public school program.

The colonial records on education during the first decade of the twentieth century refer often to the struggles to set up schools. Colonial leaders were preoccupied with the enormous challenge of physically creating buildings, recruiting students, training Filipino teachers, finding adventuresome American teachers, winning over skeptical parish priests and parents, printing and adapting textbooks, and cajoling money from the various levels of government and the local people. By around 1909–10 the schools were better able to develop an operating theory of rural and industrial "human resource" development within these broad curricular orientations.

HUMAN RESOURCE DEVELOPMENT FOR COLONY STATUS

The colonial policy of human resource development had three policy trends.[20] First, the colonial government adopted a policy to develop the rural areas and to increase agricultural production from 1907 on. This agricultural development approach viewed rural development as a prerequisite for national development and stressed keeping peasants in the rural areas through "relevant" educational programs and activities. Such early school programs became the forerunner to a variety of postwar "community development" and amelioration projects. A second approach, from 1907 to 1922, attempted to create industrial education for occupational training and a profit. This involved an elaborate and unsuccessful scheme to export the products produced by intermediate and trade-school pupils. A third policy trend, the vocational-school movement, evolved out of the industrial education experiment around 1922. The emphasis became more on preparing people for future industrial development and less on using student labor to produce export items. This third approach was championed by *both* the American blue-ribbon educational surveys and by the restless Filipino nationalists.[21]

The initial emphasis on the community and on agricultural training reached maturity in the second decade of American colonial education. Director Frank Crone (1910–13) wrote highly enthusiastic reports about the schools now being able greatly to expand their activities. The schools were to work with other government bureaus such as Public Health, Agriculture, Postal, and Lands in rural development. At first there were a variety of programs, but a conceptual definition of the schools' role was lacking. In 1913 the schools embarked on a countrywide corn-planting and producing campaign to improve agricultural methods and the Filipino diet. From 1909 on, the schools greatly expanded an earlier series of "civic-educational" lectures to enlighten the rural masses. The schools also began promoting the thrift and savings campaigns of the Bureau of Health, the land surveying and titling campaigns of the Bureau of Lands, and the tree-planting and roadside beautification efforts of the Bureau of Forestry.

By 1916 there was a growing notion that schools were some kind of organizing center. The Director of Education spoke of the school as a neighborhood social center. He emphasized how an earlier playground movement (1916) and a community library movement (1916) made the school the major rural service institution. By 1920 this concept of broad service was more fully developed, and the school was called a community center in the director's annual report:

> The Philippine public schools from the beginning have been community centers to an uncommon degree, but it is only within the last few years that they have become centers of a great general service.

He went on to cite the various recreational, library, dance, agricultural, night school, garden, furniture-making, and civic activities that were coordinated with other bureaus.

The sports, recreation, and physical-fitness activities were especially central to the American's community-service scheme. Indeed, in reading about how enthusiastically the Filipinos took to baseball, it seemed that the sport would revolutionize the entire culture. Baseball was supposed to keep the Filipino away from gambling and cockfighting, to develop his body, and, most important, to teach him the sportsmanship and fair play he lacked. These sports activities were meant for both the school and the community. An extensive regional meet system was developed for selecting a team for the Asian games. Almost every government report hailed the meet system as a way of politically unifying the country and of improving the Filipino character. All of these diverse activities were seen as coming together into this all-purpose rural school, to serve, enculturate, and improve the masses.

Closely related to the community-center concept was the gradual development of special elementary-level agricultural schools. As early as 1907 the school system, with the support of prominent Americans and Filipinos, embarked on a program to create farm schools. Each school had its own farm land. The schools were to be self-supporting and primarily for very isolated, dispersed settlements, particularly the cultural minorities. The curriculum was a little of the three R's and a great deal of practical farm work. The early schools had difficulty with high drop-out rates, but by 1919 there were 162 settlement schools for the cultural minorities and 25 farm schools for nonminorities. The great expansion in this program started around 1915 and was almost doubled by 1924 because of the Thirty-Million-Pesos Act (1919) creating a new rural school program.

The colonial policymakers also provided a more specialized agricultural school for secondary and, later, college-level work. The Central Luzon Agricultural School was initiated in 1909, but by 1914 there were only four other similar schools. As in the case of the farm schools, the major expansion of such schools occurred later in the 1920s. By 1919 there were fourteen of these self-supporting secondary-level technical schools. In 1918 the Bureau of Public Schools strongly supported the De Guzman Agricultural Education Bill. This bill created a series of secondary-level agricultural schools specializing in abaca, tobacco, sugar, coconuts, and rice. These schools were to supply manpower and technical expertise for the encouragement of plantation/commercial export agriculture.

From 1917 on the Bureau of Education sponsored a wide range of new agricultural development projects. Thousands of agricultural clubs were organized in the schools. Food-production campaigns were used to expand and promote the earlier gardening and animal-husbandry projects, which, during World War II, were called "war gardens" and "victory gardens." Dating from the De Guzman Bill, the Bureau of Education urged the legislature to support the expansion of specialized agricultural schools and the idea of self-supporting farm schools. Rural development through specialized schools, vocational curriculum, and direct community-development activities were clear policies throughout the colonial period.

Another major aspect of the colonial "human resource" development policy was industrial education. By 1910 four trade schools were operating, but they produced very little for commercial sale. From 1910 to 1914 colonial educators began to create a handicraft industry. They introduced woodworking, embroidery, lace, hat and basket-making, and weaving into the elementary, intermediate, and special vocational schools. Several fairs and exhibitions were organized to display the goods produced by the schools. By 1914 there were fourteen trade schools producing substantial quantities of commercial furniture.

In 1914 the Sales Agency for the Bureau of Public Schools was organized to institute a commercially profitable industrial education program. The provincial supervisors of industrial education were enlisted to organize hundreds of Household Centers. A School of Household Industries was organized to train leaders for the centers. Students, former students, and local community members worked in these centers. Their production was supervised by the Bureau, and their products were marketed locally or sent to the Sales Agency for exportation. Government reports from 1916 to 1921 hail this as the most significant contribution of the schools to national development. The Bureau of Education sent out several hundred designs for baskets, furniture, and embroidery and lace. Students from grades 1 to 7 worked from five to ten hours a week. Students in the special schools worked up to one half of the school day. Many of those who worked in the household centers were full-time. The major justifications for these programs were to teach the dignity of labor, support students' study, teach them an occupation, and improve the local economy.

The industrial education program encountered many difficulties. The program's local market for baskets, hats, and mats was quickly saturated, and the workers continually overproduced. The international market for lace and embroidery, despite the duty-free American trade agreement, was competitive. Their production and transportation system was also erratic, and they continually fell short of filling their contracts with Marshall Field's in Chicago. Many parents also disliked the cottage-industry programs. They suspected the teachers of using such programs to supplement their salaries. A second objection was that their children did not go to school to become carpenters and embroiderers. They sent their children to school to leave the village, not to become better tenant farmers or day laborers.

By 1922 the industrial education program was in serious trouble. The Director of Education's annual reports stopped publishing statistics on sales and began referring to industrial education as industrial and vocational education. He emphasized that no particular effort was now made to commercialize the trade schools. The elementary vocational education curriculum was described as training for "home improvement," not commercial production. This renunciation of the commercial value of education was particularly clear after the Monroe Report of 1924. The report denounced the remnants of the industrial education program as wasteful, mechanical, and economically unsound. Such criticisms set off a wave of public debates, and vocational education was rapidly "decommercialized." The Sales Agency died a quiet death in 1926, and the phrase "industrial education" was not used again in the succeeding official reports.

The mid-1920s, then, became a critical period of reevaluation of the entire vocational (agricultural/handicrafts) emphasis in public elementary education. Colonial educators had pushed hard for the expansion of the broadly conceived agricultural development approach, but the Philippine legislature had been unresponsive. The colonial reports from 1919 to 1924 continually lamented the lack of understanding, concern, and money for agricultural education. Simultaneously, colonial educators had seen their vaunted industrial education program become unprofitable and unpopular. The reports of 1925 and 1926 explicitly discussed the need for more agricultural education to replace industrial education. Meanwhile, Nacionalista party leaders grew stronger in the early 1920s and demanded political independence. The Filipino national political elite increasingly proposed government-run national development companies in such areas as banking, rails, coal, water, iron, cement, and electric power, and development policies emphasizing industrialization.[22] Increasingly, Filipino leaders began pushing for education more suited to an industrialized society. This trend was evident in elementary education and particularly in secondary education.

The early model for secondary education was considerably less vocational. Public secondary education was initially patterned after the American academic high school. Students took heavy doses of language, rhetoric, humanities, Latin, history, mathematics, and natural sciences. From 1917 on, however, public secondary schools went through a series of reforms. Several new, practical curricula for household science, commerce, and teaching and several token vocational courses in agriculture and building trades were added to the academic courses. By the late 1920s the general high-school curriculum contained approximately 15 to 20 percent vocational subjects. In 1931 the Committee on the Reorganization of Secondary Education recommended a comprehensive secondary high school with approximately 60 percent academic and 40 percent vocational studies.

Such changes in the public high schools, which were located in urban centers and serviced less than 10 percent of the population, did not affect the private, academically oriented schools of the elite. An extensive dual system of private schools from elementary through college arose to serve the urban and provincial elite. American colonial policy never attacked such inequalities. The Monroe Commission (1924), which included such notable progressives as Ruggs and Counts, ably described the private school system, but they made no comments about its obvious promotion of class differences. Meanwhile, they recommended a rural, agricultural high school as the national public secondary school for the Filipino masses.

The educational policies of the Commonwealth period (1933–46) were generally a continuation of the compromises worked out on primary, secondary, and vocational education in the previous decade. The prestigious Monroe Report had criticized the waste in elementary schools because of high drop-out rates. It argued that to achieve literacy in English takes at least five years of schooling. This prompted the Quezon Commission on Education to recommend the Compulsory Education Act of 1936. As the Commonwealth period began, the Filipinos further committed themselves to a massive and costly expansion of public education. Quezon replaced the secondary academic curriculum with the general education degree (60 percent academic and 40 percent vocational). Vocational education was redefined to include trade, agriculture, and home economics and was greatly stimulated by the Vocational Education Act of 1937. Generally, the curriculum in all special vocational schools was made more academic. Likewise, the emphasis on academic and vocational balance was restated for elementary and intermediate levels. In effect, curriculum at all levels in all types of schools became more general and less specialized. This trend suggests the profoundly politicized nature of education as myth, hope, and patronage.

Filipino leaders recognized that the masses wanted more educational credentials. At this point in history the public secondary schools were financed through provincial and municipal funds. The vocational schools were, however, financed through the central government appropriations. Consequently, the vocational schools were greatly expanded and made more similar to the academic high school; vocational schools were no longer simply workshops for building government furniture. The number of academic subjects and particularly the amount of English were greatly increased during the early 1930s. The schools became appropriate means for general social mobility, and the great majority of vocational-school graduates reportedly went into nontechnical occupations. The schemes to employ specialized agricultural graduates on public lands and on the commercial plantations and *haciendas* failed. Further, there were never enough industrial positions to absorb more than a fraction of trade-school graduates. The new vocational schools did, however, expand political patronage distribution and did symbolize hope. Some communities received these schools from their political patrons. In return for this hope and patronage, the village chieftain and his followers owed these leaders a measure of loyalty.

NEOCOLONIAL POLICIES OF EDUCATIONAL DEVELOPMENT

Postindependence policies generally followed prewar policies but with several interesting variations. Immediately after the war, educators responded like other concerned liberals to the breakdown in Philippine society. In several provinces public educators were using the schools to help rebuild war-torn Philippine communities.[23] Many of the old community-oriented improvement activities were revived. The new approach stressed more direct action and community organization. Children were no longer simply basket-weavers, lace embroiderers, and furniture makers; they were now helping hands to clean up communities, survey problems, and mobilize their parents for civic activity. Rural Filipino teachers had always been expected to stress community work, but after the war the teacher was made even more responsible for attacking community problems and for building, with parents and children, community-based curriculums.

In 1948 a UNESCO survey, with the help of several American educators like Floyd Reeves and Paul Hanna, surveyed the war-torn Philippines and was greatly impressed with the community programs in the rural schools. Professor Hanna, who actively promoted and wrote about American community schools in the 1930s, hailed what Filipino educators were doing as "one of the most significant social inventions of this epoch" and as something "the free world will hail." [24] By 1953, UNESCO created the National Community Training Center staffed by foreign experts, with jeeps, dormitories, and facilities for conferences.[25] The center was to promote community development education and serve as a showcase for local and foreign educators.

The Director of Education's reports of the early 1950s stressed that the schools added to the nationwide campaign for law and order. When the reports discussed what teachers were doing specifically, they mentioned such activities as reporting violations of ordinances, enforcing traffic regulations in school zones, displaying good citizenship posters, and holding community assemblies. Such activities are certainly not big-league counterinsurgency activities. But the schools were quite active in promoting a good image of the government and in cooperating with the various rural amelioration programs. Meanwhile, American military advisers and the Philippine Constabulary were battling the guerrilla movement (the Hukbalahaps).

By 1952 there were numerous complaints by parents and teachers about the excessive time spent in community work at the expense of classroom activities. Further, the extensive rural development efforts of other agencies began replacing the schoolmen's dream of being the center of all community activities. New agencies for agricultural extension, welfare, and community improvement circumscribed the school efforts to assist in rural development.[26] By 1959 the community-school movement had been stripped of excessive community activity, and new curric ulum movements in English, mathematics, and science wer introduced.

The community-school case is an excellent example of hov foreign aid and advisers reinforce the direction of educationa reform in developing countries. American educators such as Pro fessor Hanna, in naming the movement in 1949 and in personall publicizing it for twenty years, kept a movement alive that ha dissipated by the mid-1950s. The UNESCO Center, although i made little impact in the field, also had a great deal to do wit further perpetuating the notion that Filipino educators wer making history. Thousands of foreign educators have travele to the Philippines to see the community school in action at th Bayambang center and at other sites that the Bureau maintain for visitors. The Philippines was the demonstration center fo "progressive" American educational concepts. The same has bee true of the vocational education program, the concept of th state university, and the specialized science high school.[27] I recent years the Philippines has become the place to see nev techniques in modern mathematics, science, and teaching Eng lish as a second language.

This phenomenon of the Philippines as a regional Asian cente for displaying American educational concepts also expands to a wide variety of other development programs. Located in th Philippines is the premier center for agricultural research, th International Rice Research Institute. Further, the Center fo Asian Business Management, Asian Center for Mass Media Asian Labor Education Center, International Community De velopment Training Institute (PRRM), Asian Institute of Publi Administration, and several regional UNESCO programs (teache education) are located in the Philippines. In effect, the Philip pines, because of its location, English language, relative politica stability, and numerous public and private aid programs, ha become a major regional training center for the "developmen professions." These regional programs for training progressiv and democratic elite leaders in the latest administrative, orga nizing, educational, and management techniques are supple menting and even replacing earlier exchange programs.

The community-school movement also illustrates one othe

form of colonial influence over education that should be studied more carefully. In interviewing the leaders of the movement and in observing one regional division of schools, it became obvious that those educators who were connected with the community-school movement were disproportionately represented in higher administrative positions.[28] No detailed study of professional mobility was conducted for national-level administrators from 1950–1965, but it would undoubtedly show that being an advocate of the community school was good for professional mobility. There were numerous scholarships and study grants offered through UNESCO, and several of the community-school leaders were selected to study under AID-financed administrative exchange programs. In one region studied intensively, the superintendent, assistant superintendent, and academic supervisor had all been given scholarships in the 1950s to study community education and adult literacy. Given a time lag of several years, the products of the latest American-inspired reform movement and training program will gain a disproportionate number of the line and staff leadership positions on the local and national levels.

A second major type of postwar educational reform has been the effort to initiate reforms of the academic subjects. The earlier community-school movement stressed a problem-solving, unified curriculum approach, but this idea began losing ground to content specialists in the late 1950s. The Swanson Report (1959) commented on the post-Sputnik era and made several recommendations on improving the subject-matter areas in the elementary and secondary schools. This, of course, was not a new recommendation, and many other earlier surveys by Americans and Filipinos recognized the need for continually improving instructional quality. The American recommendations were followed by the reports of prestigious Filipino educators in step with this new wave of essentialist philosophy. The Magsaysay Committee on General Education (1960) emphasized a classic, essentialist philosophy of education. The report reviewed past Filipino thinkers who had deplored vocationalism and "empleomania" in education and showed their relationship to the views of Ortega y Gasset, Robert Hutchins, and other noted educational conservatives. The report focused on higher education but also made broad recommendations for instituting major content reforms in the lower levels of public schools. The Sinco Report (1960) also concurred with these general views.[29]

Subsequently, the content specialists have run thousands of in-service training institutes, written hundreds of new manuals and lessons, and have dominated discussion of what is wrong with the public school system. Educators, then, have turned inward and are preoccupied with new definitions of content and new methods for transmitting this content. Learning the vocabulary of modern mathematics and the laboratory approaches of discovery science has replaced sanitary toilet campaigns and literacy classes. There was an attempt by President Marcos to revive the community-school approach in the late 1960s, but this new community-school approach is far more specialized and less time-consuming for teachers. All the former rhetoric about transforming the rural areas remains, but the level of activity is far more controlled than in the early 1950s. The present educational reform effort is primarily subject-matter oriented and appears to have its origin in American surveys and in foreign-aid programs for textbooks and exchange teachers.

The third major area of postwar curriculum reform has been the continuation of the prewar vocational education program. The UNESCO Report (1948) and the joint Congressional Committee on Education (1948) concurred that the secondary schools were too academic.[30] They recommended further specialization and strategic centers: college-prep programs for the exceptional, urban schools that were "half learning and half earning," and rural schools that would become a community center and would keep rural students in the rural areas. They reiterated the old colonial view that most young people have an aversion to work and need to be resocialized. They advocated abolishing the academic high school altogether, which was, of course, a misunderstanding of the politicized nature of education in the Philippine context. Aside from being eager to experiment with the local vernaculars, the early postwar Filipino educational thinking was almost a carbon copy of the American colonial position on all issues. The basic rationales for universal public education and the need to continue educational expansion was strongly emphasized.

The United States Aid mission of that period (ICA) instituted a five-year contract for $1.5 million under the supervision of Paul Hanna and Stanford University. This involved a large Filipino counterpart fund of 11 million pesos (2 to 1 ratio in 1951).[31] The program increased the number of vocational trade schools from twenty-nine to thirty-five, created postsecondary level work in seventeen new schools, initiated an exchange program, and became an important demonstration project for others in Southeast Asia to visit. The program also stimulated considerable administrative expansion. Central Office Vocational personnel went from seven to twenty-six and regional superintendents from five to twenty-five.

In 1959 U.S. AID financed another Filipino–American survey under Chester Swanson, an expert in vocational education from the University of California. Swanson wrote a rather favorable report on the vocational trade schools and recommended they be expanded. He also suggested that general elementary and secondary schools reform their curriculum to give a better prevocational education. The general high school had still not developed an appropriate practical arts curriculum. Swanson was particularly concerned with the status of agricultural education and said that the status of instruction in agriculture was in dire need of upgrading. He went on to present the usual argument that the Philippines was a predominantly agricultural country and needed more agricultural producers. The report also viewed the work of community schools and adult education for literacy favorably and recommended that such programs be continued. In short, all the previous colonial policies in rural and vocational education were encouraged. Even the old industrial education programs for home industries were championed as capable of uplifting family and national economies.

In 1967 AID recommissioned Swanson to survey the school system and pronounce on educational policy.[32] In this report Swanson was very critical of vocational education as merely academic high schools in disguise, and he conceded that the enormous expansion of vocational schools, ninety-three in six years, was related to the pressures of parents, school personnel, and the provincial and national politicians. He also recognized that the conversion of academic high schools to trade schools and trade schools to national colleges was part of the tendency to use public education as hope and political patronage. Nevertheless, Swanson took the same policy position of earlier American progressive educators. Again, the American policymakers and experts recommended the continued expansion of vocational and general education without questioning the inequities of the continuing privilege of the Filipino elite.

Postwar American influence over textbooks and teachers' guides took on a new, more indirect form. The NEA-ICA project assisted the war-torn Philippines with a massive textbook printing campaign to produce twenty million books. The ICA program addressed itself to a real need, but as the Sinco Report (1960) stressed, the Philippines has to begin producing more inexpensive instructional materials. No thorough evaluation of the ICA project has been done, but it was a very expensive project. A second and far more important American aid program for curriculum development was the Peace Corps. For the past twelve years thousands of young Americans, sometimes called the "new Thomasites" (a reference to volunteer American teachers of the colonial period), became important resource people in the Bureau of Education's programs to develop English, mathematics, and science materials.[33] Peace Corps volunteers, like the earlier Thomasites, were neither experienced nor highly skilled professionals, but some of them became national curriculum writers for this sovereign nation state.[34] The postwar Philippines still had to accept the "technical expertise" and the cultural values of the new wave of untrained American teachers and the expensive AID-printed American textbooks.

SUMMARY AND CONCLUSIONS

The centrality of the educational system to the American development plan was clearly expressed in the early statements of American colonials. The basic policy and curriculum orientation of the public schools reflected the American colonial theory of political and economic development. The islands were to remain agricultural, and there was virtually no industrial or even general economic development plan. However, the American regime was committed to making a showcase Asian democracy, and schools, English, and a literate citizenry were central to this goal. As a result, schools were expanded into even the most remote villages. To fit the agricultural model of development, schools were designed to have a strong vocational orientation. There were various unsuccessful attempts at developing farm settlement schools, specialized agricultural schools for plantation-type crops, and industrial education programs.

The schools were also used from the beginning as an agency of community development. The idea was to expand government services to the people, to indicate the presence of a new national state. Consequently, many rural development programs were started to symbolize the concern and activeness of the new foreign and national elite. The idea of schooling and school credentials as a form of social mobility was also transmitted to the masses. Indeed, this concept was so well inculcated into the masses that they increasingly pressed for academic curricula and more postelementary schools. Expanding this vocationally and community-oriented mass-education system has continued up to the present and has resulted in considerable overexpansion.

A highly centralized, politically controlled educational system developed from this collaboration between the American colonials and the power-seeking Filipino elite. From the beginning, the American colonial rulers cooperated with a Filipino elite who politicized and used the educational system in two fundamentally important ways. First, the Filipino elite developed its own private school system to preserve its privilege and access to the colonial bureaucracy. Second, the new national-level Filipino politicians used school expansion—i.e., new buildings, teacher appointments, and promotions—as patronage to local chieftains and their followers. In return the provincial leaders and the peasantry were expected to accept the new central state and its emerging ruling class *and* to accept an inferior, vocationally oriented public school system. Understanding these policy patterns and the politicized nature of Philippine education, one finds it difficult to characterize the creation of a mass education system as a progressive, egalitarian institution.

Finally, this pattern of a dependent, Western-oriented politicized educational system of the colonial period lingers on after Philippine political independence. American educational surveys and technical assistance programs have replaced direct colonial control in influencing the direction of Filipino educational thought and curricular reforms. Striking parallels between the two historical periods can be found between 1) "Thomasite" volunteers and Peace Corp volunteers, 2) expensive American colonial texts and expensive AID-produced texts, and 3) colonial village education for rural amelioration and American/UNESCO-sponsored village education for counterinsurgency. Liberal American educational advisers of both periods retain the essentially colonialistic mentality that subscribes to a "human resource development" approach to mass education for economically dependent agricultural society.

Historically, few Filipinos have written extensively about this colonial legacy and the role of education in underdevelopment. Indeed, the recent Presidential Survey of Education (1970) is a logical culmination of this colonial legacy. This report conceptualized the educational system in the same way that American advisers have, as an input-output machine that has no historical roots and no connections with the cultural and political context. Consequently, the type reforms it suggests will not disturb the primary functions of a politicized, class-dominated mass education system. This brief paper cannot adequately describe the various patterns of Filipino educational thought and response to American educational surveys and policies, but in closing it should be noted that some recent Filipino educational leaders (The Sinco Report) and student leftists (Jose Ma.Sison, Renato Constantino) have begun to question American educational policy as impractical or as a form of cultural imperialism. One would anticipate that future interpretations of education's role in Philippine national development will further explore and test these critical perspectives.

Notes

1. Benito Legarda, Jr., "Foreign Trade, Economic Change, and Entrepreneurship in the 19th Century Philippines," (unpublished Ph. D. dissertation, Harvard, 1955; Eliodoro Robles, *The Philippines in the Nineteenth Century* (Quezon City: Malaya Books, 1969).
2. Edgar Wickburg, *The Chinese in Philippine Life 1850–1898* (New Haven: Yale University Press, 1965); John Larkin, *The Pampangans: Colonial Society in a Philippine Province* (Berkeley: University of California Press, 1972); Marshall McLennan, "Land and Tenancy in the Central Luzon Plain," in *Philippine Studies* (1970): 651–82.
3. Charles Burke Eliott, *The Philippines to the End of the Commission Government: A Study in Tropical Democracy* (Indianapolis: Bobbs-Merrill, 1917); Charles Burke Eliott, *The Philippines to the End of the Military Regime* (Indianapolis: Bobbs-Merrill, 1917).
4. Michael Cullinane, "Implementing the 'New Order': The Structure and Supervision of Local Government During the Taft Era," in N. Owens, ed., *Compadre Colonialism* (Ann Arbor: Michigan Papers on South & Southeast Asia, 1971).
5. Frank Jenista, Jr., "Conflict in the Philippine Legislature: The Commission and the Assembly from 1907 to 1913," in Owens, *Compadre Colonialism.*
6. Dapen Liang, *The Development of Philippine Political Parties* (Hong Kong: South China Morning Post, 1939); Maximo M. Kalaw, *The Development of Philippine Politics, 1872–1920* (Manila: Oriental Commercial Company, Inc., 1926).
7. Michael Onorato, "The United States and the Philippine Independence Movement," in *Solidarity* 5 (September 1970); "Manuel Quezon and His Modus Operandi," in *Asian Forum* 5 (July–September 1972).
8. Douglas Foley, *Rural Education and Nation-Building in the Philippines,* unpublished manuscript, 1975.

9. Victor Clark, "Labor Conditions in the Philippines," in *Bulletin of U.S. Bureau of Labor* 10 (May 1905); W. Cameron Forbes, *The Philippine Islands* (Boston: Houghton Mifflin, 1928).
10. Len Giesecke, "History of American Economic Policy in the Philippines during the American Colonial Period, 1900–1935," unpublished Ph. D. dissertation, University of Texas, 1974; Karl Pelzer, *Pioneer Settlement in the Asiatic Tropics* (New York: American Geographical Society, 1945); A. M. McDiarmid, "Agrarian Public Land Policy in the Philippines during the American Period," in *Philippine Law Journal* 6, no. 26 (1953): 851–88.
11. Giesecke, "American Economic Policy."
12. Harry Luton, "American Internal Revenue Policy in the Philippines to 1916," in N. Owens, *Compadre Colonialism.*
13. Cesar Majul, *The Political and Constitutional Ideas of the Philippine Revolution* (Quezon City: University of the Philippines Press, 1967).
14. David B. Abernathy, *The Political Dilemma of Popular Education: An African Case* (Stanford: Stanford University Press, 1969); Michael Katz, *The Irony of Early School Reform* (Boston: Beacon Press, 1968); Steven Hazlett, "Conceptions of Democratic Education in the Founding of the French Third Republic (1870–1890)" (Final Report, project no. 1–0627F, HEW, 1973).
15. David Barrows, *A Decade of American Government in the Philippines, 1903–1913* (New York: World Book Company, 1914).
16. Forbes, *Philippine Islands.*
17. Dean Worcester, *The Philippines: Past and Present* (New York: Macmillan, 1914).
18. Philippine Bureau of Education, annual report 1907, p. 12.
19. Lawrence Cremin, *The Transformation of the Schools: Progressivism in American Education, 1876–1957* (New York: Vintage, 1964).
20. Philippine Bureau of Education, annual reports, 1901–37.
21. Charles A. Prosser, "A General Report on Vocational Education in the Philippine Islands" (Manila: Bureau of Printing, 1930).

22. Ralston Hayden, *The Philippines: A Study in National Development* (New York: Macmillan, 1962).
23. Board of Educational Survey, *A Survey of the Educational System of the Philippine Islands* (Manila: Bureau of Printing, 1925).
24. Vitalino Bernandino, *The Philippine Community School* (Quezon City: Phoenix Press, 1957).
25. U.S. Operations Mission to the Philippines, Education Division, *The 6th Milestone: ICA and Education in the Philippines* (Manila, 1959).
26. Urban Fleege, *The Community School: Potentialities and Needs* (Bayambang, Pangasinan, Philippines: Phil-UNESCO Training Center, 1956).
27. J. V. Abueva, *Focus on the Barrio* (Quezon City: University of Philippines Press, Institute of Public Administration, 1959).
28. Harry Case and Robert Bonnell, *The University of the Philippines: External Assistance and Development* (East Lansing, Mich.: Institute of International Studies in Education, Michigan State University, 1970).
29. Douglas Foley, *Rural Education in the Philippines.*
30. Chester Swanson, et al., *A Survey of the Public Schools of the Philippines, 1960,* U.S. Operations Mission to the Philippines (Manila: Carmelo and Bauerman, 1960); Vicento B. Sinco, ed., *Report of the Committee on the Reform of the Philippine Educational System* (Manila: Board of National Education, 1961).
31. UNESCO. Philippine Education Foundation, "Fifty Years of Education for Freedom, 1901–1951" (Manila: Bureau of Printing, 1953).
32. Sidney High, Jr., *Vocational Industrial Education in Newly Developing Nations* (Comparative Education Series #1, Stanford University, 1960).
33. Chester Swanson, et al., *The Public Schools of the Philippines: A Review of a Survey* (Manila: USAID/Manila Publications, 1968).
34. Charles Lindsey III, "The Developmental Contribution of the Peace Corps in the Philippines," unpublished master's thesis, University of Texas, 1972.

Colonial Schools in Vietnam: Policy and Practice

Gail P. Kelly

This essay traces the development of schools in colonial Vietnam. It first explores the reasons the French established an extensive school system in the colony by reviewing French planning-council proceedings as well as French reactions to Vietnamese traditional education and Vietnamese attempts to develop modern schools on their own. This survey will show how the French planned the Vietnamese colonial school system in direct response to Vietnamese educational initiatives. Not only were the schools a response to Vietnamese schooling, both traditional and modern, but the colonial schools were planned to prevent the development of any modern education as the French knew it in their colony. The extent to which the intent of planners became reality is illustrated in this article. The second part of the article analyzes school curriculum to show how educational policy was translated into educational practice.

FORCES AFFECTING EDUCATIONAL POLICY

The French established an extensive school system in Vietnam because schools had traditionally played a great role in Vietnamese society and teachers in traditional schools resisted colonial rule. When French armies invaded southern Vietnam in 1858, Vietnamese schoolteachers organized and led the fight against the foreigners.[1] It was natural that such a role befall teachers. Throughout Vietnamese history they had integrated the village with the nation. The teachers provided the village with ties to the Vietnamese government. They versed the youth in

Confucian moral codes, prepared the brightest children for state service, and helped implement government policy at the local level. The Vietnamese traditional teacher was not solely a tool of the state. Teachers had national networks—independent of the government—that were formed through contacts made in the course of their studies. Time after time in the course of Vietnamese history, village teachers used these contacts to foment rebellion when government became unjust or times too difficult to bear. The teacher in Vietnam, in short, was the backbone of a political network that was capable of organizing armies. For the French there was little question that this network was effective. The teachers held out against the French for over twenty years, despite the capitulation of the Vietnamese monarchy. They frequently used village schools to recruit soldiers to fight against the French.

The role of the traditional teacher did not go unnoticed. As early as the 1860s the French admirals who administered the newly acquired territories in southern Vietnam initiated a school system of their own making to counteract the power of the traditional teachers who, the French believed, were inclined to "trouble-making." [2] Between 1860 and the turn of the twentieth century a government school system emerged in areas under French occupation. It was staffed by French-selected teachers and taught, in Vietnamese written in the roman script (developed by Catholic missionaries), moral behavior, French, and hygiene. These schools appeared in greatest number in areas where Vietnamese armed resistance had been strongest—in southern and northern Vietnam. In the areas where the Vietnamese monarchy was able to keep traditional teachers from joining the resistance, French colonial schools were almost nonexistent.

Traditional Vietnamese education was not the only factor that led the French colonial government to establish schools. Of as great a concern to them were educational reformers who developed "modern" Vietnamese schools based on neither Vietnamese educational traditions nor on the education given in colonial schools. French authorities viewed with alarm the *Dong-De* (Eastward Movement), which sponsored Vietnamese to study at military academies in Japan. In 1905 the French made expulsion of Vietnamese students from Japan a condition for its loan to that government. Around the same time in northern Vietnam, Vietnamese opened "free schools," the most significant of which was the Dong Kinh Free School located in Hanoi. The school, opened in 1907, had over one thousand students in forty classes. Its course of study included Chinese, Vietnamese, French, science, hygiene, geography, political history, civics, economics, and physical education. Attached to the school were agricultural and commercial cooperatives. The school also raised funds to send students to China and Japan to receive modern education. The school's founders tied education to regaining national autonomy. They believed that if the youth became knowledgeable in modern science they could spread their information throughout the country. Modern science, they maintained, was the key to regaining nationhood.

The Dong Kinh Free School was closed down by the French in late 1907. The French traced to the school a pamphlet urging Vietnamese not to circulate iron coins minted by the government. They considered the school "anticolonial." This charge had some basis; many people associated with the school were active in the 1908 tax protests as well as in a plot to poison the French garrison stationed in Hanoi.

Traditional education and initiatives to modernize education for the youth on non-Western lines were two factors that prompted the French to develop a school system for Vietnamese. Vietnamese pressure on French schools within the colony also affected the colonial government's policies. French schools had been established in three urban centers in Vietnam at great cost. They were designed for the children of French residents of the colony (*colons*). Vietnamese children were admitted to the schools if they performed well on entry examinations and could complete the *lycée* course if they passed prerequisite degree examinations. Places in the French schools were limited. Only three to five hundred children could be accommodated at a time in the thirteen grades in each of the *lycées*. By the early twentieth century children of Vietnamese civil servants, entrepreneurs, landed gentry, and the traditional elite began to outnumber *colon* children in these institutions. In several instances French children had been denied admission to the *lycées* because they did not do as well as Vietnamese children on entry examinations.

or were terminated from *lycée* because they flunked the French primary certificate exam. European parents complained bitterly that Vietnamese were usurping their rights to elite status by crowding the benches of French schools. They maintained that the presence of Vietnamese children in the schools lowered standards in such a way as to be responsible for *colon* children's failure on exams. Finally, Vietnamese who received French education, these *colons* maintained, would demand equality in access to government jobs, in how the government treated them, and, in the long run, in making political decisions. For these reasons a sizable number of Frenchmen in Vietnam urged the government to develop schools for Vietnamese that would place Vietnamese out of competition with them both in access to education and in the privileges that came from having received French education.[4]

Vietnamese traditional education and its role in the anti-French resistance, initiatives to develop autonomous modern Vietnamese education, and Vietnamese competition with *colons* for French education all provided a backdrop to the emergence of an educational policy and the development of a colonial school system. By 1906 the French colonial government convened a council to plan education. This body, the Council for the Improvement of Native Education, met for seven years in Hanoi. Sitting on the Council were the Inspector of Public Instruction for Indochina, the French education administrators for each of the five countries that made up Indochina, French political authorities, members of the police, directors of French schools in the colony, and several hand-picked "prominent" Vietnamese.[5] The Council's deliberations clearly indicated that colonial schools in Vietnam were developed to substitute for autonomous Vietnamese education and to preempt any independent formulations of Western, or modern, education. The meetings of the Council show that manpower needs, often thought to be the reason for developing colonial education, were not a major concern of educational planners or politicians. French civil-service administrators and the governor-general emphasized that too many educated Vietnamese were demanding jobs that were not available in either government or private industry and not likely to be available in the forseeable future. These individuals supported the expansion of colonial schools regardless of manpower needs or lack of them. Governor-General Klobukowski, in his opening remarks to the 1910 meeting of the Council, spoke only of the moral value of education, not of the government's need for trained manpower.[6]

Political concerns were dominant in development of colonial education. Council members made this clear when they spoke of the different ways Vietnamese could be educated under French rule. The Council members rejected any possibility of continuing to educate Vietnamese in traditional schools. They argued that traditional education was uncontrolable by the government and would be potentially subversive to French rule.[7] Their teachers, Council members pointed out, were anti-French, and the schools taught Vietnamese written in Chinese characters. Council members harped on the dangers of Vietnamese learning their own language written in Chinese characters. Once Vietnamese learned the characters, they maintained, they would be able to read Chinese, and that would expose the youth to anti-French, anti-Western literature as well as to Western liberal and radical tracts that had been translated into Chinese through the efforts of educational reformers and nationalists in China. Vietnamese, as far as they were concerned, would "misconstrue" the thoughts of Rousseau, Locke, and Voltaire.[8]

While Council members rejected Vietnamese traditional schooling, they were no less harsh on French schooling as the educational vehicle for colonized peoples. Except for two Vietnamese members, the Council declared French education "ill-adapted" to Vietnamese mentalities and antithetical to providing Vietnamese with ". . . a simple education, reduced to essentials, permitting the child to learn all that will be useful for him to know in his humble career of farmer or artisan to ameliorate the natural and social conditions of his existence."[9] Council members instead proposed a new type of education for Vietnamese that would consist almost exclusively of moral instruction and vocational orientation to occupations within Vietnamese traditional occupational sectors—rice farming and crafts. This education, designed for elite and mass alike, would be given in Vietnamese written in roman script to avoid the problems that teaching Vietnamese their written language in Chinese characters implied. This education was to be, according to the Council's final report, the sole educational vehicle for Vietnamese and was to replace traditional schools, private schools that taught anything other than state-standardized curriculum, and French schooling for Vietnamese youth.

The Council visualized only a seven-year educational system consisting of a five-year primary course and a two-year complementary course, described as a "compromise between primary Franco-Vietnamese education and French secondary education . . . accentuating . . . the professional nature of these schools." [10] This complementary education was to be open only to the Vietnamese elite and would emphasize farming.

The Council's recommendations did not go unheeded. By December 1917 a Code of Public Instruction was promulgated, setting up a new school system financed by the colonial government along the lines of Council recommendations. These schools, called Franco-Vietnamese schools, were to become the exclusive means of educating Vietnamese. In 1924 the government enacted a stringent private-school law that required all educational institutions in Indochina, church and otherwise, to meet state building requirements, to adhere to the government prescribed curriculum, to hire only government-trained and certified teachers, to admit only students who were in the age ranges suggested by the government for each grade level, and to open themselves to state inspection.[11] This law was responsible for closing 1,835 schools in 1924–25 alone.[12] Affected most by the law were Vietnamese traditional schools in the countryside.

In 1924 the government clearly disassociated schooling for Vietnamese from schooling for French children. It did this through differentiating Vietnamese from French school curriculum. The government also made the Vietnamese language the mandatory medium of instruction for the first three years of education.[13] This language reform insured that Vietnamese would be handicapped in entering French schools unless they began their education in them. From 1924 to 1926 this differentiation widened as the government added two years more to Vietnamese education so that Vietnamese would be too old to enter age-specific French schools by the time they completed their primary and/or secondary education. The government also introduced Vietnamese curriculum, attempting from 1924 on to replace Western-style subjects with what the government considered "Vietnamese"-style subjects. Chinese was reintroduced into the schools, replacing class time formerly allocated to teaching French. Instead of sciences, Vietnamese were given larger doses of "national" history, Sino-Vietnamese literature, drawing, and moral education. As the schools developed, they systematically cut off Western knowledge from their Vietnamese students. And, as curricular differentiation occurred, colonial authorities similarly established higher levels of education, emphasizing vocationalism, not necessarily in terms of clerkships, commerce, or industry but in terms of an orientation to farming as Vietnamese already knew it and to the study of Sino-Vietnamese literature and arts.

The preceding review of educational planning in colonial Vietnam, the conditions under which it occurred, and the school system that evolved is instructive in several ways. First, it shows that school system was planned not as a replica of French schools or a diluted version but rather as a distinct system that would be appropriate not merely to the colonized but to *Vietnamese* who were colonized. It was the peculiar circumstances in which the French found themselves in Vietnam that shaped that school system, not any policy made in Paris and standardized for all colonies. If traditional education had not been the major mobilizing link in the anti-French resistance and had it not, regardless of the resistance's failure, still retained a potential to mobilize villages across regions against colonial rule, schooling might not have become as great a government concern as it became. The French would never have spent upward of 15 percent of colonial budgets on education (which is a greater percent than budgets expended on education today in most Third World nations) had not educational policy become a matter of colonial survival.[14] Vietnamese initiative for autonomous educational reform, as exemplified in the Dong Kinh Free School, and demands for French education prompted the government to define educational policy precisely. French authorities were well aware of the use "free" schools had been put to by Chinese self-strengtheners and radicals. Such schools in China not only taught Western science and promoted liberal and/or radical ideology; they also were heavily involved in military training and the manufacture of armaments. The Dong Kinh Free School and others like it represented a political threat of a nature perhaps different from Vietnamese traditional education but nonetheless a real challenge to French authority if uncontrolled.

The Council for the Improvement of Native Education was not just a body that spun pipe dreams about what education should be, wrote its reports, and let those reports gather dust on the shelves. Its recommendations became school practice more rapidly than any individual member of the Council had foreseen or thought desirable. Late in 1917 Albert Sarraut, the Governor-General who convened the Council and who returned to Indochina for yet another term at the job, promulgated a code of public instruction that made the Council's recommendations law and set up an educational bureaucracy to carry them out. The system of schools, called Franco-Vietnamese (sometimes Franco-native or Indochinese), came into being between 1917 and 1924 and remained the major educational route for Vietnamese until the French left Vietnam in 1954. The Council's policy was translated not only into a clearly defined institutional structure and set of bureaucratic controls, but also into a distinct school curriculum. The remainder of this article analyzes Franco-Vietnamese school curriculum. I base this analysis on school textbooks and curriculum guides used in Vietnam between 1918 and 1938.

My discussion of school curriculum shows how Franco-Vietnamese education differed from French education and how, despite a heavy emphasis on teaching the French language, this education oriented students not to the European world but rather to a redefined Vietnamese culture and society.

FRANCO-VIETNAMESE SCHOOL CURRICULUM

The colonial school system that emerged in Vietnam in 1918 consisted of thirteen years of education: three years of elementary school given in Vietnamese written in roman script; three years of primary education given in French; four years of vocationally oriented primary superior education given in French; and three years of French-language secondary education leading to an Indochinese baccalaureate. A university was established in 1919 which by 1930 gave only three of its original seven courses of study. About 15 percent of the school-age population went to school. Of those enrolled, 90 percent were in the elementary grades, receiving rudimentary instruction in the Vietnamese language, moral education, Western-style computational mathematics, hygiene, and/or drawing and manual labor. The other 10 percent were in primary-through-university-level education. About 9 percent were in the primary grades and were attending schools in urban areas.

The major emphasis in schooling was language acquisition.[15] In the elementary grades, between nine and fifteen hours out of a twenty-seven-hour school week were spent on languages, mostly on teaching students Vietnamese. In the primary grades between fifteen and eighteen hours a week were spent on language-learning, mostly French. At all other levels of education the French language and literature dominated the curriculum (through university training). Secondary to language was instruction in hygiene and practical science (about three hours a week at all levels, which was about half of what French schools devoted to the sciences), mathematics (about two to three hours a week), moral education (one to two hours a week), Chinese (about two and a quarter hours a week), and physical education (two and a half hours a week). History was relegated to one half hour a week, geography to one hour.

On the surface, one might assume that these schools could not help but teach what metropolitan schools taught because of the large bloc of time devoted to French-language education. Surely one might be able to assume that in teaching the French language the school was also teaching about things French, about Europe, science, the universe, and so on. Thus, despite the un-European nature of the curriculum, in teaching so much French the schools might in fact end up teaching about France. An assumption of this kind is warranted only if one can document that in fact the French-language curriculum of the schools taught about France and about contemporary European life and science. In the pages that follow I will look into the French-language curriculum of the school to show what in fact this curriculum taught. I will look specifically at the kind of information imparted about French and Vietnamese society and culture and at the curriculum's presentation of modernity and science.

Organization of the Curriculum

The French-language curriculum was organized to develop reading, listening, speaking, and writing skills simultaneously. According to the educational journals of the period, instruction was to begin with the concrete and progress to the abstract; it was also to progress from the simple to the complex. Students were supposed to first learn about objects and persons immediately in their environment and then about events and institutions, ending finally with emotions.

The curriculum of the schools, as outlined in both textbooks of the 1918 to 1938 period and the education journals published in Vietnam (*Hoc Báo, Su Pham Hoc Khóa,* and the *Bulletin Général de l'Instruction Publique*), in all grades of the elementary and primary school were grouped into "centers of interest." These centers of interest, in the order they were presented year after year, grade after grade, were the school, the family, the human body, houses, the village, food and clothing, commerce and industry, wild and domestic animals, and atmospheric phenomenon (weather, stars, seasons, time). This progression was followed also in the first two years of the primary superior grades. In each center of interest a student was taught vocabulary appropriate to the topic (e.g., parts of the body and words relating to its care were taught in the second month of each school year), grammar (with drills relating to that center of interest), a verb and its conjugation, composition (using the center of interest for composition topics), readings on the center of interest, poems designed for pronunciation drill relating to that center of interest, and dictated readings to develop listening and writing accuracy.

Table 1 shows the central focus of the readings, regardless of the apparent center of interest contained in the titles. Table 1 treats only those materials presented for classroom use in the *Bulletin of Public Instruction* for the primary grades for the 1925–26 school year through the 1938–39 school year. It

Table 1.—Topics Covered in French-Language Curriculum Guides, Primary Grades, in the *Bulletin of Public Instruction*

	1925/26–1926/27		1927/28–1928/29		1929/30–1930/31		1931/32–1932/33		1933/34–1934/35		1935/36–1936/37		1937/38–1938/39	
	Number of Readings	% of Readings	Number of Readings	% of Readings	Number of Readings	% of Readings	Number of Readings	% of Readings	Number of Readings	% of Readings	Number of Readings	% of Readings	Number of Readings	% of Readings
Descriptions of daily life														
Vietnamese or Indochinese	146	25.8	117	29.2	98	26.7	142	31.0	117	23.0	73	22.2	36	7.7
French	55	9.7	19	4.8	68	18.5	62	13.5	99	19.5	48	14.5	110	23.4
Other	23	4.1	5	1.3	5	1.5	4	.9	0		3	.9	2	.4
Total	224	39.6	141	35.3	171	46.7	208	45.4	216	42.5	124	37.6	148	31.5
Vietnamese art and culture	9	1.6	10	2.5	2	.5	9	2.0	7	1.4	0		0	
Race														
Vietnamese	8	1.4	4	1.0	0		0		0		0		0	
Other	5	.9	1	.3	0		9	2.0	1	.2	0		0	
Morality	18	3.2	13	3.3	21	5.7	22	4.8	0		4	1.2	2	.4
Description and emulation of														

Modern and tra-ditional schools	18	3.2	14	3.5	1	.3	6	1.3	0		5	1.5	23	4.9
School behavior	26	4.6	16	4.0	4	1.1	0		0		4	1.2	8	1.7
French schools	1	.2	0		2	.5	1	.2	2	.4	9	2.8	0	
Total	45	8.0	30	7.5	7	1.9	7	1.5	2	.4	18	5.5	31	6.6
Hygiene and science	41	7.3	16	4.0	5	1.4	16	3.5	4	.8	16	4.8	32	6.8
Industry, transportation, communication	68	12.0	66	16.4	45	12.3	35	7.6	89	17.6	26	7.9	44	9.4
Political information														
Government services and structure	17	3.0	11	2.8	3	.8	0		8	1.6	4	1.2	5	1.1
Citizens' duties and loyalties	6	1.1	8	2.0	7	1.9	3	.7	1	.2	1	.3	0	
Total	23	4.1	19	4.8	10	2.7	3	.7	9	1.8	5	1.5	5	1.1
Nature description														
General	30	5.3	29	7.3	14	3.8	37	8.1	50	9.9	43	13.1	115	24.4
Indochina	27	4.8	22	5.5	19	5.2	45	9.8	29	5.7	10	3.0	5	1.1
Total	57	10.1	51	12.8	33	9.0	82	17.9	79	15.6	53	16.1	120	25.5
Miscellaneous	17	3.0	9	2.3	17	4.6	48	10.5	32	6.3	11	3.3	33	7.0
Total number readings	565		399		367		458		507		330		470	

indicates more than anything else how the curriculum of the schools tended to teach students about everyday life, family, villages, houses, food, dress, local markets, rites and festivals, etc., things that students probably already knew about before they came to school. Second, it is clear from table 1 that the curriculum taught about Vietnamese (or Indochinese) life more than it did about French life. In short, the schools taught Vietnamese children about life in Vietnam rather than about France. In teaching about Vietnam, however, the French-language curriculum taught about the country as seen through French eyes. The materials on daily life included in school textbooks and the curriculum guides of the education journals, except for one or two pieces, were written by Frenchmen or Eurasians. Some were administrators, such as Governor-General Pasquier, who glorified the Vietnamese past. Still others were anthropologists whose interest was in depicting primitive cultures. Thus, it was not unusual for the curriculum to present the child with portraits of superstitious Vietnamese women who made offerings of incense when their children got ill, petty traders, a Vietnamese family ruled absolutely and tyranically by a father, etc.[16] While the curriculum dealt considerably with the Vietnamese family's peculiar traits and customs, students were told to respect and love their families, to preserve family traditions and ways; for not only did the students owe this to their parents in return for what their parents had done for them (such as send them to school), but only in so doing would they be happy.[17]

When the curriculum brought in materials on French family life, it did so only to bolster the desirability of Vietnamese children preserving their family ways. Lamartine, Hugo, and other French writers' works were paraded for Vietnamese children to understand that traditionalism was in fact the way of modern peoples.

Illustrative of the curriculum's emphasis on Vietnamese life and the way it described French ways only to bolster the desirability of maintaining Vietnam as it was are the units on the village used in French-language instruction. When the curriculum described the village, it focused on Vietnamese villages, their economic life (primarily rice farming), political governance, and the emotions that the village of birth should evoke. It spent considerable time describing how tenuous village life had been before the French came to rule Vietnam. Not only were villages beset by pirates, famines, and floods; they were also exploited by ignorant, superstitious, self-seeking mandarins who had no concern for the welfare of villagers because they had been educated in Vietnamese traditions.[18] However, under French tutelage, villages had "modernized." Modernity was depicted as follows:

> . . . it [the village] possesses a pretty school of three classes constructed recently. You can travel there in a car via a paved road which is linked to the provincial highway.
>
> At the head of the village is a council of notables, a mayor, an adjunct, a communal secretary, and a treasurer. They are concerned with village welfare and make [the village] a happier and prosperous place.[19]

Modernity was also the absence of pirates to disturb the traditional rice farmers. Modern feelings consisted of nostalgia for the village of birth, and children were told not to immigrate to the cities.[20]

While descriptions of daily life dominated the curriculum, they were by no means the only thing handled in the curriculum. French-language instruction did contain a great deal of material on industry, transportation, and communication (the second most frequently covered category of instructional content). Science was usually included in the unit labeled "Commerce, Transportation, and Industry," although I tabulated it separately in table 1.

A close look at the materials presented for student use reveals that science, industry, technology, trade, etc., were not necessarily promoted through the schools. Rather, the school curriculum contained quaint descriptions of Vietnamese markets, general emulations of rice farming as a modern occupation, and depictions of modern transportation as something terrifying. One class lesson, typical of those presented in textbooks and suggested by school authorities in curriculum guides, described trains as "monsters":

> The monster approaches; you can already hear it slowing down; it sobs out a breath of steam that the rays from the foyer illuminate; its eyes of fire grow larger and larger, exuding a blinding light.
>
> You can make out right now the form of a beast, massive and thickset. . . .[21]

Airplanes were presented as fantastic birds. The units also presented romantic descriptions of pedicabs and sampans.[22]

The industries presented in the French-language curriculum were farming, particularly rice production as Vietnamese had practiced it for centuries, and traditional crafts such as lacquering, carpentry, and weaving. The only commerce described were petty traders in the rural markets of Vietnam, French boutiques, and Les Halles, the market center in Paris. Modern industry, thus, was what Vietnamese already had.

Science was extolled more than described in the curriculum, and the adulations of science were tinged with ambivalence. The science presented to the youth of Vietnam consisted of biographical sketches of Pasteur and Curie and emphasized their love for their rural villages and parents. While course materials told students to be "scientific," they argued for the necessity of Art and the Ideal. Each time course materials eulogized Pasteur, they praised Victor Hugo and pointed out that letters were as important as science. Such readings were attempts to put a damper on Vietnamese aspirations to "science." The curriculum never taught scientific terminology. It comes as little wonder that when the schools came to teaching science and hygiene, those classes became first and foremost courses in the French language. Science curriculum specialists complained that language teaching in the school simply failed to provide the vocabulary necessary for teachers to instruct their students in physics, chemistry, hygiene, or even general science.[23]

Taken as a whole, the course materials on science, industry, commerce, and transportation focused more on conveying images of these topics that were congruent with Vietnam as it was —a raw-material producer with little or no industry. French industry was never depicted, since it had little to do with French images of a "modern" Vietnam. The norm of modernity was perhaps accepted, but its content was transformed into crafts and farming. Likewise, the curriculum professed to promote science, but it ended up devaluing science and industry, putting it in its place, perhaps secondary to literary pursuits.

From table 1 it is clear that the third largest category of materials that the curriculum contained was grouped under nature description. This category of materials exemplified the more trivial aspects of curricular content. It abounded with sunsets, storms of every imaginable variety, starry nights, woodlands, rice fields, the beauty of animals, and the like. The materials emphasized more than anything else the wild beauties of nature, man's need to stand in awe of nature, and his unity with it.

Finally, the school curriculum spent a great deal of time recommending adult occupations to children. Table 2 indicates the type of work that the French-language curriculum commended to Vietnam's future elite. About 45 percent of all course materials on work (aggregated from 1925 to 1939) recommended that urban students attending schools on the primary level become traditional rice farmers, while about 29.2 percent suggested artisan/crafts occupations like lacquering, carpentry, masonry, and fishing. Another 13.9 percent urged manual labor and about 8.3 percent exhorted students to work at any job. Less than .6 percent of the materials suggested government jobs or literary pursuits; 3.1 percent suggested business. In short, the curriculum promoted occupations that were open traditionally to the mass of Vietnamese, precisely as Vietnamese have always done them. It did not suggest occupations in medicine, teaching, the sciences, or engineering. The difference between the occupations suggested by the curriculum and work that Vietnamese have traditionally done is that Vietnamese were being dissuaded from taking leadership in their own society or from engaging in knowledge production and dissemination. The scholar, so much glorified in Vietnamese traditions, was actually ignored as a potential role for children. The poet, however, was presented as a starving person who sat in a garret spinning out verses that no one read or heard and that had little utility for anyone.

The French-language curriculum, in short, was not a vehicle for imbuing Vietnamese youth with new ideas of anything that

Table 2.—Work Emulated in *BGIP* School Section, French-Language Lesson Readings—Primary Grades

Year	Farmer		Worker		Trader-businessman		Artisan-craftsman		Intellectual-government worker		Nonspecific occupation		Total
	Number of Readings	% of Readings	Number of Readings	% of Readings	Number of Readings	% of Readings	Number of Readings	% of Readings	Number of Readings	% of Readings	Number of Readings	% of Readings	
1925/26	10	55.5	5	27.8	1	5.6	2	11.1	0		0		18
1926/27	13	40.6	4	12.5	2	6.3	9	28.1	0		4	12.5	32
1927/28	9	33.4	5	18.5	1	3.7	9	33.3	0		3	11.1	27
1928/29	1	8.3	4	33.4	0		1	8.3	0		6	50.0	12
1929/30	16	57.2	2	7.1	0		7	25.0	0		3	10.7	28
1930/31	10	35.8	6	21.4	0		7	25.0	2	7.1	3	10.7	28
1931/32	2	14.3	3	21.4	0		8	57.2	0		1	7.1	14
1932/33	4	80.0	1	20.0	0		0		0		0		5
1933/34	23	60.5	2	5.3	0		13	34.2	0		0		38
1934/35	19	63.4	8	26.7	1	3.3	1	3.3	0		1	3.3	30
1935/36	23	56.0	2	4.9	0		12	29.3	0		4	9.8	41
1936/37	15	46.9	1	3.1	0		15	46.9	0		1	3.1	32
1937/38	15	51.7	2	6.9	0		8	27.6	0		4	13.8	29
1938/39	2	7.7	5	19.2	6	23.1	13	50.0	0		0		26
Total all years	162	44.9	50	13.9	11	3.1	105	29.2	2	.6	30	8.3	360

resembled "modern" education or contemporary French education. Rather, if the curriculum is any indication, the school countered Vietnamese aspirations to modernity by defining it as subsistence rice farming, handicrafts, affection for rural villages, gushing feelings for parents, beautiful sunsets, sampans, and pedicabs. When the schools taught the French language, they consciously expurgated how much of French culture would be taught. They presented France to the child as a country of small hamlets and people who loved their mothers. The schools rarely, if ever, taught about French cities, French political or social organization, factories, science, or technology. Rather, the schools used the French-language curriculum and the views it promoted of what it was to be modern to preempt or substitute for Vietnamese independent conceptions of these things. Of this most Vietnamese were aware. The monied urban elite sought to send their children to France for their entire education, claiming, as did Bui-Quang-Chieu, that only there could their children get a modern education.[24] Other Vietnamese concluded that no modern education could be gotten in these schools and formed independent self-study and self-education societies like the Society for the Diffusion of Quôc-Ngũ. The only complaint about the schools that most members of the Vietnamese elite and villagers shared was that they thwarted not only Vietnamese self-expression, they actually stood in the way of autonomous change. As such, the schooling offered by the colonialists condemned the nation to extinction. The only persons who supported such schools were the French rulers and the neotraditionalist elite the French kept in power. For these neotraditionalists, modernity, or any change at all, threatened their continued class positions. They would have preferred "modern" education to consist solely of memorizing a few Chinese characters that emphasized to the youth the necessity of obedience and loyalty.

There is no question that the French planned the education given in these schools as a backward education. Colonial educators agreed with politicians on the need to keep Vietnamese dependent on French rule. Vietnamese could provide raw materials such as rubber and coal—activities requiring little more than unskilled manual labor. However, in the colonial order there was no room for industrialization in Vietnam. A 1926 report on vocational and technical education said as much, as did a 1938 report on whether even French education designed for Europeans in Vietnam should follow metropolitan reforms. After all, said the 1938 report, French with technical skills and scientific training could not be absorbed by any Vietnamese industry in the near future. Further, colonial educators also saw education as a means of insuring social stability and bemoaned changes in Vietnamese society that followed the French takeover. Change, as they saw it, was bound to be negative. Thus, they felt that the schools should resurrect the old ways. Such was the reasoning of Governor-General Pierre Pasquier, as well as of Director of Public Instruction Blanchard de la Brosse, who argued that schooling should be designed to promote Vietnamese traditions —this was the mission of the schools. Nowhere was this clearer than in the village schools promoted in the 1920s and the half-day, half-farm school of the 1930s designed by Governor-General Brevie. Schools, according to French colonial officials, were to resurrect traditional culture even on the elite level. Schools could do this by redesigning Vietnamese expectations of the rewards of modernity and progress.

TOWARD A THEORY OF SUBSTITUTION AND PREEMPTION

This essay has described in some detail school policy and curriculum in colonial Vietnam to clarify our thinking about colonial education policy and the nature of colonial schools. On one level it has shown that if we wish to know what school policy in fact is, we must go beyond statements issued by ideologues of empire stationed in the metropole and the rhetoric of those who enunciate policy. To understand colonial education we must look at local planning, the factors that shape it, the institutions that evolve, and what those institutions propose to teach those who go to them. Analysis at this level gives an impression quite different from, if not at variance with, that which arises out of policy statements intended for metropolitan consumption. The methodological point is of some importance. Of more significance, however, is what analysis of this sort shows, which analysis confined to policy statements does not show.

Most of our knowledge of colonial education has centered on the intent of Europeans, influenced only by themselves, not by the colonized, or, if by the colonized, only peripherally. Even scholars like Remi Clignet, who correctly has argued that those who went to colonial schools affected them, tend to see the colonized as reactive rather than active participants in education.[25] Their role boils down to picking what the colonizer chooses to offer and assimilating it into their individual cognitive and cultural modes. While Clignet can be credited with first pointing out the influence of the colonized on the schools, that influence was far greater than he presupposed, and, in the case of Vietnam, it was not only the influence of individual colonized but the influence of the colonized's institutions. Village schools of characters, widespread in precolonial Vietnam, defied any form of foreign domination. Had there been no school system capable of organizing resistance to the French, colonial schools might not have become as great a concern on the part of the government, nor would they have taken the course they did. It was not only Vietnamese traditional education that impelled the French to develop their own brand of education; it was also Vietnamese efforts at autonomous educational change, change that would lead to modernity. The Dong Kinh Free School was a catalyst to colonial educational planning just as much as the extensive network of the village schools of characters. The Dong Kinh Free School represented Vietnamese freely sifting through European technology, science, and political ideology; Asian patterns of educational reform, particularly Japanese and Chinese; and Vietnamese traditions to educate the youth. The Dong Kinh Free School had ties not only to Westernized urban elites but also to the village schools and the village scholar tradition. Coming when they did, educational planning and the development of colonial schools were essentially a reaction to *Vietnamese institutions.* That reaction involved undermining autonomy by substituting for traditional schools and preempting any attempts at autonomous change. Developing colonial schools, in short, had little to do with training skilled workers, with "civilizing" or assimilating Vietnamese, or allowing them to develop along their own lines.

The notion that colonial schools were substitutes for indigenous traditional institutions and preempted change toward autonomy has its basis not only in the atmosphere and timing in which educational planning began; evidence for it also exists in subsequent direction of government educational efforts. In the twentieth century the government made its education the sole education available to Vietnamese, both mass and elite. It did so by shutting down the village schools of characters and sent government-trained teachers to work in the villages to counteract the influence the teachers of characters had. It also controlled other forms of education, including French schools that served urban Vietnamese, forcing these schools to adhere to government-prescribed Franco-Vietnamese curriculum. Those schools that offered French education were regulated so that their student bodies would be composed solely of Europeans and Eurasians. Additionally, travel abroad, including to France, was restricted. Such policies prevented any Vietnamese initiatives for educational change and restricted those who wished to become educated to learning what the government thought they ought to learn.

The school curriculum, more than anything else, demonstrates the extent to which schooling not only substituted for traditional education but also how it militated against change of any nature. School curriculum stressed traditional ways as the French understood them or wanted to understand them and argued that the modern world was in fact what Vietnam was under the French. It oriented students, both of the urban elite and of the peasantry, toward rice farming and indigenous trade and not to any changed economic relationships. As a student progressed in school, he learned more and more about Vietnamese antiquity and less and less about science and technology than his French peers. Even in learning French, he learned little about the European world. What he learned about it only pointed to villages based on rice farming, veneration of ancestors, and the like.,

Colonial schools thwarted autonomy, be it traditional or oriented toward change. It was the schools rather than the Vietnamese that were "reactive," for the establishment of the schools had more to do with responding to Vietnamese institutions that threatened the colonial order than with responding to the desires and defined administrative needs of the colonizer.

I have explained the development of colonial schools in terms of preemption and substitution for indigenous institutions and attempts at modernization. I have documented this in the case of Vietnam. Such an explanation is probably not solely applicable in the Vietnamese case and extends to other colonial situations. More research on education in other British, French, Dutch, and German colonies may well indicate that the rate of school development and the nature of the education imparted in them depended on the mobilization potential of indigenous educational institutions and the degree to which colonized peoples attempted autonomous educational change.

Notes

1. An excellent discussion of the role of the village teacher can be found in Nguyen Khac Vien, "Marxism and Confucianism in Vietnam," in Nguyen Khac Vien, *Tradition and Revolution in Vietnam* (Berkeley: Indochina Resource Center, 1974); Phan-Boi-Chau, "Memoires," in *France-Asie/Asia,* no. 194–95 (¾ Quartier, 1968): 3–201.
2. See Milton Osborne, *The French Presence in Cambodia and Cochinchina: Rule and Response* (Ithaca: Cornell University Press, 1969); John De Francis, *Language, Government and Writing in Vietnam* (Honolulu: University of Hawaii Press, in press).
3. My discussion of the Dong Kinh School and *Dong-De* is based on Vu-Duc-Bang, "The Dong Kinh Free School Movement, 1907–1908," in Walter Vella, ed., *Aspects of Vietnamese History* (Honolulu: Asian Studies Program, University of Hawaii Press, 1973), pp. 30–95; David Marr, *Vietnamese Anticolonialism, 1885–1925* (Berkeley: University of California Press, 1971), chap. 4.
4. Gail P. Kelly, "Franco-Vietnamese Schools, 1918 to 1938" (Unpublished Ph.D. dissertation, University of Wisconsin, 1975), chap. 2.
5. A list of participants can be found in "Conseil de Perfectionnement de l'Enseignement Indigène," in *L'Avenir du Tonkin,* 30è Année, no. 5467 (10 April 1913): 3. A report of the Council's work up to about 1909 can be found in Henri Gourdon, *L'Énseignement des Indigènes en Indochine* (Paris: Société Générale d'Imprimerie et d'Edition Leve, 1910). *L'Asie-Française* reported extensively on the Council's works.
6. See "L'Indochine—Le Congrès de Perfectionnement de l'Enseignement Indigène," in *L'Asie-française,* 10è Année, no. 115 (October 1910), pp. 434–36.

7. See Gourdon, *L'Énseignement des Indigènes;* Deletie, *L'Énseignement Traditionnel* (Paris, 1908); G. Prêtre, "L'Enseignement Indigène en Indochine," in *L'Asie-Française,* 12è Année, no. 137 (August 1912), p. 311. (This is a report prepared for the Governor-General. Prêtre was Inspector General of Schools in Indochina.)
8. See especially "La Session du Conseil de Perfectionnement de l'Enseignement Indigène en Indochine," in *L'Asie-Française,* 10è Année, no. 116 (November 1910), pp. 464–68; Prêtre, "Enseignement Indigène en Indochine."
9. "La Ville—Ouverture de la 4è Session du Conseil de Perfectionnement de l'Enseignement Indigène," in *L'Avenir du Tonkin,* 30è Année, no. 5466 (9 April 1913), pp. 2–3.
10. Ibid., p. 3.
11. See "Decret Reglementant l'Ouverture et le Fonctionnement des Establissements d'Enseignement Privé en Indochine (Promulgé 18 September 1924)," in *Journal Officiel de l'Indochine Française,* 36è Année, no. 79 (1 October 1924), pp. 1847–49.
12. Gouvernement Général de l'Indochine, *Rapports au Grand Conseil des Intérêts Economiques et Financiers et au Conseil de Gouvernement, Deuxième Partie: Fonctionnement des Divers Services Indochinois* (1925), Tableau, "Enseignement Privé en Indochine" (no page number given).
13. See 18 September 1924, "Arrêté relatif à l'Enseignement en Langue Indigène au Cycle Primaire Franco-Indigène," art. 135, in *Journal Officiel de l'Indochine Française,* 36è Année, no. 3 (November 1924), pp. 39–40.
14. See Gouvernement Général de l'Indochine, *Rapports au Grand Conseil des Intérêts Economiques et Financiers et au Conseil de Gouvernement. Deuxième Partie: Fonctionnement des Divers Services Indochinois* (1930), Tableau, "Depenses pour Chacun des Budgets de l'Indochine," 1936, p. 119. In 1922, for example, 10.05 percent of the Tonkin, 11.31 percent of the Cochinchina, and 9.70 percent of the Annam budgets were allocated to education; in 1930 the figures were 14.23 percent in Tonkin, 13.47 percent in Cochinchina, and 14.45 percent in Annam. In 1936 the percent of budgets spent on education was 13.39 percent in Tonkin,

12.22 percent in Cochinchina, and 10.96 percent in Annam. Kenya, for example, in 1967 spent 7 percent of its budget on education. See Ernest Stabler, *Education Since Uhuru: The Schools of Kenya* (Middletown, Conn.: Wesleyan University Press, 1969).

15. My discussion of the school curriculum is based on school law as published in the *Journal Officiel de l'Indochine Française* from 1917 to 1939 and curricular guides appearing in *Hoc Báo,* the Tonkinese primary school official education journal, and the *Bulletin Général de l'Instruction Publique* published by the Indochinese Office of Public Instruction from 1921 on.
16. See particularly "Enseignement primaire," in *Bulletin Général de l'Instruction Publique, Partie Scolaire,* 13è Année, no. 1 (September 1933), p. 31; 12è Année, no. 1 (September 1932), p. 34.
17. See "Enseignement primaire," in *Bulletin Général de l'Instruction Publique, Partie Scolaire,* 16è Année, no. 1 (September 1936), p. 14; Dao-Van-Minh, *La Conversation Française à l'Usage des Elèves des Cours Enfantins, Preparatoires et Elémentaires des Écoles Franco-Annamities* (Nam Dinh: Impr. Nam-Viet, 1929), p. 276.
18. See, for example, "Enseignement primaire," in *Bulletin Général de l'Instruction Publique, Partie Scolaire,* 16è Année, no. 5 (January 1937), p. 149; 4è Année, no. 5 (January 1925), p. 276.
19. *Bulletin Général de l'Instruction Publique, Partie Scolaire,* 7è Année, no. 5 (January 1928), p. 292.
20. A good example of this was a poem students were required to memorize that began: "To the voice that will tell you about the city and its wonders/Open not your heart to it, peasants my friends. . . ." *Bulletin Général de l'Instruction Publique, Partie Scolaire,* 8è Année, no. 5 (January 1929), p. 306.
21. "Enseignement primaire," in *Bulletin Général de l'Instruction Publique, Partie Scolaire,* 17è Année, no. 8 (April 1938), pp. 185–86.
22. Bui-Huy-Hue and Ha-Van-Duc, *Dictées Françaises* (Hanoi: Mai-Linh, 1936), p. 88.

23. See, for example, A. Charvet, "A propos de l'Enseignement des Sciences," in *Bulletin Général de l'Instruction Publique, Partie Generale,* 4è Année, no. 3 (November 1924), pp. 27–30; no. 4 (December 1924), pp. 39–42.
24. Bui-Quang-Chieu, "Pour le Domination Indochinoise," in *Viet-Nam-Hon,* 1re Année, no. 1 (January 1926), p. 4.
25. Remi Clignet, "The Inadequacies of the Notion of Assimilation and Association in African Education," in *Journal of Modern African Studies* 8, no. 3 (1970): 425–44.

Damned If You Do, Damned If You Don't: The Dilemmas of Colonizer-Colonized Relations*

Remi Clignet

As the legitimacy of the current social order becomes open to challenge, a number of minority groups use the colonial situation as the frame of reference around which they articulate their new claims and demands. In a recent pamphlet, for example radical students are tempted to compare their plight to that of "niggers." Once more, therefore, the time has come to reassess the variety of meanings attached to the concept of colonial situations and briefly to sketch their educational implications.

Using the writings of F. Fanon, O. Mannoni, and A. Memmi as springboards, I would like first to identify the various theoretical frameworks underlying the definitions that have been given to the term "colonial situation." [1] As a second step in the analysis, I would like to demonstrate how the perceived complementarity of the positions occupied by colonizers and colonized varies with the vicious circles characteristic of the distinctive phases of colonization. This will lead me in a final part of the essay to examine the dilemmas with which colonizers and colonized are currently confronted.

THE COLONIAL SITUATION AS AN INSTITUTIONAL FRAMEWORK

Up to the early 1950s, colonial phenomena are mostly examined in historical, ethical, economic, and political terms. In such contexts, the presence of European powers in Africa, Asia, or

* Reprinted, with permission, from the *Comparative Education Review* 15 (October 1971).

South America is justified on the basis of the overall moral physical or cultural superiority of white Nations. And it is explained or criticized at a similar level of generalization and abstraction.

Classical Marxist studies, for example, tend to reject the psychological components of the colonial situation as mere superstructures of objective historical and economic forces. Insofar as they affect the colonial situation, individual systems of attitudes and behavior are perceived as the subjective translations of the objective positions occupied in productive structures. Correspondingly, this scheme of analysis leads the observer to expect a linear, simple, and universal relationship between attitudes or behaviors and the objective status achieved in the economic organization. The more privileges they derive from such a status, the more *all* individuals sharing such an experience will be obliged to construct similar sets of prejudiced beliefs and expectations regarding the exploited categories of the population. Whatever the specific nature of these categories (workers, women, colonized) the mechanisms of exploitation do not change and there are no significant variations in the treatment meted out to them.

In brief, such a theory minimizes the specificity of the colonial situation as well as it disregards potential differences between individual and global participation in the colonial situation. Indeed, in the same way as a Marxist scholar argues that the racism of an individual increases with the significance of his privileges, he will be likely to suggest that the higher the involvement of an entire nation in a colonial enterprise, the more colonialist will be the outlook of its citizens.

Against this Marxist view of the colonial situation which stresses the significance of an economic determinism, other scholars have emphasized the role of a political determinism. But they have therefore reached parallel types of conclusions in their analysis of the colonial situation. They propose thus that the colonialist attitudes and behaviors of an individual will be determined both by the nature of the regime to which he belongs and by the position he occupies in the political hierarchy. Their conclusions are hence parallel to those of Marxist researchers. Colonialism is the subjective translation of the political forces at work in the society at large, and the mechanisms underlying the emergence of corresponding attitudes and behaviors are the same for individuals and for groups.

In the educational field, the tenets of an economic or a political determinism will emphasize the universality of the educational mechanisms by which the economically or politically dominant groups of the colonizing society generalize their power onto the colonial scene. They will thus demonstrate how the selectivity underlying the recruitment of colonial students and the nature of the curriculum imposed upon them tend to perpetuate existing patterns of domination.[2] At the same time, however, they will minimize the significance of the role played by the cultural traditions of colonial peoples in their acceptance or their rejection of the experiences attached to colonial educational systems. They will also disregard the significance of eventual variations in the relations developed between colonizing teachers and colonized students.

Yet, much evidence suggests that the empirical propositions derived from these two types of determinist frameworks do not hold true. For example, Mannoni argues quite convincingly that manifestations of racism are most pervasive and intense among the unskilled white manual workers of South Africa.[3] In this country it is equally obvious that overt manifestations of antiblack, antifeminist, and antistudent feelings are more frequent and more intense among white lower classes than among any other social group. Similarly, many black Americans report that they receive a warmer welcome in the Netherlands (whose colonial past is not a model of liberalism) than in any other European country, including those without any colonial experience, such as Sweden or Norway.

It is similarly quite clear that the relationships developed between teachers and students in the colonial context cannot be entirely accounted for by the overall economic and political structures of the colonizing society nor by the position occupied by the individual teacher within such a structure.[4] In the same vein and against the views of scholars stressing the primacy of political factors in the emergence of colonialist behaviors, Memmi has illustrated the ambiguities of the French Left with regard to the colonial situation.[5] Not only is it remarkable that the Socialist Party has been a privileged seedbed for the recruitment of colonial administrators, but the Jacobinism of the whole Left has never been able to come to terms with the nationalist aspirations of the colonized.[6] Hence the liberal colonizer is often obliged to use defense mechanisms to alleviate the tensions that he experiences because of the conflicts between his ideology and his participation in the colonial situation. Some of these liberals will argue that their liberalism is applicable only in the context of industrialized nations; some of them will adopt a messianic view of the world. Ultimately, Memmi argues that the choice of the liberal colonizer is not between the Good and the Evil but between being evil and being ill at ease.

THE PSYCHOLOGICAL COMPONENTS OF THE COLONIAL SITUATION

It is then Mannoni's main achievement to have been the first scholar to emphasize the relevance of psychological dimensions and concepts for an examination of current colonial situations. To be sure, Mannoni argues, colonization is the result of certain processes of economic and political development, but colonial enterprises cannot take place without the recruitment of particular actors who are predisposed to play the roles expected of them. This view leads Mannoni to emphasize the significance of psychological motivations, and these motivations are defined as resulting from experiences undergone during early childhood.

The participation of the colonizer in the colonial situation reflects his inability to establish an adult system of interaction with others. Regardless of the overt reasons that he gives to justify his calling (altruism, desire for travel, aspirations to upward mobility, etc.), he is in effect unable to cope with the demands of his immediate social surroundings. The loneliness that he experiences in Africa and the distance that separates him both from the colonized and from his counterparts in the metropole enable him to project onto local people the dehumanized images of charming or cruel ghosts and shadows that he has been unable to control during his childhood. In short, the colonizer is the Prospero of *The Tempest.*

The colonial situation, however, develops only insofar as the colonized accepts the demands imposed upon him by the colonizer. According to Mannoni, the social arrangements that prevail in colonized societies induce types of child-rearing practices that foster personalities characterized by marked feelings of dependence and inferiority. Initially directed toward ancestors, such feelings are easily transferred to the colonizer, who is often perceived as a source of stable—and hence reassuring—power. In short, the colonized is the Caliban of *The Tempest.*

To sum up, Mannoni stresses the importance of the role played by psychological forces on participation in the colonial situation. Colonizers and colonized are prisoners of their past and more specifically of their childhood. Their interaction therefore follows patterns of development that are independent of the political and economic components of the colonial situation. There is, however, a certain asymmetry in the impact of psychological forces on the behaviors and attitudes adopted by these two types of actors. The social differentiation prevailing among industrialized nations introduces variations in familial arrangements and hence in child-rearing practices. Correspondingly, there is a marked psychological selectivity in the recruitment of colonizers, and the "Prospero complex" only characterizes those segments of the colonizing society which choose to participate in the colonial enterprise.

In contrast, the uniform nature of the social arrangements characteristic of colonized societies leads the "Caliban complex" to be evenly distributed among all social segments of such societies. In this sense psychological determinism is more powerful in the latter case. Since the colonized is perceived as definitely and uniformly unable to be a Prometheus, the crises that occur in his interaction with the colonizer are not deemed to result from an inherent need to achieve political, economic, and psychological autonomy. Rather, such crises are said to result from the fact that the colonized feels abandoned and betrayed by his colonial master. As a consequence, colonial rebellions are not and cannot be a search for independence but rather a quest for new sets of dependence.

In educational terms, such views stress the importance of cultural relativeness. Both curricula and teaching methods must be adjusted to fit the specific psychological makeup of colonized students. On the colonizer side, efforts must be made to assure a proper psychological screening of the teachers who are candidates for a career in colonial areas.[7] Whether expressed directly or in the form of a denial, their potential "Prospero complex" cannot but have adverse effects on the attitudes and behaviors of the colonized. Thus, the followers of Mannoni in the field of education are likely to prefer a micro to a macro approach to the problems raised by teaching and learning in the colonial context. Insisting on the variety of misunderstandings that the behavior and the motivations of a teacher can evoke among his pupils, they will also attempt to identify the limits within which the object of the pedagogical communication can be effectively handled by these pupils.

Yet the conceptions that Mannoni proposes of cultural relativism remain static. Conflicts that arise among various categories of actors are independent of the institutional tensions that may cause certain segments of society to oppose one another. Rather, these conflicts are likely to be read as the cyclical repetition of deep-rooted neuroses. Conflicts do not result from inequities and from growing awareness of their existence but from the individual's inability to identify the psychological limits within which he operates. Should we believe Mannoni, there would be no room for social action and for legitimate revolutions. The only solution for alleviating any conflict consists in subjecting the particular actors or group of actors who are misfits in their roles to an intensive psychotherapy.[8]

We hope now to have sketched strongly enough the contrasts and similarities between the views of Marxist scholars and of Mannoni on the problems associated with a colonial situation. The first school stresses the universality of exploitation and disregards the necessity of distinguishing between the various mechanisms by which the masters impose their power on distinctive categories of slaves. Variations in these mechanisms are only the byproducts of variations in modes of economic or political activities. In contrast, Mannoni emphasizes the specificity of the psychological mechanisms involved in the colonial situation. Such mechanisms are, however, apparently uniform across a variety of colonial situations and are unlikely to change over time, since the effects of social arrangements on child-rearing practices are deemed to be permanent. Finally, while the Marxist scheme leaves hardly any room for individual praxis, Mannoni's framework regards concerted action as irrelevant since the dominant traits of a colonial type of interaction are independent of the fixed institutional context in which they take place. At the same time, however, these two schools of thought are alike in the sense that both are universalist in scope and both disregard the problems raised by the interaction between individual actors and the particular societal context within which the interaction takes place.

THE COLONIAL SITUATION: A BRIDGE BETWEEN INSTITUTIONAL AND PSYCHOLOGICAL VIEWS

It is, then, the great merit of both Memmi and Fanon to have shown how the colonial situation involves, in effect, dialectic sets of interaction between structure and culture on the one hand and the social status of an individual and the level, as well as the form, of his self-esteem on the other. For Fanon, but particularly for Memmi, there is no doubt that although exploitation is a universal consequence of certain types of structural arrangements, it gives birth to patterns of interaction and of ideological representations that vary both with the nature of the particular group to be exploited and with the processes by which individual actors internalize the conflicting demands imposed on them. Thus the exploitative patterns of women, Jews, and colonized are specific and cannot therefore be legitimately compared. While, for example, the crux of the exploitation of women concerns their relationships with men and children, the crux of the exploitation of the colonized is cultural.[9] For the colonized is deprived of the choices that he should have in terms of his relation to his past and his present, to himself, to his peers, and to the outside world.

The stress placed on the specific situational terms of the colonial interaction leads these two authors to differ in their methodologies from a scholar like Mannoni. Far from being universal, individual dreams reflect the anxieties that accompany participation in specific sets of situations. In the colonial context the images of guns, as they emerge in the dreams of the colonial individual, are not necessarily the images of the penis but rather of the guns used by the soldiers that colonial authorities use to repress political rebellions.[10] In more general terms, dreams are not necessarily the symbolic translation of the anxieties associated with permanent traits of the human condition but of the uncertainties that accompany active or passive participation in a situation whose political and ethical outcome is problematic.[11] The anxieties of the colonized reflect his fear of being involved in a situation in which he thinks he has no control, his fear of failing to achieve independence, or the guilt associated with his refusal to participate in the struggle. The anxiety of the colonizer is symmetric. His dreams do not reflect permanent and universal sexual phantasms as much as they reflect the various feelings associated with participation in or witnessing activities of repression. Thus in *The Wretched of the Earth,* Fanon shows how the nightmares of both Frenchmen and Algerians reflect the numerous traumas that went along with the last stages of this particular colonial enterprise.[12]

The divorce between the views of Mannoni and those of Memmi or Fanon is not only methodological but political as well. Whereas the first author perceives the colonial situation as an unescapable necessity, the last two scholars view it as a result of dynamic processes and forces that are not beyond the control of individuals and of social organizations. The relative importance attached to situational factors is, however, not the same for Fanon and Memmi. The latter stresses the variety of symptoms developed by both the colonizer and the colonized as a result of the colonial situation. The former, conversely, minimizes the differential reactions of the colonizer to such a situation. Further, for Fanon, there are no distinctions between the attitudes and the behaviors of the oppressor. Drawing some analogies between anti-Semitism and racism, he writes, "During World War II, French Jews were not likely to distinguish between the anti-Semitism of Maurras and the anti-Semitism of Hitler."[13] This, however, is to forget somewhat too easily that the anti-Semitism of Maurras was a result of his nationalist prejudices. Correspondingly, some of his followers, although few in number, gave pre-eminence to nationalism over anti-Semitism during the war. Engaged in resistance activities against the Germans, they were induced not only to cooperate with Jews but also to protect them. Lastly, and especially in his later writings, Fanon believed that the pathological symptoms of the colonizer were to disappear on the very first day of independence, and therefore he did not escape to the messianism that he decried about the writings of Marxist scholars. In contrast, Memmi views the form of interaction between colonizers and colonized as likely to persist beyond the colonial situation. Individual actors do not free themselves that easily from their past.

In brief, while Fanon views *anthropological* models (based on a simple dichotomy of the yes, no, or presence-absence type) as appropriate to describe colonial phenomena, Memmi advocates the necessity of using *sociological* models (based on the principle of differential variations).[14] Indeed, there are no perfect correlations either between the objective components of the colonial situation or between the attitudes and behaviors of the actors engaged in this particular situation.

In the field of education, these two authors, implicitly or explicitly, stress the significance of the contrasts between a colonial and a metropolitan school system. Both recognize the cultural relativeness of educational problems, and both indicate that the only significant changes to take place in the educational scene are those initiated by the colonized himself.

Insofar that both Fanon and Memmi view the colonial situation as affected by dialectical forces, I would like now to turn my attention to an examination of the processes by which the perceived complementarity of the positions occupied by colonizers and colonized varies with the vicious circles characteristic of the distinctive phases of colonization.

THE DIALECTICS OF THE COLONIAL SITUATION

In *The Dominated Man,* Memmi argues that an analysis of racism reveals the following four essential elements: a) stressing the real or imaginary differences between the racist and his victim; b) assigning values to these differences to the advantage of the racist and the detriment of his victim; c) trying to make these valued differences absolute both in space and in time by generalizing from them and claiming that they are final; d) justifying any present or possible aggression or privilege.[15] As a first step, I would like to illustrate the mechanisms by which the colonizer deals with the differences that oppose him to the colonized, and this will lead me to explore the countermoves that the colonized develops in order to reply to this particular type of strategy. As a second step, however, I would like to suggest that in contrast with the views developed by Memmi and Fanon, colonialism also involves a certain blindness to intercultural differences and the assignment of absolute values to this pseudo universality. The demonstration of this last point will of course lead me to examine the responses of the colonized to this second strategy.

a) *The colonizer in the classical colonial situation.* Speaking about South America, Paulo Freire refers to the colonial situation as a culture of silence.[16] Successfully enough, the colonizer attempts to prevent the colonized from understanding his position in time and space and hence from maintaining contact with his own past or with alien cultures. Correspondingly, the colonized is only exposed to the elements of the colonizer's culture likely to facilitate a perpetuation of the colonial order.

In this sense, the colonized experiences a double alienation. The practices, ideologies, and philosophies imposed on him are alien to his framework of reference and his own tradition. His first alienation results therefore from his exposure to educational and cultural stimuli that tend to erase the significance of his own past. But his second alienation results from the selective nature of the elements of the metropolitan culture with which he is confronted. The machinery, the books, the movies, the curricula, and the labor force exported to the colonies reflect the specific needs experienced by the segments of the metropolitan society present on the local scene. As such, they offer a distorted image of the metropolitan culture.

Thus, the educational experiences offered to the graduates of the William Ponty School in French West Africa were for a long time entirely determined by the immediate needs of the colonial administration, and the curriculum offered by such a school prevented graduates from transferring to a metropolitan school, where they could acquire the same occupational rewards and opportunities as those obtained by French students. Further, patterns of recruitment into educational institutions were defined in terms alien to local structures. Whether students were recruited from leading families or the masses, the links established between schools and the remainder of the colonial society were predetermined by the processes at work in the colonizer society rather than by those underlying the functioning of the colonized world. In concrete terms, policies of recruitment into schools were more strongly influenced by the vicissitudes of the French metropolitan system than by the objective tensions developing in each one of the colonial territories.[17]

The use of such strategies requires the colonizer, however, to adopt a particular ideological stance toward the colonized. More specifically it requires him to deny the existence of a colonized culture. Fanon stresses in this respect the significance of zoological or infrahuman references in the description that the colonizer makes of his victim. "The native is declared insensible to ethics. He represents not only the absence of values but also the negation of values and in this sense he is the absolute evil."[18]

The colonized culture was denied not only by administrators or entrepreneurs but also by intellectuals. Thus colonized societies have often been referred to as ahistorical societies, meaning societies where time is only sociological—that is, made of the cyclical repetition of rituals and patterns of action associated with the changes of seasons or generations.[19] In other words, colonized societies have been deprived of their own history.

Should the colonizer recognize the existence of a colonized culture, he is still tempted to privilege those elements of such a culture that serve his own needs. The predilection of the European surrealist movement toward African masks and dances can thus be viewed as a colonialist adventure since it has arbitrarily privileged the irrationality present in African art and translated it in terms that were only meaningful by reference to the personal frustrations and expectations of the European intellectuals of the time.

The strategies used by the colonizer in the context of the colonial situation raise, however, two questions. First, is there a colonial situation in the absence of the colonizer? In other words, does the situation only exist where concrete contacts are established between the colonizer and his victim? Secondly, does the colonial situation depend on the acceptance by the colonized of the role that is imposed on him?

According to many scholars (including Fanon and Memmi), the colonial relationship exists only at the time when the colonized integrates the discourse of his masters into his silence and his passiveness.[20] In fact, the arbitrariness of the colonial situation obliges the colonized to recognize the power and the dominance of the colonizer. It is therefore to this point that we would like to turn our attention.

b) *The colonized reaction to the classical colonial situation.* The recognition by the colonized of the inferior position imposed on him leads him to try to beat the colonizer at his own game. He attempts, then, to play whitey and hence to reduce the differences that the colonizer has defined as being at the origin of his second-class status. This reduction is attempted in terms of language. Insofar as the colonized is evaluated in terms of his distance from the colonizer's cultural model, he is tempted to speak the colonizer's language with more refinement than his "master" himself and to avoid any verbal pattern that would betray his own origin.[21] This attempt is particularly evident in the case of French colonization, since French people assign a high correlation between the status of an individual and the elegance as well as the purity of his verbal and written styles.

This reduction also is attempted in terms of clothing styles. Fanon as well as Memmi have stressed the extreme sensitivity of the colonized to metropolitan fashions. This theme has been, in fact, picked up by the new generation of African movie-makers. In *Mandaby,* Ousmane Sembene shows how the current social hierarchy of many African cities is symbolized in terms of vestiary patterns. At the lower end of the continuum, one finds the Senegalese who continue to wear the traditional *boubous* because of a total lack of exposure to European fads and practices. At the intermediate levels of this continuum, one finds the individuals who wear obsolete European dresses or equipment (a tropical helmet, for example) because their lack of financial and cultural resources prevent them from keeping up with the European Joneses, a privilege that has been acquired by the *Been to,* who maintain their privileged contacts with the metropole.[22]

Further, this reduction takes place at a higher intellectual level and affects the definition that colonized peoples give of their own culture. Since colonizers never bothered to distinguish between the various types of colonized societies, many Africans or blackmen feel obliged to assert the goodness of the undifferentiated stratum to which they have been arbitrarily assigned. Fanon denounces in this respect the theme of *Negritude* that stresses arbitrarily the unity of experiences undergone by black peoples and cannot as such lead to a concrete emancipation of the colonized society and of the colonized individual.[23] In the same vein, Fanon also complains about these African intellectuals who have called many congresses to make ultimately meaningless comparisons between coins and sarcophagi. Such intellectuals, he says, identify their social functions only by reference to the definition of the role that is assigned to their white counterparts.

Finally, this reduction is attempted at the political level. Fanon criticized many African nations for defining their developmental problems in terms of a European jurisprudence. Technologically and culturally these countries seem to admit that there is only one road toward full economic and social growth and that the way toward this road has been shown once and forever by the pioneering European nations of the nineteenth century. As stated by Memmi, the problem is to determine whether the dilemma between formal and substantive liberation—that is, between national and social independence—is really universal.[24] Fanon chastises the political leaders of many new nations for having satisfied themselves with formal liberation, and hence for having imitated the developmental patterns of many European nations of the nineteenth century. By contrast Memmi recognizes that decolonization processes necessarily involve a number of sequential steps. "It is probable that the domination of one people by another initially resolves itself into a national and hence formal liberation."

To sum up, the first vicious circle inherent to the colonial relationship leads the colonizer to deny the universality of cultural, social, and psychological processes and values, while the colonized reduces this universality to the specific forms that these values and processes take in the context of colonizing societies. This conflict in the definition of the concept of universality is not unequivocal, however. Indeed, I would like to suggest that in the second vicious circle inherent to the colonial relationship, the colonizer attempts to impose his own definition of universality, while the colonized is therefore obliged to stress the significance of his own particularism.

c) *The colonizer and the assimilationist strategy.* In contrast to the views developed both by Memmi and Fanon, I submit that colonialism does not only consist of stressing and capitalizing on the real and imaginary differences that oppose the colonizer to the colonized but also of minimizing such differences. This minimization might be partial. The early missions in Ghana, for example, imposed on their pupils the same curriculum as the one meted out to lower classes in Great Britain itself.[25] As far as French colonial policies were concerned, it is also easy enough to demonstrate how the naval officers who signed treaties with the chiefs of the lower part of the Ivory Coast did so under the assumption that such chiefs had the *same* political, social, and cultural attributes as those of European kings or noblemen.[26]

This minimization of the differences that oppose colonizers to colonized might also be global. In the early days of the French colonization in Sudan, French teachers used the same books as those used in the schools of Paris and therefore expected the same performance from their local students as they would have expected from their Parisian pupils.[27] In the same vein, this assimilation was systematized after World War II, when the French government introduced into its colonies the same educational programs, curricula, and techniques as those used in French metropolitan institutions.

The minimization of cultural differences between colonizer and colonized might be the result of ignorance. In this case, it is likely to take place in the first phases of the colonial enterprise when the anxiety of the colonizer is heightened by his exposure to an unknown and hence frightening environment. It is, however, also the result of political pressures. As the number of colonized able to "minimize differences" between their own cultural standing and that of the colonizer increases, they are likely to challenge the legitimacy of the existing social order. "Assimilation" becomes the ideological framework within which the colonizer stresses the universality of his own culture and reduces the aspirations toward upward mobility experienced by the colonized into individual rather than collective terms.

The very use of the word *assimilation* in the language of the colonizer is suggestive enough of its colonialist overtone. Indeed it is most often used in a passive form (blacks, Africans, etc., should or should not be assimilated). The use of this passive form suggests that the colonized is reduced once more to the role of an object. In fact, the colonizer attaches to his own policies an ideological value that introduces confusion between the means and the ends of the corresponding practices.[28] While the ends of such policies are the superimposition of metropolitan structures and processes, their success depends on the degree to which the colonized actively adapts his framework of analysis and action to the new legal and cultural demands of the colonizer. In its current political usage, the word *assimilation* is therefore colonialist, since it sanctions the unilateral concession of equality by the colonizer to his victim and does not differentiate between the perspectives of analysis of the two sets of actors present in the colonial situation.

d) *The colonized and the assimilationist game.* In fact, as the colonizer stresses the universality of his egalitarianism and emphasizes the value of assimilative policies, the colonized is induced in turn to claim that the differences that oppose him to his master make this universality impossible and illusory. As Senghor became an important figure in the French metropolitan political and literary Establishment, he became increasingly anxious to celebrate the specific virtues of black cultures, even though this celebration might reinforce the stereotypes held by the colonizer. Similarly, his desire to find authentically African solutions to the colonial dilemma leads Fanon to believe that African revolutionaries should move into the hinterland and work with the rural proletariat; for if the African revolution is to come it will be necessarily that of farmers who have been the most severely and cruelly exploited by the colonizers. Taking this view, which differs from those held by Marxist historians, he seems thus to suggest that violence that goes with revolutionary activities is the result of absolute rather than relative deprivation.[29] Similarly, and against the views of many African political leaders, Fanon indirectly magnifies the particularist values attached to ethnicity. Insofar as he perceives the role of the African intellectual as consisting of plowing back into his past to rediscover the golden era that has been shattered by the impact of colonization, he insists on the necessity of restoring the individual sense of national dignity and self-esteem. Yet, he has hardly addressed himself to the question of the relationship between national culture and ethnicity, and many of his writings seem likely to promote or justify types of ethnic contradictions incompatible with the processes of nation building he was so anxious to facilitate.

THE NATURE OF THE CHOICES OPEN TO THE COLONIZED

Thus far, we hope to have underlined strongly enough the nature of the dialectical processes underlying the relationships between colonizer and colonized. We hope also to have shown strongly enough how, thus far, such processes are associated with mere reversals in the relative positions held by the relevant categories of actors. Whatever their outcome, the development of such processes depends, however, exclusively on the actions undertaken by the colonized. The greatest contribution of Fanon, it seems to me, is that he sketched the legitimate aspects of historical violence in this respect and showed how the transcendence of the vicious circles associated with the various phases of colonization is a function of the extent to which the exploited effectively takes his own fate in his hands. What has been done by the colonizer can only be undone by the colonized, and this is true not only of colonial exploitation but of all forms of exploitation.

Yet the colonized remains confronted with a series of difficult choices in this respect. The first one pertains to his use of the relationships between cultural and structural factors. The second one concerns the use that he makes of time, and the third one concerns his definition of the links between social or personal status and self-esteem.

First, the governments of new African nations are confronted with a task whose requirements are apparently mutually exclusive. On the one hand, the social and economic development of these nations demands an intensive mobilization of the masses. This mobilization can only be achieved by stressing the specificity of the cultural heritage of the new nation and hence by imposing a particularist African curriculum on the variety of local educational institutions. On the other hand, however, this mobilization is only an indispensable tool for enhancing and accelerating the overall level of economic and political achievement of the entire social system and for making it more competitive in international deals and bargains. Thus African leaders must choose between the formation of a particularist elite with deep roots in the historical and social substratum of the local society and the formation of a universalist elite able to converse and compete freely with their counterparts elsewhere. Similarly, the leaders of new African nations are confronted with conflicting notions regarding the consequences attached to the present nature of ethnic differentiation. While this differentiation, which is a part of their cultural heritage, introduces particularistic systems of social interaction, for example, in the evaluation of students' or of workers' performances, the continuing but temporary presence of European technical assistants, indifferent to local history and tradition, guarantees more universalism and objectivity in such a system of interaction.[30] In short, insofar as liberation is both cultural and structural, the colonized must reconcile the diverging demands of specificity and particularism on the one hand, uniformity and universalism on the other.

This dilemma is not, however, specific to African nations, and black Americans, for example, are confronted with similar choices in this respect. On the one hand, the Black Panthers stress the primacy of political factors in economic and social decisions. They argue, therefore, that meaningful changes in the American system of race relations can only be produced by a mobilization of individual black aspirations and orientations, hence by the acquisition of a specific black power. On the other hand, a man like Bayard Rustin claims that Afro-American studies, deemed to be the tool necessary for the mobilization of black power, are not going to provide black youths with the kinds of differentiated skills necessary to take advantage of existing economic opportunities. In short, in all cases, the colonized or the exploited must recognize that independence implies both a cultural sense of self-identity and a structural sense of equal competition with others.

To reconcile the diverging demands of cultural and structural emancipation raises the second dilemma that I have mentioned and which pertains to the notion of time. The colonized must indeed recognize that the challenges he makes represent only limited phases of the dialectical processes involved in the colonial situation. For example, the stand currently taken by the Black Panthers in this country is acceptable only insofar as it is defined as a temporary, although necessary, step toward the real emancipation of black Americans.

The main problem with which colonized leaders are confronted in this respect pertains therefore to the definition of the processes by which a particular ideology or theme of mobilization becomes obsolete or irrelevant. In the field of education, for example, African leaders who had condemned the introduction of agricultural components in school curricula as a form of colonialism must recognize the value of such an introduction after they have gained a certain level of political independence. Similarly, they must select among traditional themes those which are likely to have a real and positive impact on the patterns of development that they want to pursue. To give a specific example, is polygyny relevant to the various experiences of African socialism? If so, does this institution exert a positive or negative influence on such experiences? Where are the wheats and the chaffs of their historical legacies and how can they capitalize on our past without falling into the apparently conservative trap that Mannoni was unable to avoid? Symmetrically, however, the leaders of new nations must also avoid the pitfalls inherent to a variety of messianisms. Memmi reproaches Fanon, and rightly so, for adopting a Manichean philosophy and believing much too easily that the day the colonial oppression ceases, the colonized gets immediately rid of the old man and appears entirely new before our eyes.[31]

This leads us finally to the examination of the last dilemma that we have mentioned. To bring colonization to an end is both a collective and individual adventure since it involves both structural and cultural processes, social and psychological forces. Indeed the end of the colonialist relationship requires a new definition of universality which takes into account the equality and the diversity of individual actors, as well as the differentiation between the optimal objective conditions for their participation into concerted action and the subjective conditions underlying their individual commitment to a new order. To be free is not only to be free from exploitation but also to be free from one's self. To be free is not only to reverse the terms of the social dialectics but also to recognize the significance and the limits of interdependence.

THE CHOICES OF THE COLONIZER

Clearly, the first obligation of the colonizer is to accept the notion that the abolition of the colonial situation requires the colonized to take significant and autonomous initiatives. Often enough, the former colonizer remains tempted to superimpose his own values and own strategies on those adopted by the colonized. Although they are undoubtedly conservative, the writings of Mannoni remain timely when he warns colonizers against the negative implications of those of their behaviors which are dictated by their own contradictions rather than by an appreciation of the needs experienced by the colonized. These warnings could, for example, apply to many so-called radical educators in this country who blame the current educational system for "stifling individual creativity" and seem unable to see that this reproach is both trivial and culture-bound. Indeed, the main reproach that American poor and blacks seem to make to the school system is not this one. Their view is that the system has unduly deprived them from real opportunities for upward mobility, and it is quite clear that the two reproaches are not necessarily complementary of each other. In short, radical educators seem prone to export their anxieties about their own creativity to the slum scene, rather than to listen attentively to the demands of slum dwellers.[32]

Similarly, the former colonizer must avoid generalizing his theoretical and methodological choices on an *a priori* basis to the colonial scene.[33] The main contributions of Memmi and Fanon are their stress on the specificity of each type of exploitation. Again, this contribution appears to be quite significant at a time when students or women assimilate in a "colonialist" fashion the plight of the black or of the workers to their own problems and deny therefore the fact that forms of oppression vary with each situation and each mode of institutional participation.[34]

These two pitfalls implicitly suggest the importance of cultural relativism. This importance, however, is problematic insofar as this relativism could very well constitute an excuse for maintaining the status quo. Hence, the former colonizer must also examine the processes that prevent the colonized from receiving or integrating communications from the external environment. In the field of education, for example, it is quite clear that while the necessity of an Africanization of the curriculum is recognized, too little attention is still paid to the problems raised by an Africanization of the teaching style. It looks as if cultural relativeness is an accepted notion with regard to the *content* of communications but not as far as their *processes* are concerned. Yet, is it not the task of the former colonizer to contribute to reducing the misunderstandings associated with a lack of communication? Obviously, the first aspect of Africanization is more directly appealing at the political level than the second one. But does it mean that it is necessarily more moral? The dilemma experienced by the former colonizer is perhaps, then, to reconcile the diverging demands of cultural relativeness and of planned change, of short-term political investments and of long pedagogical efforts.

CONCLUSION

In the last two sections we have briefly sketched the variety of dilemmas with which colonizers and colonized are confronted. Insofar as these dilemmas are symmetric of each other, the main problem remains to determine whether both can be solved. An African novelist gives us a pessimistic answer to this query:

> The Chinese have a game that they call the connecting link. They capture two birds and tie them together, loosely with a thin but strong and long rope. When the birds are released, they think they are free and take their flight, rejoicing in the wideness of the sky. But suddenly crack, the cord is stretched taut. They flutter and whirl in all directions, blood drips from their bruised wings while fluffers and fluff fall on the onlookers. . . . Sometimes, the cord gets tangled in a tree, sometimes it twines around the birds and they struggle as though caught in a trap, peck at each other's eye, beaks and wings and if Providence does not impale them on a

> branch, one of them dies before the game is over. Alone. Or with the other. Both of them. Together. Strangled. Blinded. Mankind is such a bird. We are all victims of the game. All of us without exception.[35]

The query is then to decide whether interactions between contradictory terms (man/woman, worker/manager, colonizer/colonized, teacher/student) constitute a collection of independent zero sum games, as the Chinese game suggests, or whether these collections of couples of "birds" can transcend the cruel game imposed on them. The beginning of all colonial situations did generate a number of myths. So does their end.

Notes

1. O. Mannoni, *Psychologie de la Colonisation* (Paris: Le Seuil, 1950); A. Memmi, *Portrait du Colonisateur et Portrait du Colonisé* (Paris: Pauvert, 1966); A. Memmi, *The Dominated Man* (Boston: Beacon Press, 1968); F. Fanon, *Peaux Noires et Masques Blancs* (Paris: Le Seuil, 1952); F. Fanon, *Les Damnés de la Terre* (Paris: Maspero, 1961); F. Fanon, *Toward the African Revolution* (New York: Grove Press, 1967).
2. For an example of such a school, see A. Monmouni, *Education in Africa* (New York: Praeger, 1968).
3. O. Mannoni, *Psychologie de la Colonisation,* p. 16.
4. It should be noted, indeed, that an implicit hostility developed between French colonial officers and teachers whom they accused of fomenting agitation in their classrooms. Many French schoolteachers have been in fact the first victims of a certain type of colonial oppression.
5. In West Africa, the most repressive administrators have often been members of the Socialist Party. Similarly it is noteworthy that the most vicious opponents of Algerian nationalism were G. Mollet, R. Lacoste, and M. Lejeune, all high officials of the French Left. Finally, it was quite clear that the Communist Party did not strongly support the efforts of the nationalists in Algeria. Thus, like other members of the French society, the French Left has been markedly influenced by the ideology pertaining to centralization. All these people perceived the nationalist aspirations of the colonized as leading to undesirable forms of social reactions.
6. A. Memmi, *Portrait du Colonisateur,* chap. 2.
7. See O. Mannoni, *Psychologie de la Colonisation,* chap. 6.
8. Obviously Mannoni is not the only author to take such a stand. It is also quite apparent that L. Feuer and B. Bettelheim tend to minimize the impact of institutional forces in

the development of student unrest. For illustrations of such positions, see L. Feuer, *The Conflict of Generations: The Character and Significance of Student Movements* (New York: Basic Books, 1969), and B. Bettelheim, "The Roots of Radicalism," in *Playboy* (March 1971), pp. 106, 177–80.

9. See A. Memmi, *The Dominated Man*, chap. 12.
10. See F. Fanon, *Peaux Noires et Masques Blancs,* chap. 4.
11. P. Naville, *Psychologie Marxisme et Materialisme,* as quoted by F. Fanon, *Peaux Noires et Masques Blancs,* chap. 4.
12. F. Fanon, *Les Damnés de la Terre,* chap. 5.
13. F. Fanon, *Peaux Noires et Masques Blancs,* p. 92.
14. See C. Lévi-Strauss, *Anthropologie Structurale* (Paris: Plon, 1958), for a discussion of the determinants and implications of such a distinction.
15. A. Memmi, *The Dominated Man,* "Racism and Oppression: Attempt at a Definition."
16. See A. Silva, "La Pedagogie de Paulo Freire," in *Etudes* 333 (December 1970): 656–72.
17. See, for example, the role played by the Popular Front and the vicissitudes of metropolitan parliamentarian politics after World War II on educational development in overseas territories.
18. F. Fanon, *Toward the African Revolution,* chap. 1; idem, *Peaux Noires et Masques Blancs.*
19. See, for example, G. Gurvitch, *The Spectrum of Social Time* (Dordrecht: D. Reidel, 1964).
20. See A. Silva, "La Pedagogie de Paulo Freire."
21. This point is raised both by F. Fanon, *Peaux Noires et Masques Blancs,* chap. 1, and by A. Memmi, *Portrait du Colonisé,* pp. 139 ff.
22. *Been to* is a popular expression referring to those who have been in England.
23. F. Fanon, *Les Damnés de la Terre,* chaps. 2 and 3; idem, *Toward the African Revolution,* chap. 20.
24. A. Memmi, *The Dominated Man,* chap. 7.
25. For a presentation of this theme, see P. Foster, *Social Change and Education in Ghana* (Chicago: University of Chicago Press, 1965).
26. See P. Atger, *La France en Côte d'Ivoire de 1843–1893:*

Cinquante Ans d'Hesitations Politiques et Commerciales (Dakar: Publications de la section d'histoire, no. 2, 1962).

27. See D. Bouche, "Ecoles Françaises au Soudan, 1884–1900," in *Cahiers d'Études Africaines* 5, no. 2 (1966): 228–67.
28. For a more thorough discussion of this theme, see R. Clignet, "Inadequacies of the Notion of Assimilation in African Education," in *Journal of Modern African Studies* 8, no. 3 (1970): 425–44.
29. For a general discussion on the determinants of violence, see P. Lupsha, "On Theories of Urban Violence," in *Urban Affairs Quarterly* 4, no. 3 (1969): 273–96.
30. A problem of interest along these lines is to determine whether variations in the number and the turnover of European expatriates affect the postindependence political development of new nations.
31. A. Memmi, *The Dominated Man*, chap. 7.
32. This is the case, for example, of the varieties of articles or books written by John Holt.
33. For an example of this limitation, see Nguyen Nghe, "Franz Fanon et les problemes de l'independance," in *La Pensée* 107 (1963): 23–26, which illustrates the misunderstandings that a certain Marxism can generate with regard to the writings of Fanon.
34. The reader will note my use of the term *assimilation*. I refer explicitly here to the fact that some students or women consider their own experience as the preexisting framework that they try to justify by borrowing selected elements of the blacks' or the workers' problem.
35. Y. Ouelegem, *Bound to Violence* (New York: Harcourt Brace Jovanovich, 1971).

Internal Colonialism

Civilization and Assimilation in the Colonized Schooling of Native Americans

Katherine Iverson

Historians use a long list of contrasting labels to characterize successive periods in the 350 years of white policy toward Native Americans. They range from civilization to removal, extermination, incorporation, assimilation, revitalization, termination, and self-determination. Formal education constituted a part of each phase. Often it was the primary emphasis. Despite shifts in informal philosophical perspectives and official policy directives, the experience of schooling in fact remained remarkably similar throughout this long period. Changes in jurisdiction and scope of educational efforts reflect policy redirection as well as the growth of the country. But the organization, curriculum, and language medium of these schools has aimed consistently at Americanizing the American Indian. The undisputed failure of the endeavor becomes understandable only in an analysis recognizing the continuity of a colonized education.[1]

Educationists debate whether schooling in America has been a means of social change or a tool for maintaining a social order. But critics and defenders of the system alike must agree that formal education for Native Americans has always aimed at radical change of Indian societies for the purpose of promoting order in the larger economic and political system. If education was intended to permit native people mobility into the mainstream, we must ask why in over three centuries it has been so remarkably unsuccessful. Experiences of international colonialism have shown how an educational tradition of a politically dominant culture, modified by assumptions about limits in the culture and capabilities of native people, serves forever to keep those people at the bottom of the social structure while maintaining the illusion that failure and dependency are due to their own deficiencies. It includes the prejudicial syndrome of blaming the victim.

The relationship of Native Americans to the United States is a prototypical case of what André Gunder Frank calls the historical development of underdevelopment resulting from worldwide European expansion. His model of constellations of developing metropolises (concentrations of economic and political power) and underdeveloping satellites, on whose resources the metropolises depend, illustrates the growing white American control and Native American dependency in political, economic, and social institutions, including education.[2] While the continent may have been undeveloped, underdevelopment of Native American societies is a consequence of a colonial concentration of power and expropriation of land and resources. Because formal education programs were initiated from the colonizers' political and economic interests, it is not possible to discuss schooling apart from those developments. However, the paradigm does not depend on conspiracies or even intentions. This essay attempts to demonstrate the pervasiveness of a colonial pattern of education in the most humanitarian efforts as well as the most exploitative designs.

INTERNAL COLONIALISM AND NATIVE AMERICANS

Something must be said about Native American societies as colonies. The case is not difficult to make; nevertheless, it is complex. Since the opinion delivered by John Marshall in *The Cherokee Nation* v. *the State of Georgia* (1832), Indian tribes have legally been considered "domestic dependent nations." Geographically, too, many occupy a distinct land area, under United States jurisdiction but retain sovereignty with respect to state governments. Efforts to levy taxes and impose law enforcement, continuing to the present in states such as Arizona and South Dakota, indicate the importance of this decision. Most critical to a colonial analysis is the extent to which the economies and cultures have been colonized by white America. As "wards" of the federal government, Indians have found the land which was finally left as reservations to be held "in trust" by the United States. The economic as well as political decisions of tribal councils are subject to the approval of United States Bureau of Indian Affairs officials. Often "tribal" businesses are initiated and administered by federal bureaucrats. The federal government is responsible for the education of most Indian children, either through funding or direct school administration. Indeed it is surprising that more scholarly work has not employed what Cherokee anthropologist Robert K. Thomas calls the BIA agents' presence on Indian reservations, "a classic model of colonialism." [3]

The complexity of colonial analysis arises not so much in the intricacies of federal, state, and tribal jurisdiction as in the multiplicity of Native American societies and their varying experience with the colonizers. There is no American Indian nation beyond the white stereotype of people Columbus called "los Indios." Except for a few, primarily urban, organizers of a pan-Indian movement, native people generally think of themselves initially in terms of their particular tribal cultural identity—Seneca, Winnebago, Yurok, etc. Moreover, they do not agree on a preferred general term, either Native American or Indian. Not being in a position to resolve the controversy, I use them interchangeably.[4]

In land occupied by the United States alone, Indian people speak at least 200 mutually unintelligible languages of at least six unrelated linguistic stocks and exhibit cultural diversity as great as existed at the time of European discovery. Duration since initial contact varies from 400 years in the East and Southwest to barely a century for some western groups. White-Indian relations in different cases involved open bloodiness, stalemated hostility, quiet exploitation, or varying patterns of all three. Some tribal populations have all but disappeared, while others have increased only recently or continually. However, and most important, Indians are not some cultural relic of a legendary past. Nor are they simply the numerical remnants of a once romantic way of life. Native American peoples and cultures persist today, more in spite of than because of their "special relationship" to the United States government. The real cultural and historical differences among Native American nations have been exacerbated by the colonial isolation and lack of opportunity to work out mutual problems in concert because of their loss of power over the direction of their own institutions.

Robert F. Berkhofer, Jr., points out the dilemmas inherent in all analyses of Native American societies, including this study: diversity versus uniformity, trend versus process, and persistence versus change.[5] Sensitivity to great diversity in Native American cultures and histories limits many writers to tribal ethnographies and individual tribal histories. On the other hand, interest in analytical generalization has produced white-centered history and excessive attention to policy rather than experience, for what Indian peoples had in common was often the American government which colonized them. This approach either leaves out the indigenous groups almost entirely or makes the actions of Native American peoples seem like compliant reactions to white control rather than innovative activity in determining their own existence. The same problems face scholars who have searched for recurrent sequences of change, or processes, in a general acculturative trend toward white American culture. Changes have not everywhere taken place in the same manner or order, even though some general patterns have been frequently repeated. This study traces a pattern of resistance to colonial education domination. But because of the problem of diversity it must be rather anecdotal in order to portray experiences at the community and personal level.

Persistence and change are additional analytic problems, for while anthropologists tend to stress persistence of indigenous culture and personality, historians usually emphasize changes resulting from white impact, and sociologists study the pathology of urban enclaves. Out of all this confusion comes the recurrent ambiguity in contemporary America about "Indianness." We somehow expect real Indians to be unchanged from those descriptions at first contact. People and tribal groups who do not exhibit unmodified ancestral customs are thought to be less Indian, even though, as Berkhofer says, we don't consider an Englishman less English although he is far removed from Anglo-Saxon culture. Americans hold a prevailing belief that Indians have all but disappeared, despite actual population increases and persistent private practice of culture patterns literally clothed in business or cowboy attire.[6]

This notion is central to two key problems in the whole history of Native American–white relations, particulary in education. They are the moral and political issue of "civilization" and the economic issue of "assimilation." European colonizers from the first contacts have wished "savages" away from perceived threats to their own civilization and to the present have imagined an assimilation process occurring without providing access to the mythical American melting pot. A colonial analysis helps explain education not merely as an element but as a central instrument—and an excuse—in a 400-year desire to acquire the resources but not the inhabitants of a rich continent.

INDIAN EDUCATION AS MORAL EDUCATION

Given the recency of widespread publicity on the paucity of education for Native Americans, one might expect the history of the effort to be short. However, colonists brought formal education to supplant the indigenous process of socializing the young with their earliest explorations. De Navarez brought four Franciscans for that purpose in 1528, and a Jesuit established a school for Florida Indians in Havana in 1568. In the seventeenth century Jesuits in the Northeast, who wanted to "Galicize and sedentarize" Indians by removing children from their families, and Franciscans in the Southwest, who pursued a more community-oriented education in the pueblos, engaged in schooling efforts. The Anglicans in Virginia began educating Indian children by 1609 with fifty missionaries sent to teach thirty pupils by 1619. King James I ordered Henrico College be built for the children of Infidels in 1617. However, hostilities in 1622 and 1644 ended the Virginians' sense of responsibility to educate Native Americans for more than a century, until the Brafferton Building for Indians was eventually constructed at William and Mary in 1723.

The change of attitude, to be played out again and again, demonstrates the centrality of preserving their European civilization as a justification for the colonists' economic desires. The Virginians recognized the natural right of the Indians to the land and at first made purchases, though of course the natives had never claimed "ownership" of land. However, the colonists always presumed that a Christian obligation to improve the land and a

Lockean notion of cultivation and property ownership gave them a superior right to that land, despite the fact that Algonquian economies in Virginia and New England were based on agriculture, supplemented by hunting and fishing. But the early writings from Virginia reflect hopes for peaceful coexistence and the recognition of some elements of civilization in the natural state of Indian life. The killing of 347 colonists changed that position completely.

> Because our hands which before were tied with gentlenesse and faire usage, are now set at liberty by the treacherous violence of the Savages, not untying the Knot, but cutting it: So that we, who hitherto have had possession of no more ground than their waste, and our purchase at a valuable consideration to their owne contentment, gained; may now by a right of Warre, and law of Nations invade the Country, and destroy them who sought to destroy us.[7]

Roy Harvey Pearce says, "The Indian became for seventeenth century Virginians a symbol not of a man in the grip of devilish ignorance, but a man standing fiercely and grimly in the path of civilization."

This case is not anomalous. The Harvard Charter in 1650 established as the purpose of the institution "the education of English and Indian youth of the Country." President Dunster was apparently serious about making Harvard "the Indian Oxford as well as the New English Cambridge." Dartmouth College originated as Eleazer Wheelock's training school to remove Indians from their natural environment and surround them with Puritan influences. The Princeton Charter also expressed a concern for educating Indians. But the drama of education and Christianization for civilization in confrontation with colonial population pressures on Native American land had the same sorry result in New England.

Given the Puritan religious vision, education and civilization were probably pursued for the greater goal of salvation. But the inextricable links between the three ideals were no less apparent. Massachusetts colonists felt a strong responsibility for the delivery of the Puritan package of theology and pedagogy, including literacy, a complicated dogma, and a drastically changed social existence to natives in the Northeast. Puritans exerted much more effort toward Indian education, reflecting the central role of education in the lives of Massachusetts' own white children.

The moral obligation carried economic and political considerations as well. Puritans saw Satanism as the core of Indian life, giving them the choice of saving a victim of Satan or destroying a partisan of Satan. But from the beginning God had shown the way for the Puritans by sending a "wonderful plague" killing a third of the New England Native American population in 1616 and 1617 to clear Puritan title to the land. When rapid expansion of the colonies caused friction, God again temporarily ended the controversy by "sending small pox amongst the Indians" in 1633. Five years later the massacre of five hundred Pequots, exterminating an entire tribe, was justified by the argument of Christian violence. The pursuit of Indian education in Massachusetts undoubtedly relates to the fact that, in contrast to Virginia, Indians rather than colonists suffered brutal losses early. "Civilization" seemed triumphant.

John Winthrop opened free common schools to Indian children in 1645 and a few participated. However, despite confident rhetoric and special buildings, Puritans met with the general lack of enthusiasm from Native Americans that educators would experience for the next three centuries. Not more than seven or eight Indian boys ever went to Harvard in the pre-Revolutionary War period. Only one finished, and all but one died of disease while at school or in King Philip's War. John Eliot was by far the most successful in attracting students. He alone knew the Algonkian language, employed Indians to teach under his supervision, and used his own translations of the catechism and both Testaments of the Bible as the chief instructional materials. But some education for the purpose of conversion also went on in each of the fourteen "praying towns" in the Bay Colony, where Christian Indians lived segregated from both pagan kinsmen and the Christian Europeans.

The war that broke out in 1675, ending education efforts in the Northeast for a century, as in Virginia, demonstrates the paradoxical problem of civilization in American white relations with the continent's natives. The bloody war of colonial demographic and political expansion resulted in the attack of fifty-two white settlements in New England and the death of 5,000 Native Americans; the rest would be placed on the forerunner of the reservation system.[8] New World military tactics of surprise attack, flaming arrows, tomahawk and war whoops seemed hideous to the colonists, but they retaliated with barbarisms of their own, offering bounties for heads, practicing scalping, selling captives into slavery. Canonchet, the captured Narraganset sachem, was quartered and his head sent to authorities in Hartford. Philip's head and those of other male and female sachems were displayed on poles in Plymouth and elsewhere for twenty-five years.

To emphasize merely the brutality of the "civilizers" would be to oversimplify the contradiction. In the wake of King Philip's War, the Massachusetts General Court passed a law in November 1675 both explaining the sins of the colony and establishing measures for prosecuting the war. The Puritans looked to themselves for an explanation of their difficulties and enumerated evidence of Puritan backsliding. But their solution, found at the end of the document, was to put the Indians on islands and make it lawful for the English to kill those found "straggling off." [9] According to Puritan ethnocentric introspection, Indian uprisings resulted not from colonial expropriation of land but from God's punishment for failing to be the civilized people they, the Puritans, must be.[10]

Yet, despite policies repressing "savagery," forbidding even non-Christian Indians from hunting or fishing on the Sabbath, the colonists came to realize that the heathens were being lowered, not raised, by contact with civilized Christians. During the Great Awakening, the high Puritan faith in the use of civilization as a means of conversion died out almost entirely. Missionaries were to convert Indians on the frontier, apart from schools and other manifestations of civilization. By the time of the American Revolution even the Christianization goal had temporarily given way to the ideal of a new social order in which the Indians were to be eliminated, not included, and only a dozen missionaries continued to carry the Gospel to the ravaged natives, while most American effort went toward their extermination.[11] The reasons for the suspension were mostly political and economic. The new status of nationhood restricted mission budgets and interest in the welfare of Indians. Even after 1819 federal involvement in Indian education amounted to only a few thousand dollars appropriated and distributed, under the "Civilization Act," to mission groups for the support of their education programs.

With the rising nationalism after the War of 1812, churchwide mission societies were organized in most denominations. More money, better transportation, and the federal policy of removing Indians to the West enabled missionaries to cross the continent in pursuit of Manifest Destiny. While the debate whether Indians should be first civilized or Christianized continued to the Civil War, in fact that argument was one of semantics. Whether missionaries thought that learning the Word and observing the Sabbath were the best way of elevating Indians to civilization or that literacy and private property were necessary so Indians could support the work of the church themselves, in practice "civilization" and "Christianity" were always linked.

Like other nineteenth-century American educators, missionaries used schools as instruments for the inculcation of American civilization, epitomized as the ideal in the unilinear development of human society. But of course educators of Native Americans had the greater job to do, for their charges were neither familiar with economic individualism, democratic republicanism and Protestantism, nor necessarily very interested in those institutions. But many did want access to the power of reading and writing. Missionaries most often used the Bible and catechism as textbooks and, later, special readers with moral themes, sometimes translated into native languages. Berkhofer described *The Osage First Book*, containing four sections—"Familiar Sentences," "Moral Lessons for Children," Scripture selections, and the Ten Commandments—plus alphabet and spelling lessons. The familiar sentence section included pronouncements on the proper use of tools, the proper female role, the importance of a cabin with a stone chimney, the significance of agriculture, the concept of private property, and the benefits of civilization.[12]

If teaching materials have since become slightly more subtle, teachers' concerns with proper habits have not. In the early 1800s, as in the late 1900s, punctual and regular attendance was seen as the most essential of civilized habits, partly for the sake of pursuing education but also because an "orderly life" was intrinsically good. But attendance of Indian students has never been either prompt or steady. Going to school, as other occupations of an Indian child's day, was usually his or her own decision, not a parental one. In addition, economic or ceremonial reasons often kept students home, as they do today. Missionary teachers for three centuries have persisted in the belief that Native American parents do not know how to raise children. A pamphlet written for Choctaw parents called *Family Education and Government* advised parents to demand obedience and not to spare the rod or be fooled by loud crying when applying it.

The experience of mission education is probably best described by students, who could set the school in the context of their own culture. Francis LaFlesche's autobiographical account of the mid-1860s in Nebraska, called *The Middle Five: Indian Schoolboys of the Omaha Tribe,* reflects the twin emphases of civilization and Christianization in a school sponsored by the Board of Foreign Missions of the Presbyterian Church. In a new student's first hours he would be given a "pronounceable" name, here William T. Sherman, Philip Sheridan, and Ulysses S. Grant.[1] Then came the inevitable haircut, bath, and outfit of white man's clothes. But the social relationships of the group of boys who called themselves the Middle Five had little to do with the daily dose of McGuffey's Readers and periodic prayers, the interminable sermons three times on Sunday and Thursday evenings, and the frequent switchings for knowing or unknowing violations of "Gray-Beard's" behavior code. The boys used the forbidden Omaha language in the events LaFlesche remembered most: the games and adventures and the death of a friend.[1]

INDIAN RESPONSES TO THE CIVILIZATION EFFORT

Meanwhile, native people carried out a variety of organizational endeavors in their changed environmental context following the devastation waged by American troops in the last two decades of the eighteenth century. A religious doctrine of moral regeneration rose in New York state among followers of an elderly Seneca called Handsome Lake. In his synthesis of Iroquois theology and Quaker morals, Handsome Lake proposed learning white ways, not through general schooling of the young but rather the delegation of two students from each of the Iroquois nations to become specialists in American ways by attending their schools. The followers of Handsome Lake successfully led the resistance to attempts in the 1820s to push the Iroquois west. Other prophets among the displaced Algonquian peoples in the Northwest Territory foretold a millennial restoration by the rejection of schools and all things European which, somewhat paradoxically, helped organize forces under Tecumseh to fight on the British side against the Americans in the War of 1812. Both nativistic movements, like messianic religious movements which frequently rise in the social disorganization of colonized societies, became established religions lasting more than a century. The Native American (Peyote) Church and the Ghost Dance Religion of the prophet Wovoka flourished in the West as white land seizure threatened Plains and Southwestern nations. All, through cultural innovation, came to represent the social factions leading the struggle against the encroachment of white civilization.

In the Southeast a more secular emphasis gave schools an important role in what Edward H. Spicer called a cultural renaissance.[15] The Cherokees realized by 1800 that relentless pressures of settlers and government to cede land necessitated formal political organization to stop the familiar pattern of treaties signed by a few headmen. In the first three decades of the century a coalition of old and young, men and women, methodically developed a system of codified laws, a law-enforcement agency, a bicameral legislature, a court system, a national printing press, and a national bilingual newspaper. A syllabary created by an unschooled Cherokee called Sequoyah aroused great interest, and the Cherokees quickly achieved a high literacy rate. In this milieu of self-directed acculturative fusion of white and Cherokee cultural elements the Cherokees encouraged missionaries to come to the Cherokee nation on the condition that they build schools. Under the vigilant watch of the Cherokee National Council six different Protestant denominations established fifteen well-attended schools but, according to most accounts, reaped few Christian converts. State of Georgia and federal government agreements to cede portions of Cherokee land in Georgia began in 1802, and Cherokee resistance became futile when gold was discovered in 1829.

Pressures by government agents, land speculators, and neighboring Georgians to open the land to whites resulted in a federal program of land allotment with the expectation of sale, though the Cherokee participants often did not understand the government's intent. But under the Indian Removal Act of 1830 most of the Cherokees as well as the Chickasaws, Choctaws, Creeks, and Seminoles, the "civilized" (meaning agricultural) nations, were moved to Indian Territory in Oklahoma. There the process of rebuilding political, economic, and educational structures began, supported by the annuities paid for land sales and taxes levied for trading and livestock grazing privileges. By 1852 the Cherokees administered their own comprehensive system of twenty-one schools and two academies that enrolled 1,100. The Choctaws, Chickasaws, and other displaced nations had begun pursuing similar efforts.

The Civil War interrupted indigenous organization once more. Both the North and the South used one Indian nation against another, and annuity payment stopped. But the measure of belief in education as a defense against white aggression was demonstrated in the reopening of schools by all the tribes immediately following the treaties of 1866. Except for the attempts by some Southern Cherokees to maintain schools in wartime refugee camps, most children had been without schools for five years and many buildings had been burned. The educational system was not only revived but expanded so that by the 1880s the Cherokees and Choctaws ran more than two hundred schools and academies and sent a sizable number of graduates to colleges in the East. The Chickasaws had reopened twenty-three neighborhood schools and four seminaries at the secondary level and provided scholarships for sixty to a hundred college students each year. The Cherokee newspaper, *The Phoenix*, remained widely read in a population with 90 percent literacy in the native language and a higher English literacy level than the white populations of nearby Texas or Arkansas.[16] The Five Civilized Tribes were still economically self-sufficient.

THE ASSIMILATION EMPHASIS IN COLONIZED EDUCATION

The Civil War is usually considered a turning point in American Indian policy, particularly in education. It marks increased commitment to education by both the federal government and philanthropic organizations whose members called themselves "Friends of the Indians." The Board of Indian Commissioners, a presidentially appointed supervisory group of ten citizens serving without pay, recognized in 1880 that statistics "proved conclusively" that the Indian population was not dying out but steadily increasing. They said, "As we must have him [the Indian] among us, self-interest, humanity and Christianity require that we should accept the situation and go resolutely at work to make him a safe and useful factor in our body politic." [17] After a century of unsuccessful attempts to obliterate the native population physically, rhetoric turned toward destroying Indianness, including tribalism, communal ownership, reservation concentration, language, and religion. In the words of a famous Indian fighter turned educator, Captain Richard H. Pratt, superintendent of the Carlisle Indian School, "All the Indian there is in the race should be dead. Kill the Indian in him and save the man." In a more pragmatic version, the Board of Indian Commissioners had said in 1880 that the "nation had learned by costly experience that 'it was cheaper to feed than to fight the Indian,' and the same commonsense teaches 'it is cheaper to teach than to feed them.'" Reverend Lyman Abbott at the Sixth Lake Mohonk Conference of Friends of the Indian in 1888 had condensed the sentiment: "It costs less to educate an Indian than to shoot him." [18]

Both strains had coexisted from the beginning, but the emphasis now shifted from "civilization" to "assimilation" and the arguments rested more openly on economic rather than moral grounds. In the same concern as that caused by the wave of European immigration, policymakers sought to "Americanize" those who had inhabited the continent for centuries. Individual allotment and ownership of tribal lands in order to eliminate reservations became nationwide under the Dawes Act of 1887, despite opposition from native societies, including the Five Civilized Tribes. When this policy was officially reversed in 1934 Indians held only one third of the land they had in 1887 (48 million acres versus 138 million acres). Indian population had increased, but no alternative economic structures existed to replace the subsistence economy.

Now schools were not simply one tool for the civilization effort but the ultimate solution to the process of assimilation into the American economy as well as the culture. Though Indians' own quiet resistance by withdrawal prevented its achievement, philanthropists and Indian Commissioners alike hoped for universal, compulsory boarding-school attendance. In three hundred year's experience the educators had become slightly less naïve. Reverend Abbott said that education provided by the government should not be a gift but "imposed by superior authority as a requirement. It is a great mistake to suppose that the Red Man is hungering for the white man's culture, eager to take it if it is offered to him. The ignorant are never hungry for education, nor the vicious for morality, nor the barbaric for civilization; educators have to create the appetite as well as furnish the food."

Under this new program supposedly built on the common-school model, classes were to follow a uniform course of study, teaching methods, and textbooks. Indian Commissioner Thomas J. Morgan wanted special attention given to systematic habits ("The period of rising and retiring, the hours for meals, times for study, recitation, work and play should all be fixed and adhered to with great punctiliousness"), habits of self-directed toil in profitable labor or useful study ("Pupils must be taught the marvelous secret of diligence"), forms and usages of civilized life ("Much can be done to fix the current of their thought in its right channels by having them memorize choice maxims and literary gems, in which inspiring thoughts and noble sentiments are embodied"). "Fervent patriotism" was to be "awakened," assuming that it lay there dormant and that it would be to the United States. The "unhappy history" of the native students could be alluded to only in contrast to a better future.

Not surprisingly, English was to be the sole medium of instruction. The 1868 "Peace Commission" of generals and philanthropists had maintained that "through sameness of language is produced sameness of thought," and for this reason the boarding schools located far from the reservations and parents were to be multitribal so that the only means of communication would be English. Moreover, students from one tribe were scattered among the ten boarding schools from Chemawa in Salem, Oregon, to Carlisle in Pennsylvania to encourage students not to return home, to promote the "disintegration of the tribes."

While even religious groups now pushed for government responsibility for Indian education, the move represented less a deemphasis on Christian conversion than the anti-Catholic sentiment of the 1890s. Since the United States had acquired the Southwest, Catholic mission schools had received the largest share of government funds for Indian education. The powerful Protestant Lake Mohonk Conferences were especially vocal in expressing the belief that "much Roman Catholic teaching among the Indians does not prepare them for intelligent and loyal citizenship" though, of course, they were not permitted citizenship until 1924. J. D. C. Atkins, Commissioner from 1885 to 1888, hinted at the importance of the Christian message for Indians as well as the usefulness of native languages when, in forbidding use of the native languages in mission as well as government schools, he noted that "preaching the Gospel in the vernacular is, of course, not prohibited." Newly appointed Commissioner Morgan in 1889 spoke of the continued urgency of consecrated mission work and of saturating the curriculum with moral ideas and the fear of God. Indeed the school itself was to be "an illustration of the superiority of the Christian civilization."

CONTINUITY IN TWENTIETH-CENTURY BOARDING SCHOOLS

These policy statements would not be so important if they did not so thoroughly reflect the shape of Indian education not only in the late nineteenth century but virtually to the present. Therefore, analysis of the twentieth century lends itself not as well to a chronology of change as to a discussion of persistence of colonial patterns of domination in federal and public-school structure, curriculum, and control. The boarding school is the ideal institution for colonial education. In promoting assimilation through segregation, the government system prepares students in isolation from both their own societies and white society and then expects them immediately to take their place as good citizens. In the 1890s educators hoped that by total immersion of all Indian children in American education, within a generation native people would disappear into the mainstream. Even if schooling could have had so great an impact, the government did not really make a large enough effort.

In 1901 there were only 16,000 Indian pupils ages 5–21 in all schools. About half of those were in off-reservation boarding schools, and all but 257 of the rest attended mission or BIA day schools.[19] In 1970 over 12,000 Native American children still attended nineteen off-reservation boarding schools, and 35,000, 25 percent of whom were under nine years of age, attended seventy-seven boarding schools on reservations.[20] Assignment is based either on educational reasons (English-language deficiencies, local school unavailability, or at least three years scholastic retardation) or social criteria (family problems or poverty, health problems, or behavior problems). In fact, over three-fourths of the students are sent to boarding schools for social and emotional reasons, but the special services needed by those students are virtually nonexistent. The BIA employs a total of one psychologist.[21] Boarding-school personnel themselves frequently call the institutions "dumping grounds."

However, despite their long-standing history of failure to meet stated objectives, boarding schools succeeded as colonized education. Though very expensive to operate, the total institution made it easier to regulate every hour of the students' day. With Americanization as the persisting goal, teachers, 95 percent of whom were and are white, could be brought in without any special expertise or training. Neither are special materials or equipment necessary. Using the same textbooks as white students in the United States, Native American students find Indians mentioned only as obstacles to the progress of national expansion by brave pioneers. To the white middle-class observer, the curriculum of federal boarding schools contains nothing unfamiliar except the very low level of expectations.

The early boarding schools were self-consciously manual, or

industrial, schools, but it is clear that from the beginning vocational courses aimed more at teaching "the marvelous secret of diligence" than specific occupational skills. In *Sun Chief: The Autobiography of a Hopi Indian,* Don Taleyesva described his work at a reservation boarding school after having been captured by agency police:

> When I returned to school in September, 1905, I was assigned to stable duty for a time. I cleaned out the manure and spread it over the fields. . . . Some time after that I was transferred from stable work to the blacksmith shop, where I learned to weld iron. Then they needed a boy in the bakery and sent me there. Later I was made a kitchen boy again and helped a little with the cooking. . . . In May, 1906, I went to Rockyford, Colorado, with a large group of boys to work on sugar beet plantations.

The next year his superior officer told fifty of the students they would go to Sherman Institute in Riverside, California. Among Taleyesva's vocational experiences there were picking cantaloupe, milking cows, and pitching hay. His reflection on returning home after the third year portrays the curriculum and its impact:

> As I lay on my blanket I thought about my school days and all that I had learned. I could talk like a gentleman, read, write, and cipher. I could name all the states in the Union with their capitals, repeat the names of all the books in the Bible, quote a hundred verses of Scripture, sing more than two dozen Christian hymns and patriotic songs, debate, shout football yells, swing my partners in square dances, bake bread, sew well enough to make a pair of trousers, and tell "dirty" Dutchman stories by the hour. It was important that I had learned how to get along with white men and earn money by helping them. But my death experience had taught me that I had a Hopi Spirit Guide whom I must follow if I wished to live. I wanted to become a real Hopi again, to sing the good old Katcina songs, and to feel free to make love without fear of sin or a rawhide.[22]

In 1928 the Meriam Report, or *The Problem of Indian Administration*, a massive study commissioned by the government, documented kidnapping children to schools hundreds of miles from home, institutional drudge work disguised as vocational education, physical abuse in punishment, and lack of health care.[23] But this landmark document represented neither the beginning nor the end of these abuses and problems. Captain Richard Pratt's memoir reported with great relish his expedition to Indian Territory and Dakota to obtain students for Carlisle in 1879. The Navajo Treaty with the United States government in 1868 stipulated that one teacher would be provided for each thirty students who could be "induced or compelled" to attend school. Not until the 1950s were many Navajos induced for more than a few weeks. Chiloco in Oklahoma even budgeted for police-department charges to return runaways. In 1970 counselors at Many Farms, Arizona, spent more than half their time retrieving runaways, officially known as "AWOLs," and posters announced "shipments" of Navajo students to Intermountain School in Brigham City, Utah.

Nor had vocational and Christian training changed very much. Hildegard Thompson, who would become director of Navajo and then all federal Indian education programs, admitted that in the late 1940s students still spent much of their half-day vocational time doing school chores. And as recently as 1970 several mentally retarded students at the high school where I worked spent most of each day in the cafeteria kitchen, for there were no special education programs available in federal schools. Missionaries made weekly appearances in the Chinle, Arizona, BIA elementary boarding-school classrooms in 1972.[24]

Some programs demonstrated more than the mere continuity of problems in an educational system alien to students' cultures and needs. One notable effort, still remembered with pride among many teachers and administrators who participated, specifically trained Navajo students in life-styles and for work at the bottom rungs of employment in positions that benefited the metropolis, not the indigenous population.

The Special Navajo Program began in 1946 out of concern that only 25 percent of the 24,000 Navajo children were in school. In addition, California had just assumed responsibility for educating the native students of that state, and Bureau officials feared that Sherman Institute would be closed. As an example of using Indian children as means to the end of money and power, the Special Navajo Program was designed to utilize the superfluous facility and staff.[25] Federal educational bureaucrats hurriedly outlined a five-year program for students twelve to eighteen years old. Three years were to be devoted to basic English, academic skills, and American middle-class manners, morals, and customs. The last two years were spent on vocational skills, girls receiving mainly home-economics training for work as domestics and boys learning painting, carpentry, and cooking. The Bureau publication, *Doorway Toward the Light,* emphasized before-and-after pictures showing improvements in grooming and eye contact.[26] While most accounts are remarkably vague about the exact curriculum, the best assessment of the program's purpose came from its director:

> Placement as a rule was in service occupations or occupations requiring a minimum of technical knowledge. The employment market at that period was in the students' favor. Many of them completed their education at a time when the Navajo Reservation school system was being markedly expanded; therefore, demand was great for dormitory aides, kitchen and dining room personnel and school maintenance staff—needed to open new schools. The training of the special students ideally fitted them for this type of employment.[27]

Obviously neither domestics nor house painters were employed within the Navajo exchange economy, and the school service personnel had little opportunity for advancement. But the program was expanded to eight off-reservation schools and an eight-year program including up to 5,800 students before sensitivity to charges against "terminal" education brought a shift toward a "regular high school curriculum."

But for Navajo and other Native American students presently in federal boarding schools the curriculum now aims neither at immediate employment nor adequate preparation for college. The mathematics program at Stewart School in Nevada provides a typical example. "The first course for 'high school' students teaches addition and subtraction. The second-level course deals with all four basic operations plus fractions. The next course is concerned with proportions for simple algebra, while the top course is finally algebra." [28] Bureau teachers or administrators confronted with this evidence would undoubtedly justify it as reaching the level the students could handle. After eight or more years of educational retardation, not to mention personal disorganization, the assessment may be correct. But that is the key to understanding boarding schools, which serve the poorest, most rural and most reluctant students, as the epitome of colonized education. The government makes what appears to be a total effort, twenty-four hours a day for many years, to raise native students from the "backwardness" and poverty of their culture. Though it is the school's failure, most Bureau teachers generally assess student failure not only as personal and cultural but racial. That "failure" is really rejection, witnessed by the concern the Bureau has always expressed that most of the students return to their homes. But government agencies can then be quite convinced that Native Americans are "not ready" to manage their own affairs, including not only schools but economic and political enterprises. Again, by self-fulfilling prophecy they are right. Students have not received the training or credentials to become teachers, attorneys, engineers, doctors, or business people—all those thousands of positions filled by white people on reservations supposedly devoid of economic opportunity.[29]

COLONIZED PUBLIC SCHOOL EDUCATION

But an indictment of federal boarding schools as colonial institutions is almost too easy. The fact is that of the 250,000 Indians, Eskimos, and Aleuts in school in 1973, 70 percent attended public schools. Since the 1890s, when "incorporation" became a policy goal, some Native American children entered public schools, though four-fifths of Indian pupils in 1926 went to federal schools. By 1937, after the passage of the Johnson O'Malley Act granting funds to public schools for education of Indians, 52 percent of the 65,000 students attended them. The movement reached its peak in the 1950s when the policy of terminating reservations was actively pursued and Indian students of nine states came under state public-school jurisdiction solely.

While less conspicuously controlled by an alien government, public-school education reflects no more, often less, sensitivity to its Native American clientele. The famous Cherokee case provides an example of its failure. Following the phenomenal success of the Cherokees themselves in the nineteenth century, the federal government assumed control in 1903 and dissolved the school system as well as the tribal organization when Oklahoma became a state in 1906. After sixty years of white control the median number of school years completed was 5.5, with a 40 percent adult illiteracy rate and a high-school drop-out rate of 75 percent. The long history of vigorous economic self-sufficiency even under illegal harassment and removal has ended. Ninety percent of the Cherokee families in Adair County, Oklahoma, receive welfare payments.[30]

Nationwide, the drop-out statistics on Native American students in public school produce a litany of failure: 87 percent in Ponca City, Oklahoma; 90 percent in Nome, Alaska; 90 percent in Klamath, Oregon. According to the 1969 *Kennedy Report,* low achievement levels reflect insensitive curricula and anti-Indian attitudes of most public schools that Indians attend. In fact the root of the problem is almost total lack of Indian control in public schools serving Indian students.

The problem of parental participation must be discussed. That Indian parents have no influence in federal boarding schools surprises no one. Even in reservation boarding schools today the only time parents come near the premises (most often a dormitory) is to take a child home or to return him or her to school. It is not only possible but quite probable that a BIA classroom teacher might spend several years at a school without ever speaking to an Indian parent.[31] Federal day schools operate similarly because of their isolated locations and administrative subservience to Bureau area offices. Teachers in both cases live in government housing in the school "compounds," separated, usually by a high fence, from the people they serve.

But public schools that Indians attend exemplify the colonial pattern of unofficially continuing past practices, despite the notion that public-school experience would integrate Native Americans in the mainstream. For one thing public schools on reservations were often opened to educate the children of white landholders, business people, Bureau administrators, and Bureau teachers. Housing ghettos built for teachers in these schools are as circumscribed as the federal compounds. Here local school boards exist, but recent studies have found any Indian representation to be a rarity, and white retribution for attempts to gain election is frequent.[32]

Inclusion of Indian-oriented curricular materials is even more infrequent than in federal schools, for the public schools, even where Indian students form a majority, exist primarily for white students. Moreover, state educational guidelines can be used to prevent initiation of special programs. English-language problems of the native students make segregation by tracking a general rule. Federal funds designed to help public-school districts pay for the education of Indians are generally used for general operating expenditures rather than for the special needs of Indian children. In fact these funds often aid non-Indian landowners, demonstrated by the lower-than-average tax rate in school districts receiving these federal funds.

Federal support for public schools comes from two major programs. The Johnson-O'Malley Act of 1934 began as the federal government's primary means of transferring responsibility for Indian education to the public schools. However, in 1951 the BIA began limiting the funds to "federally recognized" Indians living on reservations in conjunction with its policy of reservation termination. At the same time Congress passed legislation in 1950, primarily aimed at military bases. This "federal impact aid" was expanded in 1953 to include Indians under federal jurisdiction "in lieu" of tax revenue lost because of federal property. In addition to notoriously poor accountability in the use of these funds, some states have reduced state aid to districts that receive Johnson-O'Malley or impact-aid money.[33]

This federal support excludes at least 30,000 Native American children living in urban areas. None of the children of the 80,000 California Indians qualifies for Johnson-O'Malley assistance, and among the 45,000 Native Americans in California cities the dropout rate in some public schools approaches 70 percent. Minneapolis, where an estimated 10,000 Indians live, reports a 60 percent Indian drop-out rate in the public schools.[34] The figures are likely underestimates, for Native American urban residence is highly fluid. Many are never counted, and many children do not enter school and therefore are not counted as drop-outs.[35] Most of these urbanites too are part of an official government program called "relocation," but the lack of access to economic security, subjection to racial prejudice, and lack of cultural supports has made twenty-five years of this effort no more successful than other attempts to assimilate Indians while expropriating their resources.

COMMUNITY SCHOOLS—IMPOSED AND LOCALLY CONSTITUTED

One anomalous effort, during the reform movement of the 1920s and 1930s, must be noted. The appointment of John Collier, a vocal critic of American assimilation policies, as Indian Commissioner in 1933 permitted an attempt to revitalize native cultures and economies. Collier stopped the allotment, hence loss, of Indian lands and pushed legislation to renew tribal political sovereignty. His community day school program aimed at land and livestock management, community family health, and native arts and literacy, all to be experienced and ultimately controlled by Indian communities. He enlisted two presidents of the Progressive Education Association, William Carson Ryan and Willard Beatty, as the first Directors of Indian Education. But the Congressional appropriations, administrative structure, and teaching personnel did not change very much. Collier's haste in implementing his vision, bureaucratic as well as Indian suspicion of his intent, and personnel and materiel demands of World War II doomed the experiment, leaving it mostly forgotten or remembered with scorn.

The program focused on the huge Navajo Reservation, where only 15 percent of the population had ever been to a school in 1937, trachoma and tuberculosis rates in boarding schools had reached epidemic proportions, and livestock overgrazing had become locally and nationally critical.[36] In the faith shared by many development theorists that educational reforms were the best solution to the social and economic problems of the indigenous population, fifty new community day schools were built on the roadless plateau of the 25,000-square-mile Navajo Reservation. Thirty-nine opened in September 1939 alone. The curriculum was to be oriented toward agricultural and health problems as well as academic skills, but teachers had little training and few materials to pursue these cross-cultural issues. In addition to formal education for children, the schools did provide valuable water sources, carpentry and blacksmith shops, sewing and washing facilities, health-care clinics, local government meeting places, and Navajo literacy centers. Collier's interest in supporting native arts and religion was interpreted as mystical romanticism. Yet this was only one part of a far more comprehensive plan for political and social reform.

But at the same time the government's insensitive reduction of the Navajo sheep population caused resentment still felt bitterly forty years later. Expression of outrage included withdrawal from the schools, which Navajos (correctly) identified as "Washingdoon's." Most were closed during the war, and some were later converted to boarding schools.[37]

Ironically, several Navajo communities have begun in the last ten years schools very similar to the despised Collier's model. Schools like Rough Rock Demonstration School, Rock Point School, Borrego Pass School, and Ramah Navajo High School on the Navajo Reservation, as well as Rocky Point School in Montana, have through contracts with the BIA created bilingual, bicultural schools. The major difference from the 1930s experiment is that these schools are controlled by local school boards of native people, an effort that followed rather than preceded the opening of community schools in the Collier era.

That recent educational literature still describes the same half-dozen "experimental" or "demonstration" schools points to the problem of continued dependency on federal or foundation funding as an impediment to widespread expansion.[38] The Navajo Nation, as it is officially called, is planning a comprehensive education system under its control. But unless it succeeds in really controlling its own sixteen-million-acre wealth of resources, including coal, oil, uranium, timber, and precious Colorado River water, its schools will remain dependent on outside funding, therefore external control and external capriciousness. The

Speaker of the Arizona House of Representatives in 1975 left no doubt about the interests of the "metropolis" when he explicitly proposed contributing to a bankrupt Navajo public-school district because of the need for power and water in metropolitan Phoenix.

However, this collectively richest of Native American peoples, in a growing sense of nationalism, was the first to open its own independently controlled college.[39] It has also embarked on a large-scale native teacher-training program and is instrumental in the formation of an Indian medical school, an important step in ending the colonial isolation of Indian communities from each other. Moreover, these institutions are essential in providing professionals and technicians who can be employed within Native American institutions rather than continuing the colonial pattern of supplying unskilled laborers who must outmigrate to the metropolis for employment. High demands for trained Navajos exist in the Navajo Nation's own governmental bureaucracy, in legal service and health-care programs, in elementary and secondary education, in Navajo agricultural, timbering, and small-business enterprises, as well as in the federal bureaucracy and extractive industries of the metropolis that still operate on Navajo land. Navajos have for a long time been disproving the colonizer's myth that opportunity is to be found only in the city—demographically, by their high reservation return rate from government urban-relocation programs and distant boarding schools, and organizationally, by support and development of self-generating, self-perpetuating contemporary Navajo political, social-service, and economic programs.

It is ironic, though, that some Navajo students should also be studying in their college the culturally important native arts of weaving and silversmithing, increasingly lucrative enterprises now that the products have become metropolitan fashion. A colonized boarding-school education prevented many young Navajos from learning those skills from parents. But colonizers' whimsical taste can also eliminate large-scale remuneration for the craftsmanship. For some indigenous knowledge, interest by colonial powers has come too late. The Menniger Foundation has discovered what Navajos have known for centuries—that their community-centered healing ceremonies are sophisticated forms of psychotherapy. But many of the chants have been lost because young apprentices have not been able to spend the years necessary to learn them from the healer-singers.

No discussion of colonized education should fail to point out that the greatest disservice of a colonial relationship is the emphasis on education as a general cure to the economic, political, and cultural devastation that is either greedily planned or unknowingly pursued. Anthropologist David Aberle put education in a different perspective in a study for the Joint Economic Committee of the U.S. Congress in 1969:

> Economically speaking, the Navajo constitute an underdeveloped group. They are an underdeveloped, internal U.S. colony. They show the marks of it. Their poverty and their undereducation are not causes of their underdevelopment but results of it. The underdevelopment results from their relations with the larger society, which limit the economic options open to them, drain off their resources, and fail to provide them with the education, the technological base, and the organizational forms necessary for satisfactory development.[40]

A number of Navajo leaders, including Tribal Chairman Peter McDonald, have lately used the rhetoric of having been "colonized" and are proceeding from that new consciousness. But most other Native American societies have far greater problems. They have been parted from their land and economic resources, from legal protection by treaty rights, sometimes from language, traditions, and pride. Where colonization has been internalized, the conflicts between the new indigenous elites, "the Indian bureaucrats," and both the militant youth and traditional old create the self-destruction exemplified by the Pine Ridge Sioux Reservation. There Dakota people in 1976 were literally waging a shooting war with other Dakota people, while white ranchers controlled 75 percent of reservation land.

Native Americans have been schooled in boarding schools, day schools, public schools, mission schools, academies, and praying towns. Their teachers have been missionaries, military officers, philanthropists, and civil-service employees. Curriculum has ranged from purely religious to classical, common school, industrial, and college preparatory. For most of four centuries Native Americans have been interested in education but not very enthusiastic about the schools. The problem lies in a history of teaching civilization while creating violence and expecting assimilation while practicing segregation. But since one form of schooling seems to have been hardly more effective than another, educators still ask: What do Native American peoples want? The answer must certainly be: They want the right and the means to do it themselves. That is the core of a decolonizing education in the view of writers such as Paulo Freire and Albert Memmi.[41] Yet the general omission of education in the solutions proposed by many analysts of colonialism points to the limitations in possibilities and consequences of educational change without political and economic self-determination. The world has discovered that a diluted metropolitan education will not catapult Third World peoples into an industrial mentality and instant "development," even within the United States. But a locally controlled education system is one necessary means by which a colonized people can address their own cultural and economic needs. The political implications of that control make realization an exceedingly difficult process.

Notes

1. No analytic study of the whole history of American Indian education exists elsewhere. The best bibliographical source is Brewton Berry, *The Education of American Indians* (Washington, D.C.: Government Printing Office, 1969).
2. See André Gunder Frank, "The Development of Underdevelopment," in James D. Cockroft, André Gunder Frank, and Dale L. Johnson, eds., *Dependence and Underdevelopment: Latin American Political Economy* (New York: Doubleday, 1972). For one of the few applications of this model to the Native American situation, see Joseph Jorgensen, "Indians and the Metropolis," in Jack O. Waddell and O. Michael Watson, eds., *The American Indian in Urban Society* (Boston: Little, Brown, 1971).
3. Thomas is concerned with the colonial impact of specified legal bureaucracies first on the decay of peoples' own institutions and second on the social isolation of communities from other communities and the physical environment. Robert K. Thomas, "Colonialism: Classic and Internal," and "Powerless Politics," in *New University Thought* 4 (Winter 1966–67).
4. The source of both terms, after all, is Italian exploration. Like any term that is not entirely pejorative, the word *Indian*, after several centuries of use, has gained a certain validity. It is still used by the militant American Indian Movement as well as by the more established National Council of American Indians.
5. Robert F. Berkhofer, Jr., Preface to paperback edition, *Salvation and the Savage: An Analysis of Protestant Missions and American Indian Response, 1787–1862* (New York: Atheneum, 1972).
6. The U.S. Census counted 237,196 persons as Indians in 1900 and 792,730 in 1970, up 51 percent from 1960, when the

total was 523,591. Some of the growth is purely statistical; more people were willing to identify themselves as Indians. Other reasons include very high birth rates combined with lower infant mortality. *Akwasasne Notes* 5 (Early Autumn 1973): 2. The cultural persistence is discussed in Albert L. Wahrhaftig and Robert K. Thomas, "Renaissance and Repression: The Oklahoma Cherokee," in *TRANS-action* (February 1969); also in Howard M. Bahr, Bruce A. Chadwick, and Robert C. Day, *Native Americans Today: Sociological Perspectives* (New York: Harper & Row, 1972), pp. 80–89.

7. Edward Waterhouse quoted in Roy Harvey Pearce, *Savagism and Civilization: A Study of the Indian and the American Mind* (Baltimore: Johns Hopkins, 1967), p. 11.
8. Alvin M. Josephy, Jr., *The Patriot Chiefs: A Chronicle of American Indian Resistance* (New York: Viking, 1958), chap. 2.
9. "King Philip's War: The Puritan Explanation," in Jack P. Greene, *Settlements to Society*, vol. 1 of *A Documentary History of American Life* (New York: McGraw-Hill, 1966), pp. 174–79.
10. A more complicated analysis of the conflict may be found in Richard Slotkin, *Regeneration through Violence: The Mythology of the American Frontier, 1600–1860* (Middletown, Conn.: Wesleyan University Press, 1974).
11. Berkhofer, *Salvation and the Savage*, chap. 1, "The Grand Object."
12. Ibid., chap. 2, "Nurseries of Morality," p. 32.
13. In his autobiography, Don Taleyesva said names were not always bestowed so ceremoniously. His sister was called Nellie the first year she attended Keams Canyon (Arizona) Boarding School in 1905. But the next year the teachers couldn't remember what they had called her, so she became Gladys. Leo W. Simmons, ed., *Sun Chief: The Autobiography of a Hopi Indian* (New Haven: Yale University Press, 1942), p. 89.
14. LaFlesche provides valuable insight but an atypical example. He earned a law degree and a post in the Bureau of American Ethnology. One sister was an M.D. and another

a lecturer. David Baerreis, ed., *The Middle Five* (Madison: University of Wisconsin Press, 1963).

15. Edward H. Spicer, *A Short History of the Indians of the United States* (New York: D. Van Nostrand, 1969), pp. 58–64.
16. Special Subcommittee on Indian Education of the Committee on Labor and Public Welfare, United States Senate, *Indian Education: A National Tragedy—A National Challenge* (Washington, D.C.: Government Printing Office, 1969), hereafter referred to as the *Kennedy Report*.
17. Quotations of late nineteenth-century Indian policy are taken from government documents and Proceedings of the Lake Mohonk Conferences included in Francis Paul Prucha, *Americanizing the American Indian: Writings by the "Friends of the Indian" 1880–1900* (Cambridge: Harvard University Press, 1973), pt. 4, "Indian Education," pp. 191–292.
18. Abbott was a leader in the powerful and tightly unified Protestant group started by Albert K. Smiley, a Quaker member of the Board of Indian Commissioners.
19. Even if there were only 137,000 Indians in 1900, this enrollment represents only 15 percent of that population. See Estelle Fuchs and Robert J. Havighurst, *To Live on This Earth: American Indian Education* (Garden City, N.Y.: Doubleday, 1972), p. 8.
20. These represent almost a third of the 152,000 Indian children under federal jurisdiction. *Kennedy Report*, p. xii.
21. Testimony of Senator Walter Mondale in "Education as War," in Edgar S. Cahn, ed., *Our Brother's Keeper: The Indian in White America* (New York: World, 1969), p. 29.
22. Simmons, *Sun Chief*, pp. 108–9, 134.
23. Lewis Merriam, *The Problem of Indian Administration* (Baltimore: Johns Hopkins, 1928).
24. Hildegard Thompson, *The Navajos' Long Walk for Education* (Tsaile, Navajo Nation, Ariz.: Navajo Community College Press, 1975), p. 101. I taught at Many Farms (BIA) High School and the tribally operated Navajo Community College from 1969 to 1972.
25. This syndrome is described in Cahn, *Our Brother's Keeper*,

pp. 45–49. See George Boyce, *When Navajos Had Too Many Sheep: The 1940s* (San Francisco: Indian Historian Press, 1974), pp. 197–200, and Thompson, *Navajos' Long Walk*, pp. 88–117, for the origins of the Special Navajo Program, in which both authors had key roles.

26. L. Madison Coombs, *Doorway Toward the Light* (Washington, D.C.: Bureau of Indian Affairs, Department of Interior, 1962).
27. Thompson, *Navajos' Long Walk*, p. 107.
28. Subcommittee on Indian Education of the Committee on Labor and Public Welfare, United States Senate, *The Education of American Indians: A Compendium of Federal Boarding School Evaluations* 3 (Washington, D.C.: Government Printing Office, November 1969): 258.
29. Eighteen percent of Indian high-school graduates go to college (compared to 50 percent of white graduates); 3 percent of Indians and 32 percent of whites graduate. One of 100 Indian college graduates receives a master's degree. *Kennedy Report*, p. xiii.
30. *Kennedy Report*, p. xii.
31. See Murray L. Wax and Rosalie H. Wax, "The Enemies of the People," in Bahr, et al., *Native Americans Today*, p. 187.
32. NAACP Legal Defense and Education Fund, *An Even Chance* (New York: NAACP Legal Defense and Educational Fund, 1971).
33. Both the *Kennedy Report* and *Even Chance* document the misuse and unequal distribution of Johnson-O'Malley and impact-aid funds.
34. Berry, *Education of American Indians*, p. 29.
35. Drop-outs should really be considered "push-outs," according to work by Rosalie Wax, "Warrior Dropouts," in *Native Americans Today*, p. 146.
36. Part of the concern resulted from the erosion of Navajo land into the Colorado River, threatening to fill the newly built Boulder Dam. See Katherine Iverson, "Progressive Education for Native Americans: Washington Theory and Reservation Practice" (submitted for publication); also Margaret Szasz, *Education and the American Indian: The Road to Self-Determination: 1928–1973* (Albuquerque: University of

New Mexico Press, 1974); Phelps-Stokes Fund, *The Navajo Indian Problem* (New York: Phelps-Stokes, 1939); and Boyce, *Too Many Sheep*.

37. Collier himself soon came to the painful decision that his administration had "erred profoundly" by not vesting responsibility in the local communities. John Collier, *On the Gleaming Way* (Denver: Sage Books, 1946), pp. 65–67.
38. For a detailed analysis of the legal and economic problems in implementing Native American community schools, see Daniel M. Rosenfelt, "Indian Schools and Community Control," in *Stanford Law Review* 25 (April 1973): 492–550.
39. Navajo Community College received full accreditation by North Central Association in 1976. For a description of the early stages of the school's development, see Fuchs and Havighurst, *To Live on This Earth*, pp. 264–72.
40. David Aberle, "A Plan for Navajo Economic Development," in *Toward Economic Development for Native American Communities*, a compendium of papers submitted to the Subcommittee on Economy in Government of the Joint Economic Committee, Congress of the United States, vol. 1 (Washington, D.C.: Government Printing Office, 1969), p. 228.
41. Paulo Freire, *Pedagogy of the Oppressed* (New York: Seabury Press, 1970); Albert Memmi, *The Colonizer and the Colonized* (Boston: Beacon Press, 1967).

The Colonial Mentality: Assessments of the Intelligence of Blacks and of Women in Nineteenth-Century America

Charles H. Lyons

There is a general debate about whether blacks and women in the United States could be considered as having had a colonial experience in the same sense as, say, Asians and Africans did until some twenty or so years ago. While acknowledging the obvious differences among particular situations, still one ought not let those differences obscure certain commonalities. The treatment of blacks and women in our society has in many ways resembled that meted out to other groups commonly considered as colonized.

Colonialism is a phenomenon broader than the mere conquest and political domination of one nation by another. Rather, the concept has to do with certain basic relationships that exist among people, relationships that can exist in many different settings. Colonialism can even exist within a single country in which one class, ethnic group, race, or sex dominates others through certain patterns of behavior that are identifiable as colonialistic. Some scholars have even coined a special expression for this: "internal colonialism." [1]

One thing that distinguishes the colonialistic from other forms of human behavior is the particular mind-set of the person in power—that is, the colonizer. The general point is that the colonizer—no matter the particular setting in which he operates—feels a psychological justification to rationalize his subjugation of others. He feels compelled to reason that the colonized belong to (in the words of Martin Carnoy) "a different *category* of being."[2] He feels the need not only to put a distance between himself and his subjects but to convince himself that that distance is natural and inevitable. Thus, it is quite common for colonizers to describe the colonized as savage, heathen, backward, and so on, and then to develop elaborate theories to describe why this is so. There is a tendency for colonizers to go even further: to deny the very humanity of those under their power. To do so requires the denial to the colonized of that aspect of humanity that makes men at once superior to brute creation and equal to one another: human intelligence. Again, elaborate theories are called for if that denial is to be maintained and believed.

A fascinating thing for the historian to observe is the similarities such theories have had as they were applied to different groups. Consider the rationalizations put forth in the nineteenth century to "prove" the mental inferiority and hence to justify the subject positions of blacks and women.

COMPANIONS MEEK FOR MEN

To many antiblack and antifeminist writers of the nineteenth century, Biblical tradition offered potent rationalizations for their positions. The most frequently cited source for antiblack sentiment had to do with the various traditions surrounding the curse Noah pronounced on Ham and his descendants. Antifeminists saw in the Bible numerous reasons why females were inferior to males, reasons ranging from the creation of woman from man's rib and Eve's sin to the position of women in the Old Testament and the lessons of the Gospels with reference to female submissiveness. While such Biblical messages provided primarily a rationale for social subjugation, they also contributed to the creation of stereotypes that tended to stress, among other things, the inferiority of the mental capacities of blacks and women.

The legend of Ham has a curious history. Genesis tells us that Noah fell down drunk one day. His son Ham took this occasion to ridicule his father, who, on becoming sober, pronounced a fateful curse—a curse curiously not on Ham but on Canaan, Ham's son, and on Canaan's descendants. "Cursed by Canaan," intoned

Noah. "A servant of servants shall he be to his brethren." To the early church fathers St. Jerome and St. Augustine this passage was interpreted to be a Biblical justification of slavery. Further, as Genesis points out, Canaan and his descendants settled in Egypt on the continent of Africa; hence, Africa was frequently referred to in many Western sources as the land of Ham. In later Jewish commentaries—in the Midrash Rabbah, the Babylonian Talmud, and the mystic Zohar—the meaning of the curse on Ham took on decidedly racial overtones. In these various commentaries, one can see references to Ham's being "smitten in his skin," to Noah's saying to Ham "your seed will be ugly and dark-skinned" and to Ham's being the father "of Canaan who darkened the faces of mankind." Further, one sees in the commentaries numerous references to the beastlike nature of Canaan and his descendants.[3]

Probably because of the interest in Hebrew sources displayed in Renaissance Europe, these Jewish commentaries became known in the Christian world from the sixteenth century onward. Consequently, one can find numerous references in early American sources to these various legends. Indeed, the stories took on a great popularity as there seemed to be contained in them a divine sanction for holding black Africans in bondage. The Bible condoned slavery; black men were cursed in the eyes of God; black men were animal-like; black men were, in short, natural slaves.[4]

This belief in the Biblical justification of slavery and in the divinely ordained inferiority of the black race persisted with some intensity well into the nineteenth century. In 1843, for example, the Reverend Josiah Priest published in Albany, New York, his *Slavery as It Relates to the Negro,* a book that, in various titles, was reprinted five times in the era before the Civil War. Because of the curse of Ham, he declared, religious men must concede the inherent inferiority of the black man. Similarly, the Louisiana physician Samuel A. Cartwright asserted in a popular proslavery tract of 1843 that the anatomical evidence brought to bear to show the physical and mental inferiority of the black man could be explained by the Biblical curse on Canaan. The Reverend John Bachman of South Carolina asserted much the same thing in 1850. Just as the Bible had prophesied, he said, the black man is "still everywhere the 'servant of servants.'" Surely, this is proof that the sons of Ham are "accursed" in the eyes of God. Slavery was not only justifiable but part of God's divine plan. From this position, "we have been irresistably brought to the conclusion," Bachman said, "that in intellectual power the African is an inferior variety of our species." Because of this fact, he needed the "protection and support" which the more intelligent and unaccursed races could supply.[5]

One problem with the Biblical justification of slavery, however, was that the essential message of the Bible, with its emphasis on the unity of mankind and the brotherhood of all men, seemed more suited to the anti- rather than the proslavery cause. The Bible, after all, was the major source of inspiration for abolitionist thought and equalitarian sentiment. A recent work by the historian H. Shelton Smith, however, shows that, in the South, when the chips were down, churchmen were prepared to sacrifice religious orthodoxy for racial orthodoxy. "With rare exceptions," he writes, Southern churchmen "affirmed the inferiority of the Negro race and defended the traditional pattern of white supremacy." During the days of slavery, the churches, "far from cutting their ties with the institution of human bondage," actually admitted more and more slave owners to the church. In the process, Southern religion "became captive to the slavocracy." After the Civil War, this pattern continued. The church, Smith observes, "became the first major southern institution to establish the color line; and, tragically, the clergy generally took the lead in justifying it."[6]

In order to justify slavery and racism, Christian publicists of the nineteenth century were compelled to fabricate elaborate theories in order to square their social beliefs with their religious faith. Some of these theories make the mind boggle. Consider the theory of pre-Adamite races. Any orthodox reading of the Bible confirms that all men stemmed from Adam and Eve, the first pair. This belief, called monogenesis, meant, of course, that all men are brothers and hence the equal of one another in the sight of God. To deny this equality to blacks without flaunting the Bible, some hypothesized that there were races of men that existed prior to the creation of Adam and Eve, the so-called "pre-Adamite" races. Samuel Cartwright, for example, suggested in 1860 that blacks and Indians were created before Adam and Eve and were included among the "living creatures" over whom Adam was given dominion, a version of Biblical history that enjoyed great popularity with Southerners prior to the Civil War. Indeed, Jefferson Davis was of this particular pre-Adamite belief. After the war, in 1867, a Nashville publisher, Buckner Payne, asserted that the pre-Adamite race, the blacks, were little removed from the animal kingdom; they were "beasts." In 1900, this pre-Adamite theory was still very much alive—witness Charles Carroll's *The Negro a Beast,* a virulent attack on the black man published by a religious publishing house in St. Louis.[7]

Antifeminists did not need to go to such lengths to find Biblical proof for their position; the Bible is fraught with explicit and implicit explanations as to the inferiority of women to men. In 1837, for example, the Reverend Jonathan F. Stearns of Newburyport, Massachusetts, sermonized on the duties of women. "Let us turn to the Bible for a moment," he declared, "and see what we can gather from the teachings of inspiration." The Bible tells women to be silent in the house of worship, to subject herself to her husband. Such injunctions "are designed not to *degrade,* but to *elevate* her character . . ."; they are designed to "give a useful direction to the energies of the feminine mind. . . ." He reminded his congregation that "there is a natural *difference,* in the mental as well as physical constitution of the two classes. . . ." Men's intellect is one of aggressiveness, women's one of submissiveness. This does not mean that women are inferior to men in intellect but rather that their intellect is adapted "to a different sphere," the home. Also in 1837 the Congregational clergy of Massachusetts condemned the outspoken Sarah and Angelina Grimké by reminding its female adherents of "the appropriate duties and influence of woman [as] are clearly stated in the New Testament." "When the mild, dependent, softening influence of woman upon the sternness of man's opinions is fully exercised, society feels the effects of it in a thousand forms. . . . But when she assumes the place and tone of a man as a public reformer . . . her character becomes unnatural."[8]

Indeed, the constraints of Biblical tradition pressed down on American women of the nineteenth century so firmly that most

God-fearing women unquestioningly believed that their inferior status was part of the divine plan. As one woman observed in 1849, God placed woman on the earth to be "a help, a *meet* for man." It was Eve, not Adam, who committed the first sin, and as punishment God declared "and thy desire shall be to thy husband, and he shall rule over thee." To the devout pioneer in women's education, Catherine Beecher, "heaven has appointed one sex the superior, and the other to the subordinate station," and that was simply that.[9]

The power the Bible had over women led at least one extremely militant feminist, Elizabeth Stanton, to question the Bible itself. Unlike most other feminists, she was outspokenly anticlerical. To her, "every form of religion which has breathed upon this earth has degraded woman. Man himself could not do this; but when he declares, 'Thus saith the Lord,' of course he can do it." She objected to the fact that women were asked to accept the male nature of God and that men were not brought up to see Her female side as well. "Why Should We Not Pray To Our Mother Who Art In Heaven," she wrote in 1868, "As Well As To Our Father?" Since most feminists were loathe to throw the Bible out in order to gain their objectives, so Elizabeth Stanton set to work writing a *Woman's Bible* in which the anti-feminine parts were challenged and expurgated. The work appeared in the 1890s. In her version of the Scriptures, the story of the removal of Adam's rib was merely the addition of an imaginative editor; in any case, this was "a petty surgical operation." The God of the Jews, a male figure, simply guided and directed "that people in all their devious ways. . . ." Lot's daughters were omitted as they were unworthy of a place in a *Woman's Bible*. Understandably, the Stanton Bible did more harm than good for the cause of feminism.[10]

It is interesting to note that there exists in the literature of abolitionism an indicative pairing of women and blacks with respect to religious understanding and their place in society. Abolitionists, one must remember, held some strong stereotypes of blacks, stereotypes more favorable than antiblack publicists' to be sure, but stereotypes nonetheless. The antislavery preacher William Ellery Channing, for example, saw the black man as "so affectionate, imitative, and docile that in favorable circumstances he catches much that is good." Senator Charles Sumner of Massachusetts remarked in 1862 that "the African is not cruel, vindictive, or harsh, but gentle, forgiving and kind." These qualities, of course, were qualities that were also prized in women, which led some abolitionists and philanthropists to eulogize the black in the same terms nineteenth-century men eulogized the ideal woman. Dr. Samuel Gridley Howe, the famed New England physician and reformer, remarked on visiting a Canadian center for refugee blacks that the refugees were "a little effeminate, as though a portion of their grit had been left out of their composition . . . with their African blood, they may have inherited more of womanly than manly dispositions; for Africans have more of womanly virtues than fiercer people have. Indeed, it may be said that, among the races, Africa is like a gentle sister in a family of fierce brothers." [11]

Being gentle, meek, kind—in short, feminine—blacks were, like women, frequently portrayed as "natural Christians." The Reverend James Freeman Clarke said in 1842 that "in some faculties [the black man] probably *is* inferior"; however, he was superior in "a strong religious tendency." James Russell Lowell of Boston similarly remarked that the African's "gentle, loving" traits were appealingly "feminine." As such, Africans, like women, excelled in "noble, Christian virtues." Similarly, Harriet Beecher Stowe saw blacks as "confessedly more simple, docile, child-like and affectionate than other races." It followed, then, that "the divine graces of love and faith, while inbreathed by the Holy Spirit, find in their natural temperament a more congenial atmosphere. . . ." The literary critic Helen Papashvily has pointed out that "although Uncle Tom . . . was male, it was not too difficult for feminine readers to identify themselves with him. . . . He had the virtues—meekness, piety, humility, endurance—commonly assigned to women in exchange for independence." If the meek were indeed to inherit the earth, then it would be blacks and women who would be there for the reading of the will.[12]

THE ANATOMY OF PREJUDICE

Though religion continued its important role as a source for antiblack and antifeminist thinking right through the nineteenth century, scientific thinking gradually supplanted religion as the major source for believing in the intellectual inferiority of blacks and women. To many scientists of the nineteenth century, physiological differences between the races and sexes seemed to explain what they presumed to be mental differences. For example, much of the evidence used to support the belief that black or female mental capacities were inferior to the white or male came from detailed investigations of the human brain. Though now largely discredited,[13] it was widely assumed in the nineteenth century that the size of the brain was an index of human intelligence: the larger the brain, the greater the potential intellect. Moreover, it was also assumed that the relative size of the brain provided an index in the animal kingdom as to where—either in the "Great Chain" of Being or, later, on the evolutionary scale—the species or varieties should be ranked. The lesser the brain size, the more beastlike the subject.

In the first half of the nineteenth century perhaps the most outstanding American investigator of the differences in the relative cranial capacities of the various races was Professor Samuel Morton, curator of the Natural History Museum in Philadelphia, a museum dubbed the "American Golgatha" because of its vast collection of human skulls and bones. Morton's magnum opus was his *Crania Americana* of 1839, a book that raised the measurement of cranial capacities to a new height in painstaking precision and had an astounding impact on race-thinking in America. Comparing the skulls of the "Caucasian," "Mongolian," "Malay," "American" (Indian), and "Ethiopian" races, Morton found that the mean internal capacities in cubic inches of the skulls were, respectively, 87, 83, 81, 80, and 78. From this investigation Morton concluded that the "Caucasian" race undoubtedly had "the highest intellectual endowment," while the "Ethiopian" race was characterized by "a singular diversity of intellectual character," with certain blacks constituting "the lowest grade of humanity." In a later work, his *Crania Aegyptiaca* of 1844, Morton checked his findings with specimens sent to him from Africa. Again, the Caucasian scored the highest: 85 cubic inches. The "unmixed Negro" scored 71 and his "mulattos" 80. More significant, he noticed through his investigation of "twenty embalmed heads from the Egyptian catacombs" that the relative brain capacities—and hence intellectual ability—of the black and white races was the same for centuries, a fact that led him to affirm his belief in polygenism, that quite un-Biblical theory of the separate origin of the races, and to remark that, as the ancient Egyptians kept blacks as slaves, so from time immemorial the black race has been inferior and degraded.[14]

Morton's work was carried forward, just prior to the Civil War, by Josiah Clark Nott and George Robin Gliddon, both polygenists and proslavery polemicists. Making use of Morton's findings, their quite popular *Types of Man* (1854) argued, the title notwithstanding, that the different "types" of man were in fact distinct species. The black man was biologically and intellectually closer to the chimpanzee than to the "Caucasian." To them, the black species could never advance to civilization because they were inherently and permanently inferior in mental ability. Thus, slavery had to be the natural relationship between the races.[15]

The legal emancipation of the black man hardly emancipated him from such degrading investigations and comparisons. In 1869, for example, Dr. Sanford B. Hunt, a surgeon with the United States Volunteers, published his findings based on 405 autopsies of white and black soldiers killed during the Civil War. Hunt concluded from brain-weight analysis that the brain of the "full-blooded" black man weighs some five ounces less than that of the white and that an infusion of "white blood" would "determine a positive increase in the negro brain, which in the quadroon is only three ounces below the white standard."[16]

This type of comparison between the brain sizes and cranial capacities of the various races continued throughout the remainder of the nineteenth century—and indeed into the twentieth as well. But the charge could be made—and was frequently made—that the assumption on which such findings of mental differences were based was erroneous—that brain size is not necessarily indicative of mental ability.[17]

But with the rise of evolutionary theory there emerged some scientific reason for believing in the connection. Charles Darwin himself declared that among "civilised nations" the size of the brain appeared to enlarge due to "greater intellectual ability." Moreover, as the brain grew larger and as the size of the jaw diminished "from lessened use," so the "general appearance" of civilized man in comparison with the savage races "underwent remarkable changes." The British anthropologist E. B. Tylor similarly observed in 1881 that, as civilized man called into play his higher intellect, so the frontal lobes of his brain enlarged, thereby changing the shape of his skull.[18]

The shape of the skull was thought to be extremely important in determining the relative evolutionary position of the various races. Indeed, the notion of ranking humans and animals according to skull shape long antedated the advent of evolutionary theory. During the eighteenth century, classificatory-minded biologists and anthropologists ranked the skulls of animals and men according to a variety of measures, the most popular of which was the facial angle, a measure of the degree to which the jaw juts out from the rest of the skull. The greater the angle, the higher the forehead, the greater the skull capacity, and consequently the more intelligent and "human" the specimen. The smaller the angle, the more intelligent and beastlike the creature. In eighteenth- and nineteenth-century rankings, the skull of the European invariably ranked the highest, that of the black African somewhere below. Indeed, the black skull was placed just above that of the ape, presumably the most intelligent member of brute creation. Such rankings tended to generate questions as to whether the black man was more brute than human.[19]

Indeed, in the popular as well as the scientific mind, the association of blacks with apes was a strong and persistent one. The historian Winthrop Jordan points to the "strange and eventually tragic happenstance" that early European voyagers to Africa discovered apes and blacks sharing the same habitat. Consequently, there arose persistent beliefs that blacks and apes had common ancestors, that blacks indulged in bestial relationships with simians, that menlike beasts produced beastlike men. Such ideas neatly complemented opinion that blacks possessed such beastlike qualities as sexual excess, volatile passion, instinctive rather than rational minds.[20]

With the rise of Darwinism, such ideas were translated into a belief that the black man was in an evolutionary position somewhere below the white man and somewhere above the ape. Indeed, in the popular literature of the nineteenth century, the so-called "missing link" was invariably presented with an appearance resembling the physiognomy of the black race. Scientists asserted that the black man's overdeveloped sex organs indicated his brutish nature, that his unfavorable facial angle was more beastlike than human, that his very brain structure closely resembled that of the ape.[21]

Of course, one need not have been a scientist or an evolutionist to consider the black an animal. Under slavery, the black was frequently portrayed as little more than a domesticated animal with little, if any, human sensibility. Later, in the spate of "Negrophobia" that engulfed the end of the nineteenth and the beginning of the twentieth century, the black man was pictured as a dangerous, rape-crazed brute. Charles Carroll's *The Negro a Beast* saw in the black man "the savage nature and murderous instincts of the wild beast and the cunning lust of a fiend." Thomas Dixon's *The Clansman* (1905) saw the black as "half child, half animal, the sport of impulse, whim and conceit . . . a being who left to his own will, roams at night and sleeps in the day, whose speech knows no word of love, whose passions, once aroused, are as the fury of the tiger."[22]

Female brain power was also the subject of anatomical investigation. In 1888, for example, *Popular Science* magazine carried an article saying that the cranium of a woman is smaller than that of a man and that the weight of the average female brain was some six ounces less than that of a man. These facts meant that women did not have the intellectual energy to compete with a man and that, consequently, women should be educated to stay at home in their traditional role. Similarly, in 1900 Professor Henri Marion of the University of Paris observed that "the cranium of the woman, in all ages, is smaller than that of the man, and this fact is even more true in the more civilized peoples. . . . The brain of the woman is, on average, less voluminous and weighs less; the weight is 1100 to 1300 grams in the woman, 1200 to 1400 in the man." Further, the ratio of the weight of the brain to the weight of the body is 1 to 44 in the woman and 1 to 40 in the man—"and the difference increases with age." These facts led Professor Marion to urge that women not be subjected to the rigors of an education more suited to boys, an education that would unsuit her for her true calling. The woman "is organized essentially for the maternal function which is her *essence*."[23]

On the whole, however, less seems to have been said about the quantitative differences between male and female brains than was the case with regard to the differences between black and white brains. One might suspect that the issue of relative brain sizes and weights was so bound up with racial comparison that pushing any kind of quantitative comparison could prove embarassing; white women were, after all, members of the white race. Instead, physiological discussion about women's abilities tended to emphasize the qualitative rather than the quantitative differences between the mental abilities of the sexes.

Alexander Walker, for example, saw some great qualitative differences between the brains of men and women. A British physician who visited the United States in the 1840s in preparation for an American edition of his *Woman, Physiologically Considered* (1842), Walker asserted that "there is a vast difference between the brain and mind of man, and the brain and mind of woman—a sexual difference. . . ." In a woman, "the whole brain and the intellectual functions considered generally are . . . less, even at birth, than those of a man; she has, even at that period, with larger organs of sense, a larger forehead and more powerful observing faculties. . . ." This "natural inferiority of intellect in women is compensated by a vast superiority in instinct. . . ." Such was nature's design, as "love, impregnation, gestation, partuition, lactation, and nursing (the principal acts of woman's life) [are] almost entirely instinctive. . . ." Having a "smaller cerebel," the woman has an understandable "incapacity of reasoning —generalizing, following trains of connected ideas, judging, perservering . . ." and she has a "feebler capability of attention." [24]

Such ideas received something of an *imprimatur* in the writings of Charles Darwin. In his *Descent of Man* (1871) he took issue with those who said that there exists no "inherent difference" between the sexes in the qualities of their mental attributes. "No one disputes that the bull differs from the cow, the wild boar from the sow, the stallion from the mare. . . ." The woman, "owing to her maternal instincts," has a more highly developed faculty of sense and feeling; she is a warmer, more docile creature than the man. The man, on the other hand, "is the rival of other men; he delights in competition. . . ." He must "hunt for their joint substance." But to hunt and compete, to outwit animals or other men, "requires the aid of higher mental faculties, namely, observation, reason, invention or imagination. These faculties will thus have been continually put to the test and selected during manhood." As proof for this assertion, Darwin compared man's intellectual achievements to woman's. "If two lists were made of the most preeminent men and women in poetry, painting, sculpture, music . . . history, science, and philosophy, with half a dozen names under each subject, the two lists would not bear comparison." This proves that men's faculties of "deep thought, reason or imagination" were much more highly developed than those of women. In sum, Darwin intimated that women lagged behind man in evolution, as their intellects had not developed to the same high standard as man's.[25]

Were women then to be considered beasts? Certainly not in the same sense as blacks were considered, inasmuch as white women belonged to the same species as white men and hence were undoubtedly human. However, there is plenty of evidence to demonstrate that many nineteenth-century men did think that there was something animal-like in the female nature and for reasons similar in some ways to those given for considering blacks animal-like. The woman, like the black, was considered to be ruled by passion, passion whose seat lay in her reproductive organs. As the historian Andrew Sinclair has described the typical nineteenth-century view, "the seat of a woman's reason lay in her womb. . . ." Consequently, the nineteenth-century girl was "more emotional than boys, and therefore more in the need of control." And the way to control those emotions, and thus female purity, was through training in ladylike behavior.[26]

Being made a lady was rough on the girl. She was to be segregated from boys and their temptations. She was to avoid drinking coffee or other stimulating drinks. She was to avoid lying on too soft beds or on too soft chairs. She was to take frequent cold baths to diminish "the sensibility which otherwise might do mischief." Heaven forbid that she should cross her legs or ride a seesaw, practices that would stimulate her passions. She was to be taught to wear an uncomfortable corset whose purpose was, quite literally, to girdle her passions. The dangers were omnipresent. Boarding schools were, to Alexander Walker, "a hot bed of vice to all who have reached puberty." Remember, advised Henr Marion, with puberty the emotions are enlivened in the girl much more so than in the boy: "hate, vengeance, anger . . . as well as the tender emotions so fundamental in the woman. . . ." Without self-control, remarked George Naphey in 1810, her passion would lead her to "the grave, the madhouse, or, worse yet, the brothel." Even the confines of marriage were no sure safeguard for the woman. The emotional character of the female nature, re marked Alexander Walker, made the married woman prone to infidelity; her instincts were just too strong.[27]

THE PERILS OF PUBERTY

For some obvious—and some not so obvious—reasons, physiolo gists of the nineteenth century saw puberty as a time of grea importance in the development of mental ability in both blacks and women. It was widely assumed that the intellectual potentia of the black man evolved only to a certain point—that is, that his mental development for some reason became "arrested" with the onset of puberty. It was also assumed in many quarters tha women, with the onset of menstruation, became intellectually weakened as nature focused their energies away from the devel opment of the brain and more to the development of the repro ductive organs. Great physical harm, wrote many, would occur if either postpubescent blacks or girls were educated in the same rigorous fashion as white boys.

The notion of the declining intellectual powers of pubescen blacks was present from the beginning of the nineteenth century and indeed the origin of the idea probably dates from a much earlier time. There are countless accounts from teachers, mis sionaries, and officials in Africa, the West Indies, and the Ameri can South that testified to the fact that the black child, up to the age of puberty, was every bit as bright as a white child of the same age, but, with the onset of puberty, his intellectual energies rapidly decreased. Winwood Reade, British explorer of West Af rica, observed that, "respecting the precocity of Negro children there can be no doubt"; but a missionary friend confided in him that black children "had not such retentive memories [as white children] and that . . . they came to a status quo about 16, and after that slowly forgot all they had learnt." Another Briton, Sir Charles Lyell, observed the same phenomenon among the blacks of the American South during the 1840s; he, however, ascribed fourteen as the "status quo" age. Similarly, General S. C. Armstrong, the founder of the Hampton Institute, observed in 1872 that the black man is "capable of acquiring knowledge to any degree, and, to a certain age, at least, with about the same facility as white children; but . . . [he] does not have his steady development of mental strength up to advanced years." For this reason, Armstrong said, the black man should not be given the same sort of education given to white youth; instead, he should be given a "special" kind of education in vocational subjects—hence Hampton's "industrial" philosophy. In similar fashion, the argument of the declining intellectual power of the black man was used in opposition to black education in the North.[28]

To many, if not most, concerned whites, then, the issue was not whether blacks suffered from declining intellectual powers but rather why such a phenomenon took place. Opinion was moderately divided. Some thought that it occurred because of the oppressive effects of tropical climate on tropical races: "the ravages of climate," observed one thinker of 1862, gradually injures "the brain so much as to cause an idiotic vacancy in the features, an inability to express thoughts into words. . . ." Others were of the opinion that in the tropics vegetation seems to mature much more quickly, and so it was with the blacks. Richard Madden, a British physician who visited West Africa in 1842, hypothesized that "the effects of climate act on the mental energies [of Africans] . . . bringing [them] sooner to perfection and sooner to decay." General Armstrong held a similar view: "the Negro matures sooner than the white . . ." he said, because "he is a child of the tropics, and the differences of the races goes deeper than the skin."[29]

During the second half of the nineteenth century, however, it was anatomical evidence that was primarily used to explain the nature of arrested development. European scientists led the way in this research. In 1856, the Frenchman Gratiolet advanced the theory that in the brain of the African the coronal suture closed at an early age, generally at puberty. In effect, the black brain became stunted as further intellectual growth became impossible. Similarly, the British scientist Robert Dunn in the 1860s observed that "whilst in the white man the gradual increase of the jaws and the facial bones is not equalled, but exceeded, by the development, or rather enlargement of the brain, the reverse is the case for the Negro." Indeed, "the central frontal suture closes in the Negro in early youth. . . ." Thus it happened that black and white children were equal to one another in mental ability in childhood but quite different after puberty. Portentously, Dunn observed that this same sort of arrested development happens in the orangutan: With puberty both they and the blacks are marked with a projection of the jaw (which gave the characteristic unfavorable facial angle) and the closing of cranial sutures. In 1896 the respected British ethnologist E. H. Keane observed that "the development of the negro and white proceeds along different lines. While with the latter the volume of the brain grows with the expansion of the brain-pan, in the former the growth of the brain is on the contrary arrested by the premature closing of the cranial sutures, and lateral pressure of the frontal bone." [30]

While it was European science that led the way in this type of research, American scientists and publicists followed it with keen interest and were quick to pick up on the implications. The popular philosopher and historian John Fiske, for example, was intimately acquainted with the writings of people like Robert Dunn. To him, explanation of arrested development in the brains of certain races also explained why it was that those races had become "arrested in an immobile type of civilization. . . ." Only white peoples demonstrated that "persistent tendency to progress" that was necessary for human advancement. Similarly, under the influence of the closing-cranial-suture school the biologist Edward Drinker Cope of the University of Pennsylvania in 1890 saw the black man as "susceptible of education in his youth, and bright and intelligent to a considerable degree." But with the closing of those sutures, the mind of the black man underwent "more or less an eclipse." For these reasons, Cope said, educating blacks was a waste of time and effort. It was also dangerous physiologically, argued others. Education would, some said, lead to the enlargement of the frontal lobes of the brain of the black man and this enlargement would put undue pressure on the skull.

The result would be anything from massive migraines to an impaired sense of balance that would make it impossible for the educated black to stand erect.[31]

The notion of the declining powers of black intellect dovetailed quite neatly with the theories of Social Darwinists. Herbert Spencer himself noted with some interest the reports of travelers to Africa and elsewhere as to the "great precocity among savage and semi-civilized peoples, and on the early arrest of their mental progress." This was "in conformity with the biological law that the higher the organisms the longer they take to evolve." Thus, "members of the inferior races may be expected to complete their mental evolution sooner than members of the superior races." What this meant was that the "savage and semi-civilized peoples" were in fact adult in body and child in mind. "How the races differ in respect of the more or less developed structures of their minds will be best understood on recalling that unlikeness between the juvenile mind and the adult mind among ourselves. . . ." In fact, he declared, the mind of the primitive is so much like the mind of the civilized child that to understand the one would be to understand the other.[32]

Following Spencer, the American psychologist G. Stanley Hall similarly argued that primitive races were in an early stage of evolutionary development. He was also influenced by Ernst Haeckel's Biogenic Law, which stated, first, that the development of the individual represents a recapitulation of the development of the race (i.e., the individual "evolves" from childhood to adulthood in much the same fashion as his race has evolved from a "child race" to a mature or "civilized" race); and, second, that primitive culture must be considered as being in the arrested stages of childhood or adolescence. This led Hall to a kind of benevolent paternalism when it came to the question of black education. Blacks, being a "child-like people," must be educated under the watchful eye of the more civilized race, and that education should be suited to their particular evolutionary stage. Hence, he, too, championed that special, separate type of education, industrial education, for the black man.[33]

Interestingly, Hall also advocated a special, separate kind of education for adolescent girls as well. He thought that, as evolution had advanced, so the differences between the sexes became more marked, so marked in fact as to warrant a separate system of education for girls who had reached puberty. Prior to puberty, the intellectual qualities of girls and boys were essentially the same. However, with adolescence, girls underwent such a metamorphosis that they quickly and quite naturally lost interest in intellectual pursuits and became more concerned with such petty things as dress and appearance; further, they became less aggressive and more domestically inclined than boys. Girls' education, therefore, should not consist of hard academic subject matter; rather, it should stress the development of such idealized feminine virtues as gentleness and warmth, qualities of the home. Boys' education, on the other hand, should aim to develop such male qualities as competitiveness and aggressiveness, qualities necessary in the struggle for existence.[34]

Hall's views of women's education were very much those of the Victorian man whose ideal woman was the warm, compassionate, submissive housewife and mother. He shared this feeling with another Victorian, Charles Darwin. Darwin felt that with an increase in education for girls, so the traditional intellectual differences between men and women might diminish. Like Hall, he thought that prepubescent boys and girls were alike, intellectually, and that the major differences in mental constitution came about during the period of adolescence. However, if an adolescent girl were given an education comparable to that given an adolescent boy, then things would change. If a woman wished to "reach the same standard as man, she ought, when nearly adult to be trained for energy and perseverence, and to have her reason and imagination exercised to the highest point. . . ." Then she would be able to "transmit these qualities . . . to her . . . daughters," thereby improving the intellectual strength of her sex. It could be done, said Darwin, but he implied it would be done at a great price. The man's competitive urge, which "leads to ambition which passes too easily to selfishness," needs to be tempered by the "greater tenderness and less selfishness" of the woman.[35]

It would be done at an even greater price, argued others, because it was probable that the pursuit of a rigorous academic education would result in great physiological harm to the woman. Though these Victorian gentlemen were reluctant to talk with any precision about such a delicate subject as menstruation, what was going through their minds was that education for adolescent girls interfered with menstruation: Energies that were required for menstruation and the building of the female reproductive organs were being devoted to the development of brain power instead. This would lead, then, to a physiological impairment of the female anatomy.

Perhaps the most interesting dispute over the effects of puberty on a girl's scholastic ability came in 1873 with the publication of Edward H. Clarke's *Sex in Education; or, a Fair Chance for Girls.* Clarke, a Boston physician and a onetime teacher at the Harvard School of Medicine, wrote this book just at the time when the issue of coeducation was being hotly debated in Boston, Cambridge, and several other New England towns and cities. Clarke noted that "the delicate bloom, early but rapidly failing beauty and singular pallor of American girls and women have almost passed into proverb. . . ." Too much education of the wrong sort was the cause of this and other maladies: "those grevious maladies which torture a woman's earthly existence, called leuccorrhoea, amenorrhoea, dysemenorroea, chronic and acute overitis, prolapsus uteri, hysteria, neuralgia . . . are all caused by a neglect of the peculiarities of a woman's organization. The regimen of the schools fosters this neglect." Girls have a tremendous task getting their sex organs in shape, he said, though not so indelicately. "The growth of this particular and marvelous apparatus in the perfect development of which humanity has so large an interest, occurs during the few years of a girl's educational life." Boys, on the other hand, face no such crisis as their human development is one of a steady progression to manhood. "The muscles [of the reproductive organs] and the brain cannot functionate in their best way at the same moment." To choose to send blood to the brain instead of the uterine area would result in "monstrous brains and puny bodies; abnormally active cerebration, and abnormally weak digestion; flowing through and constipated bowels; . . ." If the reader did not believe him, Clarke went into the clinical histories of the sorry effects of education on female scholars. There was a "Miss D," for example, at Vassar. She began her "catamenial function" at age fifteen; yet, in school, her "regimen was . . . nearly that of a boy's regimen." She fainted in the gym, graduated with "fair honors and a poor physique" at about the age of nineteen, and then went to see Dr. Clarke. "The evidence was altogether in favor of an arrest of the reproductive apparatus. . . ." There was nothing the good doctor could do for her now.[36]

Coming at the time of the political debates over coeducation, Clarke's book quickly drew counterattacks. Mrs. E. B. Duffy of Philadelphia called "Dr. Clarke's book . . . the last struggle of the opponents of co-education." It was a desperate and dastardly attack by those who preyed on women's fears of "weakness and invalidism. . . . They trust to the ignorance of the community to maintain their position, knowing too well how readily women accept what is told them concerning themselves by a man, and a physician at that, even when they *know* better." Remarking on the general issue of physiological harm due to education, Mary Livermore observed in 1883 that "one would suppose in reading [books by certain physicians] that women possessed but one class of physical organs, and that these are always diseased. Such a teaching is pestiferous. . . ." [37]

Dr. Clarke had some influential supporters, however. In 1874, for example, the National Education Association extended to the doctor an invitation to address the Association's annual convention; he was warmly received. In 1877 the influential John Philbrick, Superintendent of Schools in Boston, cited Clarke's findings repeatedly in his successful effort to keep Boston's high schools from going coeducational. Surprisingly, perhaps, given his wife's interest in the higher education of women, Harvard's Louis Agassiz advertised that he was "prepared to subscribe to every one of [Clarke's] propositions." Similarly, another Harvard man, President Charles W. Eliot, wrote a glowing review of Clarke's book, commenting from his stance as a Social Darwinist that higher education was unfitting the daughters of the better classes for the maternal function. "The women who are morally and physically best fitted to perpetuate and improve the race," he remarked, "are precisely those who are physically least likely to do so." Clarke, he reminded his readers, was a man of authority, a former professor at Harvard and a member of its Board of Overseers, and his views were supported by "all the medical physiologists of the world." [38]

CONCLUSION

Colonization is as much a state of mind as it is a political action. Those who hold power over others, as students of the psychology of colonialism have suggested, feel a need to justify their position, to rationalize their behavior. In this essay we have discussed how, in nineteenth-century America, whites and males developed elaborate theories in order to render legitimate their social, political, and economic domination over blacks and women.

To summarize, many resorted to religious hypotheses in order to rationalize the superiority of white males. Both blacks and women were depicted as having meek, humble, docile natures; consequently, their minds were thought to be soft, gentle, and simple. Paradoxically, perhaps, religious theories were also used to portray blacks as savage, brutal, and inhuman. This portrayal was more powerfully developed in scientific circles. Anatomists of the nineteenth century saw the black as animallike, possessed of an inferior brain, which, as many scientists said, was like that of an ape. They reasoned that the black possessed powerfully developed senses of instinct and passion and thus lacked developed faculties of reason and self-control. They said the same thing about women, who were portrayed as being motivated more by passion than intellect. Females, they theorized, were filled with an animal passion that had to be girdled.

A point to remember is that we are all children of history and thus heirs to its ideas and institutions. While the form of expression may have changed, still many basic ideas have not. We now use sophisticated IQ tests to demonstrate the mental inferiority of blacks. We have developed intricate tests of personality that glibly assert that certain human characteristics are more "male" or "female" than others. In the contemporary world, as well as the historical, we should perennially question not only what people say but why they say it.

Notes

1. For "internal colonialism," see Erwin H. Epstein, "Education and *Peruanidad:* Internal Colonialism in the Peruvian Highlands," in *Comparative Education Review* 15 (June 1971): 188; Albert Memmi, *Dominated Man* (New York: Orion Press, 1968); and Martin Carnoy, *Education as Cultural Imperialism* (New York: McKay, 1974), pp. 19–21, 233 ff.
2. Carnoy, *Education as Cultural Imperialism*, p. 26.
3. Genesis, 9:22–23; Winthrop D. Jordan, *White over Black: American Attitudes toward the Negro, 1550–1812* (Chapel Hill, N.C.: University of North Carolina Press, 1968), pp. 17–18, 35–37; Edith R. Sanders, "The Hamitic Hypothesis: Its Origin and Functions in Time Perspective," in *Journal of African History* 10, no. 4 (1969): 521–22.
4. Jordan, *White over Black*, pp. 36, 41–43, 200–201, 245–46.
5. Josiah Priest, *Slavery as It Relates to the Negro, or African* (Albany, N.Y.: C. Van Benthuysen, 1843); Samuel A. Cartwright as cited in George Frederickson, *The Black Image in the White Mind* (New York: Harper & Row, 1971), p. 87; John Bachman as quoted in Thomas F. Gossett, *Race: The History of an Idea in America* (New York: Schocken Books, 1968), pp. 62–63.
6. H. Shelton Smith, *In His Image, But . . . : Racism in Southern Religion, 1780–1910* (Durham, N.C.: Duke University Press, 1972), pp. vii–viii.
7. Frederickson, *Black Image*, pp. 86–87, 188–89, 277.
8. Jonathan F. Stearns, *Female Influence, and the True Mode of Its Exercise . . .* (1837), and "Pastoral Letter of the General Association of Massachusetts (Orthodox) to the Churches under Their Care," August 11, 1837, both as contained in Aileen S. Kraditor, ed., *Up from the Pedestal: Se-*

lected Writings in the History of American Feminism (Chicago: Quadrangle, 1968), pp. 48–49, 51.

9. [Anon], *Woman as She Was, Is, and Should Be* (New York: S. W. Benedict, 1849), pp. 15–16; Catherine Beecher (1840) as quoted in Merle Curti, *The Social Ideas of American Educators* (Totowa, N.J.: Littlefield, Adams, 1959), reprint of 1935 ed., p. 189.
10. Andrew Sinclair, *The Emancipation of the American Woman* (New York: Harper-Colophon, 1965), pp. 198–201.
11. Channing, Sumner, and Howe as quoted in Frederickson, *Black Image*, pp. 106, 107, 163–64.
12. Clarke and Stowe as quoted in Frederickson, *Black Image*, pp. 110 and 170; Lowell as quoted in Martin B. Duberman, *James Russell Lowell* (Boston: Houghton Mifflin, 1966), p. 79; Helen Papashvily, *All the Happy Endings: A Study of the Domestic Novel in America, the Women Who Wrote It, the Women Who Read It, in the Nineteenth Century* (New York: King's Crown Press, 1956), p. 73.
13. See Ashley Montagu, *Man's Most Dangerous Myth: The Fallacy of Race* (New York: Meridian Books, 1964, 4th ed.), pp. 85–87.
14. Samuel Morton, *Crania Americana, or a Comparative View of the Skulls of Various Aboriginal Nations of North and South America* (Philadelphia: John Pennington, 1839), pp. 3–9, 40, 260; Samuel Morton, *Crania Aegyptiaca, or Observations on Egyptian Ethnography* (Philadelphia: John Pennington, 1844), pp. 59–62. See also William Stanton, *The Leopard's Spots: Scientific Ideas toward Race in America, 1815–1859* (Chicago: Phoenix Books, 1960), pp. 59–62.
15. Josiah C. Nott and George R. Gliddon, *Types of Man, or Ethnographical Researches . . .* (Philadelphia: Lippincott, Grambo, and Co., 1854), pp. 457–59. See also Stanton, *Leopard's Spots*, pp. 161–73, and Gossett, *Race*, p. 65.
16. Hunt as quoted and cited in John S. Haller, *Outcasts from Evolution: Scientific Attitudes of Racial Inferiority, 1859–1900* (Urbana, Ill.: University of Illinois Press, 1971).
17. Ibid., pp. 37–39.
18. Charles Darwin, *The Descent of Man* (New York: Mod-

ern Library edition, n.d., published together with the *Origin of Species*), p. 530; E. B. Tylor, *Anthropology: An Introduction to the Study of Man and Civilization* (London: Macmillan, 1881, rev. ed. 1904), p. 60.

19. Information for this and the following three paragraphs is derived from Charles H. Lyons, *To Wash an Aethiop White: British Ideas about Black African Education, 1530–1960* (New York: Teachers College Press, 1975), chaps. 1–4.
20. Jordan, *White over Black*, pp. 28–29.
21. For black men and "missing link," see Christine Bolt, *Victorian Attitudes toward Race* (London: Routledge and Kegan Paul, 1971), pp. 133–34.
22. Quotations from Carroll and Dixon as cited in Frederickson, *Black Image*, pp. 277, 280.
23. A. Hughs Bennell, "Hygiene in the Higher Education of Women," in *Popular Science Monthly*, February 1888, as cited in Sinclair, *Emancipation of the American Woman*, p. 124, fn. 13; Henri Marion, *Psychologie de la femme* (Paris: Libraire Armand Colin, 1900), pp. 53, 57 (translations my own).
24. Alexander Walker, *Woman Physiologically Considered, as to Mind, Morals, Marriage* . . . (New York: J. and H. G. Langle, 1839; new ed. 1842), pp. 4–5, 6, 37.
25. Darwin, *Descent of Man*, pp. 873–74.
26. Sinclair, *Emancipation of the American Woman*, p. 121.
27. For this general description of the training of the nineteenth-century lady, see ibid., pp. 121–23; Walker on boarding schools as quoted in ibid., p. 122; Marion, *Psychologie de la femme*, pp. 103–4; Walker on infidelity, in Walker, *Woman Physiologically Considered*, p. 168.
28. Winwood Reade, *Journal of the Anthropological Society of London* 2 (1864): xl; Charles Lyell, *Second Journey to the United States* (London: J. Murray, 1849), p. 105; S. C. Armstrong as quoted in Henry Allen Bullock, *A History of Negro Education in the South from 1619 to the Present* (Cambridge, Mass.: Harvard University Press, 1967), p. 76.
29. J. F. Napier Hewitt, *European Settlements on the West Coast of Africa* . . . (London: Chapham and Hall, 1862), p.

71; Richard Madden, "Report of Her Majesty's Commissioner on the State of British Settlements on the Western Coast of Africa," in "Report from the Select Committee . . . on the West Coast of Africa," *Parliamentary Papers,* 1842 (551), pp. xii, 430; Armstrong as quoted in Bullock, *History of Negro Education,* p. 76.

30. For Gratiolet, see Charles S. Johnson and Horace Mann Bond, "The Investigation of Racial Differences Prior to 1910," in *Journal of Negro Education* 3 (July 1934): 329–30; for Dunn, see Haller, *Outcasts from Evolution,* pp. 34–36; A. H. Keane, *Ethnology* (London: Cambridge University Press, 1896), p. 266.

31. For the effects on American race-thinking of European research and citations of and quotations from Fiske and Cope, see Haller, *Outcasts from Evolution,* pp. 36, 138, 198–99; for statements regarding physiological harm of black education, see Gossett, *Race,* p. 263.

32. Herbert Spencer, *Essays: Scientific, Political, and Speculative* (New York: D. Appleton, 1892), pp. 335, 355–57.

33. For Hall, Haeckel's Law, and recapitulation theory, see Richard Hofstadter, *Social Darwinism in American Thought* (New York: George Braziller, 1944; rev. 1959), p. 193; for Hall's support of industrial education, see Curti, *Social Ideas of American Educators,* p. 413, and Dorothy Ross, *G. Stanley Hall: The Psychologist as Prophet* (Chicago: University of Chicago Press, 1972), p. 415.

34. Ross, *Hall,* pp. 301–302; Curti, *Social Ideas,* pp. 419–20.

35. For Hall as a Victorian gentleman, see Ross, *Hall,* p. 423; Darwin, *Descent of Man,* pp. 874–75.

36. Edward H. Clarke, *Sex in Education; or, a Fair Chance for Girls* (Boston: James Osgood, 1874, 5th ed.), pp. 21, 23, 37, 40–41, 79–85.

37. E. B. Duffy, *No Sex in Education; or, an Equal Chance for Both Boys and Girls. Being a Review of Dr. E. H. Clarke's "Sex in Education"* (Philadelphia: J. M. Stoddard, 1874), pp. 36–37; Mary A. Livermore, *What Shall We Do with Our Daughters? Superfluous Women, and Other Lectures* (Boston: Lee and Shepard, 1883), p. 22.

38. Clarke's invitation from and address to the NEA is contained in Edward H. Clarke, *The Building of a Brain* (Boston: Houghton Mifflin, 1874, 5th ed.), pp. 7–9, 13–65; [Charles W. Eliot], "Clarke's Sex in Education," in *Nation* 17 (November 1873): 324–25; Agassiz's remarks are contained in the advertisement for Clarke's *Building of Brain* in Clarke, *Sex in Education*, facing title page.

Female Education in Patriarchal Power Systems *

Bonnie Cook Freeman

> The first division of labor is that between man and woman for child breeding. The first class antagonism in history begins with the development of the antagonism between man and woman in individual marriage, and the first class oppression is that of women by men. The individual marriage is the cell of civilized society in which we can study the antagonism and contradictions which develop fully in the society.
>
> —Friedrich Engels, *The Origins of the Family, Property and the State*

That women are a subordinate group need hardly be disputed. It has been clearly documented that women within almost every society lack political and economic power.[1] In the United States they receive less education than men, are paid less for the same work, and are normally relegated to unpaid labor outside the money economy or to the least prestigious positions in the occupational structure. Women are virtually excluded from positions of power or responsibility in business, government, and education. They are denied equal protection of the laws, not only in marriage and family codes but in employment (protective work legislation), athletics, and criminal and education law as well. And from the beginning of their lives they are told that all this is right and proper, that it has always been so, and that it can never change. The school is one institution that both perpetuates the myth of women's inferiority and helps to transform the myth into a reality.

This essay argues that the relation between men and women in this society is a colonial relationship involving, as it does, the domination of one group by another and that the primary proc-

* I wish to acknowledge Gary Freeman for his comments on an earlier draft of this article.

ess by which this relationship is perpetuated, once it is established in the legal and institutional framework of the society, is through the colonization of the female's identity.[2] The educational system plays an important role in this process, and it is to an examination of the educational process that my attention will be devoted. Before proceeding, however, it is necessary to specify more clearly the meaning of colonization as it is used here.

In their introductory essay to this volume, Kelly and Altbach pose the question whether colonialism, when it is applied to such groups as blacks, other minorities, and women living in the country of the dominant group, can be meaningfully distinguished from either oppression or inequality. They suggest that the use of the colonial vocabulary in such instances may be no more than a metaphorical device. I would like to argue that the situation of women shares basic characteristics with that of groups more traditionally thought of as colonial and that, therefore, one is justified in going beyond the use of "mere" oppression to describe it. Furthermore, an analysis that is satisfied to point out inequalities between the sexes but fails to link those differences to a theory of the domination of one sex by the other is clearly inadequate. Inequality is a static concept. Colonialism provides us with a set of ideas with which to fashion a theory to explain the origins and transformation of the patterns of interaction between males and females. The subjugation of women by men within a particular national context may be understood as one instance of a more general and pervasive pattern of domination—white over black, rich over poor—but all rooted ultimately in the basic biological divisions of labor and power.

Among the characteristics Kelly and Altbach isolate as essential to a colonial relationship, and especially to the colonial educational process, are the following:

(1) the colonized group is assumed to be intellectually, morally, and physically inferior;

(2) the colonial educational system is controlled by the dominant group and is detached from the culture of the colonized and colonizer as well;

(3) the history of the colonized is either denied or reinterpreted in such a fashion that colonial education constitutes a fundamental assault on the identity of the colonized group;

(4) the substance of the colonial education is different from that given the colonizer;

(5) a plausible outcome of the colonial situation is that the colonized began to identify with their oppressor, to assume the superiority of his values and knowledge, to see themselves as weak and ignorant, and, finally, to depend on the colonizer for a definition of the situation, "protection," and other resources. Thus the relations (based on unequal resources) involve reciprocity since the colonized begin to demand protection and exploit (at least marginally) the guilt or good will of the colonizer.[3] And the colonizer must fulfill the expectations of the colonized by attempting to prove his superiority ("manliness") in order to legitimize his greater access to privileges, rights, and resources.[4]

The purpose of the remainder of this essay is to demonstrate that on all of these counts the situation and education of women in the United States meet the requirements of a colonial relationship. Traditionally, women have been considered the inferiors of men everywhere. This has been used as a justification for the differences in educational opportunities available to men and women. When women have been schooled, it has been under the guidance and control of men or women who are given the opportunity to do so by men through political and financial support.[5] The relationship between the cultural context of women's education and that of males is rather complex. There are at least two ways in which the education of women is distinct in substance from that of men. First, there is the obvious point that women have traditionally been encouraged or forced out of formal education to learn domestic skills at home. Later, women were encouraged to attend schools where a curriculum was established for women's special needs.[6] Secondly, and more subtly, the education women have received has been biased in such a way as to deny to them a full appreciation of their own history.[7] That is, they have been taught about the world through men's eyes. In a real sense, they have had a male culture foisted on them, but they have not been invited or allowed to become a part of that culture except in a very few notable instances. Kelly and Altbach suggest that in internal colonial situations the purpose of the educational system is the eradication of the minority culture and the assimilation of the group to the dominant culture. This analysis applies only marginally to women and other internal groups. A full and valid women's culture is repressed in the colonial education system, but full assimilation is not permitted either. The purpose of the educational system seems to be less to eradicate a distinct women's subculture than to create and perpetuate a culture of femininity (read "weakness" and "wiles") and motherhood (read "bearing" or "rearing"). Such a culture provides for the dominant males a submissive, supportive, succoring class of human beings that enhances considerably the rewards of being male.

The terms *oppression* and *inequality,* although certainly descriptive of the male-female bond, are not adequate by themselves. Clearly, most aspects of male-female interchange do not bear the overt marks of the oppression of the acculturated. In the same way, women appear to be the beneficiaries of a multitude of apparent "privileges" and "pedestals" that are accorded to them as members of the "fairer sex." Likewise, inequalities should be taken as the evidence, but not the essence, of the sexual relationship. The assault on the identity and culture of the female, the mechanisms by which subordination are created and facilitated, and the ideologies by which they are justified, all lead us to the conclusion that a more fundamental and systematic phenomenon—the internal colonization of women by men—is taking place. It is to an analysis of this phenomenon as it is expressed in the educational system in one country, the United States, that the rest of this essay is devoted.

In it I plan to show the following: (1) that human knowledge has been molded and fitted to the ends of males (i.e., the colonizers); (2) that when educational opportunities were granted to women it was for the purpose of preparing them for clearly subordinate societal roles that served the interests of men; and (3) that today the educational system is structured in such a way that women still have less access than men, are the victims of many forms of discrimination both subtle and overt, intellectual and physical. I begin by examining briefly the general process by which human knowledge is socially structured. I then turn to the status of women as students and teachers in public elementary and secondary schools today. And finally I review the present status of women as students and faculty in institutions of higher education.

COLONIZATION OF KNOWLEDGE

I begin this part of the essay with a discussion of the general process by which human knowledge, and particularly that dealing with women, has been molded and fitted to the ends of males, since it is central to my argument that the education of women represents a colonial process. The destruction or suppression of the history and culture of the colonized is typical of the colonial relationship. In their place the colonizer imposes his own version of reality. In this version the colonizer plays the central role, makes history, and embodies all good things. The colonized becomes invisible or objectified, almost property, a contingent being, in the words of Simone de Beauvoir, "the other." Women have a part to play in this scenario only as they are given an identity and a name by men. The male bias of knowledge is not limited to the writing and teaching of history. Nor is it simply a matter of neglecting or ignoring certain facts about women. Rather, it is built into the very way we think about the world, the concepts we use, the assumptions we make, the questions we ask.

An example of the overt distortion of knowledge through selective attention to the facts has been offered by Jessie Bernard. She notes that when it was believed that brain size was related to level of intelligence, the fact that women have, on the average, a smaller ratio of brain tissue to body weight was repeatedly emphasized. However, once it was established that beyond a minimum size complexity and not weight was the decisive variable, the brain size of women almost disappeared as a subject of scientific discussion.[8] A more subtle form of sexism in the development of knowledge can be found in the tendency of political scientists to assume that power and politics are naturally a male preserve and consequently to fail to anticipate, explain, or comprehend the rise in female participation in the 1960s.[9]

Why is it that knowledge exhibits this male bias? Systems of thought reflect the social and economic conditions within which they arise. This is the basic truth to which Marx pointed in his writings on ideology.[10] Ideologies express the interests and needs of the dominant groups in any epoch but in terms that have the appearance of universal applicability. Marx was particularly interested in the class origins of ideology, but it seems clear that in every epoch males have held a near monopoly on elite positions and, therefore, this monopoly has been reflected in the ideology, religion, and philosophy of each period.

In order to justify his privileged position, the colonizer must establish the inferiority of the colonized. The accepted ideas and values of the day must underline the rationality and justice of continued male dominance. Just one early example of such an ideology can be found in the Biblical myth of the Garden of Eden. It was Eve, the woman, who ruined the earthly paradise and introduced evil into the world by eating of the fruit of the tree of life. A more recent and much less profound example can be found in the pseudo-psychological argument that in the matriarchal family women emasculated the American male by excessive "momism." [11]

The colonization of knowledge is not simply a devious attempt on the part of males to mystify women. The seriousness of the problem is to be found, for the most part, in the fact that the half-truths and outright distortions are not perceived either by males or females. They serve as one's definition of reality; and until competing and alternative interpretations are available, they go unchallenged and exist as history, tradition, culture, nature, truth. Until they are altered or supplanted, the ideas and values of a male-dominated society are transmitted as valid human knowledge to each new generation. In this process both the family and the school have their function.

SEX-BIASED SCHOOLS

Before the child enters the formal public school, a good deal of sex-role socialization usually has already occurred. Wittingly or unwittingly, the family has had an impact on shaping the young child to his or her appropriate sex role. Most parents have encouraged their children to adopt the "normal" behavior appropriate for how boys and girls should behave. Even those who claim equal treatment of their children communicate sex-appropriate expectations in ways they may not realize—e.g., nonverbal behaviors. Children observe the different behaviors and roles (based on sex) of the parents (mother v. father). The sexual division of labor in the family promotes the separation between work that men do and get paid for and household labor that women perform and are not paid for. Such sex typing in the family tends to encourage the submission of the next generation of women to their inferior status, either in a role at the bottom of the wage-labor system and/or in the unpaid role of mother, wife, and domestic worker—an option frequently perceived not only as inevitable but attractive as well. For the most part, the school, as a public caretaking institution and socializing agent, tends not to counter the forces of parental socialization but becomes implicated in reinforcing traditional sex roles introduced by the family.

Entrance into the Public Elementary School: The Beginning

Not unexpectedly, the patterns of interaction that emerge between teachers and students in the classroom vary according to sex. Schools assist in maintaining society, not changing it, by keeping some groups and values dominant and others subordinate. Teachers carry on the work of inculcating and reinforcing appropriate sex-role behavior the parents start at home. Teachers tend to support the dominant values of their culture, even when they are unaware of what they, like parents, take for granted. Teachers, both male and female, respond to children in terms of their sex-role ideals and consistently reinforce these sex biases in the classroom.[12] Many teachers interpret their role as seeing to it that children adjust to their appropriate sex-role behaviors because that is what is considered the healthy, natural criteria for success in their future role in society. Although women experience differential treatment because of their sex throughout their educational careers, the nature of that treatment changes as they progress from one level of school to another and as some move from student to teacher status.

The effect of elementary school on the sex-role identity of girls has been to communicate some fundamental expectations of what a good female student is. She is informed in subtle ways to inhibit verbal and physical aggression, to be submissive, passive, dependent. Exactly how these behaviors are taught and reinforced is not clear, but they do represent together the embodiment of the good student. Most observers of classroom interaction report that boys receive both more positive and negative feedback from the teacher than do girls and that the teacher devotes a greater share of all her time to boys than to girls.[13]

Evidence from studies of political socialization indicates that children, some as early as preschool, have learned and accepted the "propriety" of a sex-based, highly traditional division of labor in which women have serving and helping roles in the home and in outside jobs and men are outside the home in highly prestigious, high-paying professional positions.[14] At the end of elementary school the vocational aspirations of boys and girls begin to differ significantly. One study reported that by the fifth grade, boys and girls believe that men ought to be doctors, bosses, taxi drivers, mayors, factory workers, lawyers, college professors, and clerks and that women ought to be cooks, teachers, nurses, and house cleaners.[15] When asked about their own career aspirations, boys express desires to become engineers, scientists, sportsmen, and pilots; girls say they wish to become teachers, artists, stewardesses, and nurses. Asked to describe their future lives, the girls give extensive and detailed accounts of their housewifely routine. Even when they desire a career, domestic activities in the home are more salient than careers. The girls have learned their lessons well: Positions of high power and status are rightfully monopolized by men, and women should occupy the private sphere of the home, where they will achieve their highest fulfillment as wives and mothers.

While children learn about what is appropriate for their sex role, there are some indications that young girls are not always satisfied with female role expectations. It should come as no surprise that girls perceive that the list of female career opportunities is shorter than the equivalent list for males and that there are more girls who wish to have the opportunities of the male sex role than there are males who indicate preference for the female sex role.[16] It appears that learning that takes place in the elementary school serves to communicate and expose young women, even if they are better students, to the notion that women are less valued by society than are men. The transition to high school represents a categorical increase in exposure to lower self-evaluations and greater restrictions on possible outlets for achievement needs.

The Transition to High School—Striving for Mediocrity

> In light of the social expectations about women, it is not surprising that women end up where society expects them to; the surprise is that little girls don't get the message that they are supposed to be stupid until they get into high school.—Naomi Weisstein [17]

While women experience all through their lives training and reinforcement for the acceptance of a lower station in life and for selective stupidity, the transition to high school for female adolescents represents the period in their life when they will be exposed to the greatest dosage—to a continuing narrowing of space, contradictory cues, and the physiological changes in their bodies associated with puberty. They are encouraged to give up their "tomboy ways," which usually means relinquishing degrees of autonomy, independence, self-interest, and physical activity in order to conform to the expectations of being a "woman" in American society. And presumably to encourage and facilitate conformity to that stereotype, books are written for the uncertain young woman seeking guidance. Consider the following excerpt from a book for teenage girls:

> When you know the deep, true love that a woman feels for a man, when you experience the tremendous joy of comforting, sustaining, and understanding a man you love, when you know the happiness of childbirth—*you will be acting the role you were created for*. . . . The teen years are the perfect time for learning to be a woman . . . for turning from dolls and sandlot ball games to the *feminine skills* of cooking and sewing and prettying yourself. . . . It's time to practice the feminine role of the woman pursued by the man—by your first dating experiences, by practicing your newly discovered womanliness on boys your own age. . . . If you learn

> from your dating years how to like boys, to cope with their moods, to understand them . . . then you are well on your way to learning how to be a good wife and a mature and contented woman. . . .[18]

One of the most interesting developments in high school that is sex-related is the tendency for the academic performance of girls to decline relative to their measured abilities. It seems reasonable to attribute this phenomenon to social pressures related to the passage from girlhood to young adulthood. In high school, the student role becomes incongruent with a girl's other roles but congruent with a boy's other roles. Expectations of femininity conflict with expectations of achievement. A gap grows between the behavior demanded of a good student and that demanded of a young woman. Consequently, a great number of young women become labeled as "underachieving" and "boy crazy."

There are striking differences in the age period that underachievement becomes a serious problem for boys and girls. Girls who are underachievers usually begin to be so labeled at about the onset of puberty. Boys, on the other hand, normally are recognized as underachievers earlier in their educational careers before puberty. Also boys and girls tend to approach their school work differently. Girls tend to perform uniformly in all their school subjects whether they like them or not. The role concept of a "good girl" is extended to that of a "good student." This reinforces the generalist ability of women ("Jill of all trades, Jack of none") versus the specialist-technical orientation of boys, who are more likely to concentrate their energies on their favorite courses and a specific vocational career interest. Furthermore, girls place a different emphasis on various high-school roles and statuses than do boys. Girls, for example, ascribe greater importance to being a good student than do boys. But achievement for girls is not conceived in purely academic terms but also as popularity—being liked (primarily by men). The consequence of this achievement orientation for young women is that their intellectual interests and potentialities are criticized and consequently repressed as they come to represent "unfeminine" competitiveness. High-school girls learn that they should not be too smart, competitive, or achievement-oriented.

Although adolescent peer groups have been considered to be unique unto themselves, they are actually a microcosm reflecting the exaggerated images of sex roles in the larger society. The qualities necessary for high-school success for girls tend to be ascriptive—things they cannot change. James Coleman, in his classic analysis of adolescent peer groups in the late 1950s, suggests that the girls' culture derived from the status system of the boys. He says:

> The girl's role is to sit there and look pretty, waiting for the athletic star to come pick her. She must cultivate her looks, be vivacious and attractive, wear the right clothes, but then wait—until the football player whose status is determined by his specific achievements comes along to choose her.[19]

The girl takes her social identity from the man who chooses her. In order to ensure that she will be selected, she spends her time trying to improve her physical appearance and deemphasizing her intellectuality so as not to scare off her prospective buyers. From parents and peers girls learn that it is best for them to hide their intelligence. Coleman found that the brightest girls (as measured by IQ tests) did not acquire the label of brightest student; they were "smart" enough at that point to avoid being considered a female egghead.[20]

It is not enough, however, simply to veil one's intellect. If social norms prohibit a young girl from being a brilliant student, they also dictate against her being stupid. The general values of the school and the society favor achievement, and girls are not immune to these pressures. The Catch-22 situation, in which women are pressured to fulfill conflicting expectations, has been labeled the "double-bind." Faced with contradictory cues, the young woman finds it difficult to react meaningfully, to be true to herself, or to fulfill the contradictory expectations of others. In the oppressive context of high school, for a girl to achieve is to fail.[21]

It is not only with respect to academic achievement in the high school that the woman learns subordinate behavior. Perhaps more important in the long term is the way in which women are channeled out of certain career streams. Few individuals can igmore consistently negative feedback from significant others. Parents, teachers, and counselors communicate their concern that a girl not pursue a path that will preclude the fulfillment of her "natural" destiny as wife and mother. They encourage her to find some practical vocation that is compatible with a married life that assumes the priority of the husband's career. This usually means that interest in careers defined as traditional male domains will be discouraged.

The result is that a girl may trim her sails to fit the demands of her socially defined subordinate role and wait for her contingent identity, which she will obtain from the man who chooses her and gives her his name. The option of fighting ascriptive categorization, developing one's own interests, and fulfilling achievement needs is fraught with difficulty. Her needs threaten her socially defined femininity, so she takes the route of least resistance and maximum socially defined rewards. Not only does her own self-esteem suffer, however, but the unarticulated assumption that women are, or should be, subordinate to men is projected onto other women as well. Young girls not only evaluate their own work as less distinguished than that of their male counterparts, but they also evaluate the work of women in general as lower in quality than that of men.[22] Furthermore girls are likely to say that their own work is of lower quality than a relatively objective evaluation indicates. And boys are more likely to evaluate their work accurately. When one considers the combination of a low sense of efficacy and achievement and the fact that counselors (male and female) and teachers tend to be more enthusiastic about the career aspirations of males and females who aspire to hold traditionally sex-appropriate career goals,[23] one is not surprised that women experience difficulty in attaining academic excellence and getting started on academic careers and in other "serious professions."

It is important that we do not overemphasize the impact of socialization on young girls' real opportunities for success. Although it is correct that, properly conditioned, women often become their own worst enemies and accept defeat without even trying, it is not at all obvious that the fight would have been worth it anyway. There is a tendency for analysts operating fully within the sex-socialization framework to attribute all or most of the inequalities between the sexes to differential self-images and aspirations. This leads to an implicit exoneration of males of any responsibility for keeping women in their place—a view that fails to take account of two important facts. First, the system of sex-role socialization, especially as it works through educational institutions, is not entirely or even principally a natural development. It is the result of human invention. Books are written, curricula developed, pedagogical theory spun, teachers trained. The sexist bias of the educational process is literally *built into it*. Secondly, one must ask what might be the result if all women at once shucked off their feminine roles and began to compete in earnest with men. The unavoidable conclusion is that serious resistance would be and has been generated in the major institutions of the society. This makes clear the symbiotic relationship between socialization and discrimination and suggests that the elimination of only one of these would not eradicate the effect of the other.

COLONIZATION OF THE PHYSICAL SELF

Up to this point I have emphasized the impact of schooling on a young woman's attitudes toward education, academic achievement, and occupational roles. There is another aspect of the problem that is of such importance that it deserves at least a brief discussion. The colonization of women in family socialization and the formal educational processes affects not only the mind but the body as well. It should come as no surprise that there is a relationship between some degree of body control, physical coordination, and self-confidence in other areas.[24] At home and in school young women are informed that they are physically inferior when compared with their male peers. Unequal physical strength is partially caused by purposeful training for female weakness. Parents are more likely to inhibit young girls from physical activities ("Don't play, you might get hurt," or "Don't play, you might get dirty"). Such warnings, frequently made without explanation, suggest to females that they are more vulnerable than boys to physical harm, that they are in need of protection, and that special efforts should be made to keep clean. Some young girls develop a psychological dependency on others, are uncertain about their cleanliness and purity, and restrain themselves from exploring their environment for fear of attack. Rather than develop a sense of self-sufficiency, young women are led to believe that they should seek out some parental or patriarchal figure who will protect them from danger.

In books on physical education, both sexes are informed that women are physically inferior in weight, height, muscle mass, reaction time, metabolism, energy level, pain threshold, etc.[25] Because of the greater perceived frailty and the inferiority documented in "scientific" study, boys and girls are separated during physical activity at schools. Young women do not receive the same extensive training that young men do. Greater attention and resources are invested in physical education for men. The consequence of such lopsided physical education not surprisingly is to increase the gap in physical achievements of young men and women and also to discourage integrated physical activity. There are particular prohibitions for men—unarticulated assumptions that if they play with girls they are "unmanly." Furthermore, men in single-sex sports may feel compelled to organize against feminine influence and integration to preserve an aura of "masculinity." The consequence of exclusion and discouragement over a span of years for young women is the failure to develop physical fitness and strength. As a result, women as a group do have much less motor control and muscle coordination than men.

Their weakness presumably makes them more feminine and physically attractive, but this must be coupled with good grooming and the achievement of slim figures. To be weak, dependent, delicate, and vulnerable are some aspects comprising our traditional cultural conceptualization of the term *femininity*.[26] Physical activities such as exercises to flatten the tummy or to build the bust are desirable, as they lead to more attractive figures, whereas excessive swimming is presumed to give too much width and muscularity to the shoulders and thus a masculine appearance. It should come as no surprise that a prime motivation of some women in athletics is the preservation of a good figure and/or the development of graceful movement, both of which are believed achieved through dance, figure skating, and gymnastics.

Women receive conflicting signals about their bodies. While they are socialized and trained to concentrate on developing attractive exterior images, they are also informed that their bodies invite sexual attacks and that they are consequently at fault and responsible for allowing such situations to occur. While young women are supposed to please and be pleased with themselves as they develop women's bodies, they also learn their body parts and processes are not "sugar and spice and everything nice" but rather connote shamefulness and uncleanliness—particularly taboos surrounding the monthly menstrual flow. Anthropological literature indicates numerous instances in which menstruating women have been separated from others on the basis that they are unclean. That we no longer do so does not mean that the effects of myth and taboo no longer affect the negative ways in which women think of themselves.

While young boys also experience guilt feelings about their own bodies and sex, negative communications are not nearly as strong as those that women receive. Young boys may feel guilty about masturbation; however, they are more likely than girls to know what it is, to engage in it, and to accept their sexuality. At the same time many men still hold a double standard for women. Our culture inculcates in women stronger prohibitions in sexual experience and exploration of the physical self. Not long ago a young single woman was assumed a virgin until she married; and if she remained single, she was assumed an unfortunate, sexually inexperienced, unattractive old maid (quite unlike the image of her male counterpart—the bachelor). At marriage she was introduced to sex by her husband (presumably with heterosexual experience), and if she was lucky he would assist her in achieving pleasurable sexual feelings. In contradiction to all previous learned behavior, she was now allowed to indicate her interest in sex, as it was with the one, right man in her life. That there are enormous inconsistencies and contradictions in our culture—the double standard, conflicting expectations of women before marriage and after marriage—does not preclude its long-term effects on young women, even those of the current day who are more experienced in sexual relationships than earlier generations and who are more informed about birth control techniques to prevent unwanted pregnancies.

Studies, while not always in agreement, indicate that the sexual revolution of the 1960s and 1970s may mean increased numbers of young people engaging in premarital sex and generally holding more liberalized attitudes, but it does not mean that the double standard has disappeared, that young men and women approach sex with the same attitudes or expectations, or that sex exchanges of youth are indiscriminate and insignificant.[27]

Just as there are different reactions and meanings attached to the sex of the person engaging in premarital sex, so too there is a double standard by sex in regard to admissions to college. Up until very recently sex was at least as important as intelligence in determining admission to college.[28] And it is to that double standard I turn now.

WOMEN IN THE UNIVERSITY

Undergraduate Women

> We are all for women, but Yale must produce a thousand male leaders every year.—Yale alumnus, 1970

The problems of women in the university begin before they arrive. As the last section of this essay suggested, there are many barriers erected in front of women who wish to attend college. They are unusually successful. One source estimates that "from 75 to 90 percent (depending on the study) of the well-qualified students who do not go to college are women."[29] They fail to matriculate because they have come to believe that they do not belong in college and because administrators, for a variety of reasons, do not admit them. In this section I will discuss how the structure and process of higher education in the United States colonizes even those who are daring or naïve enough to embark on a student career in higher education.

It was two hundred years after the establishment of Harvard in 1636 before women were able to attend a college in this country.[30] It was the costs of the Civil War (declining enrollments and reallocation of resources to the war) that forced male educational leaders to reconsider earlier denials of women's applications for admissions. Some institutions began reluctantly to admit qualified women.[31] However, women were rarely admitted to the most prestigious institutions, which remained male preserves until very recently. Although many more women attend college today, they do not escape discrimination, even in the admissions process. Elaine Walster and her colleagues found in their study of college admissions, in which they sent bogus applications to a sample of 240 colleges across the country, that males were accepted more frequently than females, with qualifications identical in every respect except gender.[32]

According to Jencks and Riesman, "except at Negro colleges and normal schools very few admissions offices allow their female:male ratio to rise above 50:50 despite better performances by women on college entrance examinations and high school grades."[33] The rationale for this policy is that it is necessary for the well-being of the school to preserve a male majority and that to admit students purely on merit would constitute discrimination against men. This is a strange argument, since it is clearly necessary to discriminate against women to maintain male predominance. Since the passage of Title IX of the 1972 educational amendments, sex discrimination in the admission of students to institutions of higher education that receive federal financial assistance is prohibited by law.[34]

In addition to the assumed need to preserve male student majorities, there may be an assumed priority to award available financial support to male students over female students. In a 1969–70 study of the finances of college sophomores, women on the average received smaller grants and scholarships, took out larger loans, and, if they worked, received less pay than men.[35] The average annual amount of scholarships and other financial aids is $518 for females and $760 for males.[36] These figures on differential financial aid may be an especially serious problem because parents with limited incomes have and continue to put first priority on investing in the education of their sons.[37]

Women in Graduate School

> Too many young women are casually enrolling in graduate schools across the country without having seriously considered the obligation which they are assuming by requesting that such expenditures be made for them. And they are not alone to blame. Equally at fault are two groups of faculty—undergraduate instructors who encourage their

> women students to apply to graduate schools without also helping them consider the commitment that such an act implies, and graduate admission counselors who blithely admit girls with impressive academic records without looking for other evidence that the applicant has made a sincere commitment to graduate study.[38]—Edwin C. Lewis, assistant to the vice-president for academic affairs and professor of psychology at Iowa State University (1970).

Graduate school for women is more controversial than undergraduate education. A liberal-arts degree, after all, may be "useful" for a future mother educating her children in a general way. Graduate education, on the other hand, is perceived as serious professional training. And graduate and professional schools serve as ports of entry to careers of prestige, power, and financial reward. Women do not misread the messages they receive, and therefore they account for a smaller proportion of graduate than undergraduate students. Furthermore, a greater proportion of women than men enroll in terminal M.A. programs.[39] Because the academic profession has been dominated by men, and because it is the members of the profession who determine its standards and control access, women have been considered outsiders who do not or cannot share in the common norms of the profession.[40]

There is a marked tendency for women to apply to graduate school in fields more conventionally sex-appropriate if their undergraduate degree is in a nontraditionally female field. Furthermore, as women move through their graduate-school careers they tend to switch into female-typed specialities, so that the proportions of women in such fields grow with each year of graduate training. Finally, as women leave school to take college teaching posts there is another decided shift to feminine fields. Psychologists and chemists, for example, often end up teaching in schools of home economics (see table 1). They tend to concentrate on pursuits such as research on infants and children, education, and anthropology, rather than engineering or political science; they study kinship rather than kingship. This pattern is no doubt the result of several factors, but it probably reflects counseling decisions to some degree. Some women simply realize that the effort required to succeed in "male" fields is out of proportion to the rewards associated with success. They enter, therefore, less controversial and less visible fields and, within disciplines, choose subspecialties where competition with men may not be so keen and where their role may not look so inappropriate.

Table 1
Percent of Discipline That Is Female from the B.A. to the Faculty Level [41]

Percent of Discipline That Is Female	B.A.[a]	Graduate[b]	Faculty at all institutions[c]	Faculty at Quality I institutions[d]
Electrical Engineering	.4	.6	.6	.35
Mechanical Engineering	.4	.6	.5	.45
Civil Engineering	.5	.9	.1	0.0
Chemical Engineering	1.0	.9	.9	0.0
Agriculture/Forestry	3.1	5.6	.9	1.47
Law	—	5.8	4.3	3.07
Physics	5.9	4.8	3.6	1.53
Dentistry	—	1.1	*	*
Business	8.2	4.0	16.3	2.04
Architecture	4.3	11.7	4.3	1.94
Geology	10.4	7.9	4.2	1.04
Chemistry	18.3	14.1	9.3	5.99
Medicine	—	8.8	7.7	7.66
Mathematics	37.6	23.2	13.6	6.09
Biochemistry	24.8	22.6	6.6	7.02
Economics	10.6	10.6	5.9	5.04
Political Science	20.8	18.7	10.7	4.68
Educational Administration	—	22.7	9.4	—
Bacteriology	47.2	30.8	16.6	12.92
Physiology	24.2	21.1	10.0	10.88
Zoology	21.9	23.9	7.3	6.75
Philosophy	22.3	17.8	11.5	2.96
History	35.3	28.2	11.3	3.50
Botany	34.7	16.2	9.0	5.88

Table 1 (continued)

Percent of Discipline That Is Female	B.A.[a]	Graduate [b]	Faculty at all institutions [c]	Faculty at Quality I institutions [d]
Geography	21.6	15.6	10.7	2.63
Psychology	43.1	33.8	18.5	11.7
Journalism	40.7	30.8	10.1	4.10
Anthropology	57.6	41.4	13.4	11.26
Physical and Health Education	40.8	34.3	40.9	38.65
German	59.4	51.6	27.7	16.88
Sociology	61.1	35.6	20.2	11.21
Educational Psychology	35.0	47.0	21.4	—
Speech	58.5	49.5	23.4	18.27
Spanish	75.5	57.3	39.2	20.0
Art	67.9	51.0	20.7	14.53
Dramatic Arts	58.5 [e]	49.5 [f]	23.4 [g]	18.27 [h]
Music	57.3	44.1	23.5	15.10
Secondary Education	60.8	45.5	39.7	
Social Work	80.5	61.5	43.1	39.06
English	67.6	54.4	33.5	13.46
French	82.7	68.7	45.0	26.98
Library Science	93.6	81.8	60.2	42.46
Elementary Education	90.7	78.9	39.7	
Nursing	98.6	98.5	96.1	93.91
Home Economics	97.3	90.6	89.2	92.10

* Dentistry was not separated from Medicine in the Carnegie data.

[a] Source: Feldman, pp. 43–45. Taken from Chandler and Hooper, 1969.

[b] Source: Feldman, pp. 43–45. Taken from Hooper and Chandler, 1971.

[c] Source: Feldman, pp. 43–45. Information based on General Faculty Survey, 1969.

[d] Source: Elite Faculty Sample, analyzed by the author.

[e, f, g, h]: Speech and Dramatic Arts were not separated in the data.

There are a few new twists added at the graduate level to the discriminatory admissions policies discussed earlier. Some policies that appear on the surface to be fair, in fact are highly prejudicial to the opportunities of women. For example, the "equal rejection" procedure for dealing with applications judges applicants not against the total pool but against members of their own sex or category. This means that if 90 percent of the applicants were males and only 10 percent were female, the group admitted will be 90 percent male, etc. By this method a large number of males could be admitted whose qualifications were below those of female applicants who were not admitted. Since women applicants normally have academic records better than the typical male applicant, it is clear that the equal rejection procedure is not based on merit.[42] In fact, in her study of graduate education, Ann Heiss concluded: "Not excluding academic qualifications, sex is probably the most discriminatory factor applied in the decisions whether to admit an applicant to graduate school." [43]

The story of financial aid is similar to that of admissions. Many foundations agree to award most of the fellowship grants to males. Furthermore, women often fail to apply for aid because they lack the information about available resources and because they have not been encouraged to apply. It has been common academic practice for information about aid as well as employment opportunities to be passed along through "old boy" networks.[44] Data collected from the 1969 Carnegie Commission Survey of Faculty and Student Opinion showed

> that a slightly larger percentage of male than of female graduate students (17.7 versus 15.0 percent) currently had some income from a fellowship, while a slightly larger percentage of men (31.1 versus 30.0) also had teaching or research assistanceships.[45]

Since female graduate students as a group have better qualifications than their male peers, one would expect them to receive greater support (according to the meritocratic rationale) and to be highly prized as students. In fact, they are in many instances not appreciated. Many male faculty believe that male students comprehend the material better than female students.[46] Furthermore, women are likely to be subjected to questions about their commitment and intentions, such as "Why do you want a Ph.D. anyway?" rather than respected for the obstacles they may have overcome to be in graduate school. And they will find their personal lives the subject of open scrutiny—a situation that almost never applies to male students. Thus, in order to demonstrate commitment, women students frequently become one-dimensional and subordinate other aspects of their lives to academic work. In doing so, however, they are likely to be labeled neurotic and compulsive.

The ambivalence that male academics feel toward women who invade their turf is evident in the problems a women encounters in finding an adviser who will give her career assistance rather than the nearest exit from the building. For professional success, a collegial, close relationship with one's major professor has been considered crucial in facilitating research and in developing a professional self-image. According to the Carnegie Survey of Faculty and Students, women are less likely than men to enjoy the benefits of close working relationships with their professors. This is true even for women who managed to become professors at elite institutions.[47]

In many ways the relationship of a faculty adviser to a graduate student resembles that of a patron to a client or a skilled craftsman to an apprentice. The relationship is important to a graduate student because it is through it that many crucial trade secrets are learned (the rules of the game, norms of professional behavior, academic protocol). A positive experience with one's patron can be an important factor in achieving success at each of the initiation rites through which the student must pass—the M.A., prelims, Ph.D. Frequently patrons also have control over small fiefdoms, which allow them to dole out rewards that serve as graduate support for the client during the years of graduate-student poverty.

Professors may be reluctant to accept females as student clients or, if they do, to take them as seriously as their male students. The reasons for this can be quite complex. The professor may perceive a woman first as a woman—a different sort of human being—and he may feel that a woman is less likely to be intelligent, use her degree, distinguish herself, and, by implication, to bring honor to his name as his protégé. Also women add the complicated sexual dimension of male/female relationships. The professor may believe that the woman is manipulating him sexually, or resent the fact that she attempts to avoid all interaction of an erotic nature.

While it is clear that the bulk of the problems between male faculty and female students are a result of the more general attitudes of the former toward women, it is nevertheless true that the fear, for example, that female students as a group will drop out of school is anchored in reality. Available data indicate that women who are admitted to Ph.D. programs are somewhat less likely to complete their doctorates than are their male counterparts.[48] But this information requires closer scrutiny before concluding that women are indeed poorer educational investments. First, the statistical differences between male and female attrition rates are not nearly as impressive as the myth of female failure would predict. Secondly, it is not entirely clear that the acceptance of the myth by male professors is not at least in part the reason that women decide to leave academia. Thirdly, those who drop out do not do so because of an inability to do the work. In a study of drop-outs from graduate school fewer women than men were found to report that absence of academic ability would prevent them from continuing their graduate education.[49]

Although it is not surprising in light of general studies of women's lower self-esteem, there is evidence that both graduate and faculty women tend to have poorer academic self-images than men. One study has demonstrated that women are less likely than men to see themselves as the best students in their departments.[50] Women are less likely than males to consider themselves intellectuals as well. And these lower evaluations are shared with and confirmed by the perceptions of significant others. The Carnegie study reported that 20 to 25 percent of the faculty and graduate students in American universities believe that women graduate students are not as dedicated as men graduate students.[51]

Faculty Women

Those women brash enough or innocent enough to push on through graduate school and to find a job in a university are still not considered successful. In myth and literature academic women are portrayed as unattractive people.[52] As Arlie Hochschild notes, "Most academic women have been socialized twice, once to be women (as housewives and mothers) and once again to be like men (in traditional careers)."[53] They are haunted by their earlier colonization as well as their present hostile professional context. What are the costs of their assimilation? They "cause" problems in their departments, disciplines, universities, as well as problems for themselves.

As Mary Ellman notes:

> Their real problem in teaching is not that they cease to be women. The academic woman, as she enters her profession, is visualized by sociologists as wheeling before her, in a mental grocery cart, all the stock impedimenta, the staples of her feminine role. Far from losing them, she cannot get rid of her passivity, her diffidence, her compliance, her leniency, her "conserving, stabilizing, appeasing" nature.
>
> If she speaks as inoffensively seldom as possible, her colleagues find her "withdrawn." If she teaches part-time in order to tend husband and children as well, her colleagues feel she is not seriously "involved" in the profession. If she teaches full-time and devotes herself to the nurture of students, she reveals a new shortcoming: a tendency toward momism in what the academic men believe should be as stark and rigid a training as that of the Coldstream Guards. If she consults members of her "field" freely, they assume that she is making advances. If she keeps a decorous distance, they consider her outside the real pulsing life of the subject. Even if she speaks eloquently, she finds it difficult to hold undivided attention.[54]

As an individual, the faculty woman is divided against herself by her dual socialization. There is conflict between her ascribed status and her achieved position, a conflict that is reinforced by those who interact with her on the basis of her sex; she is not "academic man." She is in every sense a "marginal woman" who, as Helen Hacker describes it, is

> torn between rejection and acceptance of traditional roles and attributes. Uncertain of the ground on which she stands, subjected to conflicting cultural expectations, the marginal woman suffers psychological ravages of instability, conflict, self-hate, anxiety, and resentment.[55]

Her position is in many ways unenviable. She is neither accepted by her colleagues nor by their wives, who are likely to be threatened by her. Male faculty may indicate to her in various ways that she is not part of the "club" by excluding her from male-only facilities and from professional committees. In her daily interaction she is likely to be mistaken for the departmental secretary, addressed in correspondence as Sir or Mr., and treated as a department token and oddity. Always unsure of her reception, the woman academic becomes very self-conscious. She resembles a stigmatized person who feels that she is always "on," "having to be self-conscious and calculating."[56]

Some women who are very ambitious and desiring of acceptance overperform, "rate-break," and overconform to professional role expectations. They become what is now described as "dutiful daughters" or "Aunt Sallys." In such a position women deny any sex discrimination in their own careers since to raise that issue opens the possibility that one is not just like everyone else only more so. A great deal of personal sacrifice occurs this way. Because women are internally colonized, even the most self-confident women have doubts about their ability to do creative work.

Also, because of the confusing signals that occur in interaction between males and females, many male faculty find that they have no basis of communication with females other than a sexual one. They have few norms for dealing with female overachievers, and though they often deny it, it is common practice in the academic community to terminate or not hire persons who cause embarrassing or uncomfortable situations or don't "fit in."[57]

The question of discrimination against women in academia is controversial and thorny. There is no question that there is discrimination in hiring[58] and that serious inequalities exist between male and female academics. The proportion of female professors in many universities and academic fields is far smaller than either their proportion of the total population or their share of all Ph.D.s (see table 1). Only a few years ago employing agents, if they advertised a position, openly indicated a preference for men. In his study just before the development of affirmative action guidelines, Lawrence Simpson found that recruitment agents would express their preference for a male over an equally qualified female.[59] However, under the new federal guidelines, universities are now required to advertise all positions publicly and indicate that they are an Equal Opportunity employer on the job announcement. However, many positions still are not publicly listed. Other openings are listed only after the decisions have been made about who will fill them, openly admitting discrimination is out of vogue but not out of practice. Although they may feel a cramp in their old style, the informal "old boy" networks continue to operate. Many male academics, and some females as well, believe that the claims of discriminatory practices made by many female academics are exaggerated; and they are also hostile because of the imposition meeting federal requirements constitutes and because they oppose other reforms designed to assist qualified women in obtaining positions (e.g., abolishing antinepotism rules).[60]

After a woman is hired as a faculty member, she is still treated unequally. University report after report on the status of women document the fact that women are paid less than men of similar rank and qualifications.[61] In a recent report the National Center for Education Statistics indicated that the faculty salary gap has widened between men and women in the same academic rank. They reported: "On the average, faculty women earned $3,096 less than faculty men during 1975–76 compared with a differential of $2,820 in 1974–75."[62]

Women also are concentrated in the lower level of university administrative positions, in research institutes, extention schools, specialist jobs, and the ranks of the unemployed. Most studies of academic careers find that the quality of the institution from which one receives one's degree is related to the quality of college or university at which one receives one's first job. This finding does not, however, apply to women. More often than men, their first academic jobs are at institutions of lower prestige and quality than would have been predicted by the institution from which they obtained their highest degree.[63]

It is important to compare the productivity of academic men and women if one is to evaluate their inequalities, but productivity is not easy to measure or define. First of all, women are more likely than men to express more interest in teaching than in research.[64] In today's university, teaching alone is not counted as sufficient evidence of professional productivity or competence. As quality of teaching is difficult to measure and is unacceptable as a substitute for research, the dedicated teacher is vulnerable to the charge of failing to meet professional expectations of scholarship. Furthermore, even in this field where women tend to make their greatest effort, the rewards are often meager. In one experiment the same lecture was presented to students by members of the different sexes who were matched for voice tonality and other communication skills. The students evaluated the presentation by the male teacher as superior to that of the female teacher.[65] Thus the sex of a teacher can be a handicap to a woman and an asset to the authority of a male. And her efforts may be unappreciated by the prejudiced; they are closed to hearing what a female has to say.

There is considerable evidence that female academics participate less actively in professional associations and publish fewer books and articles than their male counterparts. And this evidence, as in other instances, is used to demonstrate the unworthiness of faculty women. Inquiry into the structural, disciplinary, and contextual constraints and incentives may assist in explaining the existence of such evidence and the pressure on women leading to such patterns of behavior. In order to be an active participant in professional associations one must be invited to give papers and to run for offices or to serve on committees. Until recently women have been ignored in their professional associations.[66] In regard to publication, when one controls statistically for discipline, the gap in publications between men and women is nearly insignificant. Men and women in the same areas publish approximately the same, with a slight lead for men (and this is with women who as a group carry heavier teaching loads and who receive fewer incentives or rewards than do their male peers in the way of promotion or income increases). Women publish up to the expectations of their areas. Some areas are more concerned with publications, and others are more concerned with training students to enter practitioner fields. These professional orientation differences account for most of the variance in publication by sex.[67]

Perhaps the accusations against women should lead us not to apologize but to reverse the line of questioning. Why are women always as a group put on the defensive in their pursuit of professional careers? Is there evidence that academic men wish to have women in their ranks and as leaders in their fields?[68] There seems to be little evidence to indicate such support.

As one looks back on Caplow and McGee's famous study of academia in the 1950s, one sees how little things have changed. The authors of *The Academic Market Place* concluded that faculty women were not even inside the male academic status system.[69] In sum, it did not matter how hard women worked or how much work of what quality they produced. Men simply used different evaluative criteria when they judged the work of women.[70] The result of this is a tautological trap of the cruelest sort. Women have not achieved eminence in academic life because eminence depends not on merit alone but on the willingness of one's colleagues to recognize and honor one's efforts. Women have been set on the path to mediocrity and oblivion because to become successful someone would have to notice, to care. Such an outcome is rarely a real possibility for women because the academic rules of the game are rigged against them from the outset.

CONCLUSION

This review of the educational status of women in the United States has been very sketchy and has attempted to cover all the major institutional stages in the educational process. I chose to take such an approach at the risk of being overly brief because I felt an overview would demonstrate just how pervasive the problem actually is. The documentation would necessarily be thin in any case, because sufficient studies have not been completed on the subject of the educational experiences of women.

In this essay I have addressed myself to three tasks:

(1) to demonstrate the extent and persistence of inequalities in educational opportunities that exist between men and women; to show that female education differs from that provided for males in content and quality; and to point out that there are serious ways in which women receive hostile and humiliating treatment at the hands of those who operate our educational institutions;

(2) to suggest the way in which basic sexual socialization, both in childhood and later, molds and shapes the attitudes, aspirations, and expectations of women concerning the kinds of education they should receive; and

(3) to spell out the formal and informal mechanisms that operate through our educational institutions to reinforce and perpetuate those culturally induced values.

The evidence I have presented, it seems to me, follows such a general pattern that it supports the thesis that women are a colonized group and that the educational system is one of the primary means by which this situation is created and maintained.

Although I have suggested how the colonization of women is beneficial to males taken as a group, I have not systematically explored the question of how women's educational opportunities are linked to the class system and the economy. This relationship needs to be spelled out at length, and all I can hope to do here is to speculate about some possibly rewarding avenues of inquiry. It seems clear that housework and child-raising are essential functions in any society and that they have been largely performed by unpaid labor in capitalistic systems. By excluding women from educational institutions and from the labor force as well, a large supply of free labor is made readily available. It could be argued, I think, that the recent weakening of the barriers against women who wish to pursue degrees and occupational careers is directly related to the economy's temporary ability to absorb a larger supply of trained "manpower" (sic) and the corresponding decline of the centrality of the housewife's role due to the development of labor-saving devices and the trend toward smaller families. It should be possible to trace the rise and fall of opportunities for women in the various stages of capitalist development. However, I do not agree with those who believe that the oppression of women is purely a result of the evils of the system of private property. As I pointed out at the beginning of this essay, I see sexual differences as a more fundamental and pervasive conflict that is likely to be expressed in one way or another in any society, capitalist or not.

When one is dealing with an advanced capitalist, class-stratified society such as the United States, it is necessary to analyze the differences in the life experiences of women belonging to the various classes. I have not treated this problem for lack of space, but a few comments may be in order. First, it is obvious that women who enjoy higher socioeconomic status also enjoy greater educational opportunities and always have. But it is not true that they are in any way equal to those available to men of the same class. Within each class, women find themselves at the bottom of the educational heap. Furthermore, those women of the upper and middle classes who have been educated or pursued careers have often done so only because working-class women were available to perform household tasks at very low pay. While the sex-based provision of educational opportunity is certainly complicated by the cross-cutting effect of social class, the latter in no way eliminates the profound effects of the former.

My own preference is to approach the colonization of women as primarily a psychological and cultural process—a matter of consciousness (with material consequences). If this point of view is useful, then one needs to look beyond the economic imperatives of a particular period to grasp the possibilities for changing the status of women. In this respect, the women's movement, with its emphasis on raising the level of women's awareness of their oppression, is crucial. Simply recognizing discrimination for what it is will not cause the discrimination to desist. But it may lead the victim to cease cooperating in her victimization. As I have shown, force has never played a critical role in the subjugation of American women, and therefore the withdrawal of voluntary acquiescence to the sexist imperatives of the system is the vital first step toward its transformation.

Notes

1. For a good review of the modern parameters of the debate, see the papers from the conference "Women and the Workplace: The Implications of Occupational Segregation," sponsored by the Committee on the Status of Women in the Economics Profession of the American Economic Association, published in *Signs* 1 (Spring 1976). Two other very important works on the subject of social structure of the sexual order are Michelle Zimbalist Rosaldo and Louise Lamphere, eds., *Women, Culture and Society* (Stanford, Calif.: Stanford University Press, 1974); and Claude Lévi-Strauss, "The Family," in *Man, Culture and Society*, Harry L. Shapiro, ed. (New York: Oxford University Press, 1971).
2. Jean Lipman Blumen, "Toward a Homosocial Theory of Sex Roles: An Explanation of the Sex Segregation of Social Institutions," in *Signs* 1 (Spring 1976): 16.
3. O. Mannoni, *Prospero and Caliban: The Psychology of Colonization* (New York: Praeger, 1964).
4. Albert Memmi, *The Colonizer and the Colonized* (New York: Orion, 1965).
5. Thomas Woody, *A History of Women's Education*, vol. 1 (New York: The Science Press, 1929), p. 516. Woody discusses how the male power structure sponsored teacher education for women so that the public schools could be supported by cheap labor. Also see Elaine Kendall, *Peculiar Institutions: An Informal History of the Seven Sister Colleges* (New York: Putnam, 1976), chap. 3, for a good description of the unintentional ways in which financiers (e.g., Matthew Vassar) ended up founding and financing women's colleges.
6. Woody, *Women's Education*. Women are kept at home for a domestic education from their mothers.

7. Joan Kelly-Gadol, "The Social Relations of the Sexes: Met odological Implications of Women's History," in *Signs* (Summer 1976): 810.
8. Jessie Bernard, *Women, Wives, Mothers: Values and O tions* (Chicago: Aldine, 1975), p. 11.
9. Bonnie Cook Freeman, *A New Political Woman* (Madiso Wisc.: University of Wisconsin diss., 1975), chap. 1; B. Freeman, "Power, Patriarchy, and 'Political Primitives,'" *Beyond Intellectual Sexism*, Joan I. Roberts, ed. (New Yor McKay, 1976).
10. Karl Marx and Friedrich Engels, *The German Ideolo* (London: Lawrence and Wishart, 1964).
11. See, for example, Philip Wylie, *Generation of Vipers* (Ne York: Farrar and Rinehart, 1942).
12. Jean D. Grambs and Walter B. Waetjen. *Sex: Does It Ma a Difference?* (North Scituate, Mass.: Duxbury Press, 1975 p. 171.
13. Betty Levy, "The School's Role in the Sex Role Stereotypi of Girls," in *Sexism and Youth*, Diane Gersoni Stavn, e (New York: R. R. Bowker, 1974); Pauline Sears and Dav Feldman, "Teacher Interactions with Boys and with Girl in *And Jill Came Tumbling After*, Judith Stacey, et al., ec (New York: Dell, 1974), pp. 150–52; Nancy Frazier a Myra Sadker, *Sexism in School and Society* (New Yor Harper & Row, 1973), pp. 89–90. However, not all studi are consistent in their findings on this point. Patricia Ca Sexton in *The Feminized Male* (New York: Vintage, 196 argued that the needs of male students were not bei adequately attended to in the schools. O. L. Davis and Slobodian, "Teacher Behavior toward Boys and Gi during First Grade Reading Instruction," in *American Ed cational Research Journal* 4, no. 3 (May 1967): 261–6 found no differences in the amount of interaction betwe teacher and male and female pupils. Reports of conflicti data suggest that this area is in need of more researc with special attention paid to research method used, pr udices of authors, and social and economic forces ("t time") in which an investigation was conducted.

14. Lynne B. Iglitzin, "The Patriarchal Heritage," in *Women in the World*, Lynne B. Iglitzin and Ruth Ross, eds. (Santa Barbara: Clio Books, 1976), p. 15.
15. Lynne B. Iglitzin, "The Making of the Apolitical Woman: Femininity and Sex Stereotyping in Girls," in *Women in Politics*, Jane Jaquette, ed. (New York: John Wiley, 1974), pp. 27–28.
16. Lenore J. Weitzman, "Sex-Role Socialization," in *Women: A Feminist Perspective*, Jo Freeman, ed. (Palo Alto, Calif.: Mayfield, 1975), pp. 112–13.
17. Naomi Weisstein, "Psychology Constructs the Female," in *Radical Feminism*, Anne Koedt, et al., eds. (New York: Quadrangle, 1973), p. 195.
18. Mary McGee Williams and Irene Kane, *On Becoming a Woman* (New York: Dell, 1964), pp. 22 and 46, cited in Jean B. Elshtain, *Women and Politics* (Waltham, Mass.: Brandeis University diss., 1973), pp. 285–86.
19. James Coleman, *The Adolescent Society* (New York: The Free Press of Glencoe, 1961), p. 42.
20. Ibid.
21. Matina Horner, "Femininity and Successful Achievement: A Basic Inconsistency," in *Feminine Personality and Conflict*, Judith Bardwick, et al., eds. (Belmont, Calif.: Brooks/Cole, 1970), chap. 3.
22. Philip Goldberg, "Are Women Prejudiced against Women?" in *And Jill Came Tumbling After*, Judith Stacey, et al., eds. (New York: Dell, 1974), pp. 41–42.
23. John Pietrofesa and Nancy R. Schlossberg, "Counselor Bias and the Female Occupational Role," in *Woman in a Man-Made World*, Nona Glazer-Malbin and Helen Youngelson Waehrer, eds. (Chicago: Rand McNally, 1972), p. 221.
24. Joan Roberts, "Pictures of Power and Powerlessness: A Personal Synthesis," in *Beyond Intellectual Sexism*, pp. 55–56; and Ellen W. Gerber, et al., *The American Woman in Sport* (Reading, Mass.: Addison Wesley, 1974), chap. 14, "Physical Performance."
25. Gerber, et al., *American Woman in Sport*, pp. 446–54.
26. Judith M. Bardwick and Elizabeth Douvan, "Ambivalence:

The Socialization of Women," in *Women in Sexist Society,* Vivian Gornick and Barbara Moran, eds. (New York: Basic Books, 1971), p. 147.

27. Grambs and Waetjen, *Sex,* pp. 198–200.
28. Ibid., p. 181.
29. Frazier and Sadker, *Sexism in School and Society,* p. 147.
30. Pamela Roby, "Women and American Higher Education," in *The Annals of the American Academy of Political and Social Science* 404 (November 1972): 110–39. But when the economy did not require their tuition, the population of qualified women was shuffled back to home and hearth. Similar to the process of "Last hired, first fired," women's access to education has continued to ebb and flow with the ups and downs of the nation's economy, as well as with times of war and peace.
31. Lionel S. Lewis, *Scaling the Ivory Tower: Merit and Its Limits in Academic Careers* (Baltimore, Md.: Johns Hopkins, 1975), p. 124.
32. Elaine Walster, et al., "The Effect of Race and Sex on College Admission," in *Sex Differences and Discrimination in Education,* Scarvia Anderson, ed. (Worthington, Ohio: Charles A. Jones, 1972), p. 80.
33. Christopher Jencks and David Riesman, *The Academic Revolution* (Garden City, N.Y.: Anchor Books, 1969), p. 295. There is some recent evidence that the increasingly large numbers of women taking the college entrance examinations have brought down the average scores of women. Malcolm G. Scully noted that women now make up 55 percent of the high-school students taking the exams. A wider cross section of women are now considering college; and female test-takers include more than exceptional women. See Malcolm G. Scully, "What's Causing the Drop in College Entrance Scores?" in *The Chronicle of Higher Education* (February 17, 1976), p. 3.
34. Carnegie Commission on Higher Education, *Opportunities for Women in Higher Education* (New York: McGraw-Hill, 1973), p. 55.
35. K. Patricia Cross, "The Woman Student," in *Women in Higher Education,* W. Todd Furniss and Patricia Albjerg

Graham, eds. (Washington, D.C.: American Council on Education, 1974), p. 32.
36. Frazier and Sadker, *Sexism in School and Society,* p. 147.
37. Cross, "The Woman Student."
38. Edwin C. Lewis, as quoted in *Chronicle of Higher Education,* February 9, 1970.
39. Carnegie Commission on Higher Education, *Opportunities for Women,* p. 81. However, there is evidence that female enrollment in graduate programs is on the increase for M.A. and Ph.D. programs.
40. Cynthia Fuchs Epstein, *Women's Place: Options and Limits on Professional Careers* (Berkeley: University of California Press, 1970), pp. 167–68, 170. See also Jessie Bernard, *Academic Women* (University Park, Pa.: Pennsylvania State University, 1965).
41. Bonnie Cook Freeman, *New Political Woman,* p. 81.
42. Pamela Roby, "Institutional Barriers to Women Students in Higher Education," in *Academic Women on the Move,* Alice Rossi and Ann Calderwood, eds. (New York: Russell Sage Foundation, 1973), p. 43.
43. Ann Heiss, *Challenge to Graduate Schools* (San Francisco: Jossey Bass, 1970), pp. 93–95, cited in Carnegie Commission on Higher Education, *Opportunities for Women,* p. 93.
44. Carnegie Commission on Higher Education, *Opportunities for Women,* p. 95.
45. Ibid.
46. Alan E. Bayer, *Teaching Faculty in Academe: 1972–73* (Washington, D.C.: American Council on Education, 1973), p. 30.
47. Freeman, *New Political Woman,* chap. 3.
48. Saul D. Feldman, *Escape from the Doll's House* (New York: McGraw-Hill, 1974), p. 9. Michelle Patterson and Lucy Sells, "Women Dropouts from Higher Education," in *Academic Women on the Move,* p. 85.
49. Patterson and Sells, "Women Dropouts," in *Academic Women,* p. 86.
50. Feldman, *Escape from the Doll's House,* p. 95.
51. Carnegie Commission on Higher Education, *Opportunities for Women,* pp. 96–97.

52. Ellman, "Academic Women," in Stacey, et al., eds., *And Jill Came Tumbling After.*
53. Arlie Hochschild, "Inside the Clockwork of Male Careers," in *Women and the Power to Change,* Florence Howe, ed. (New York: McGraw-Hill, 1975), p. 50.
54. Ellman, "Academic Women," in Stacey, et al., eds., *And Jill Came Tumbling After,* p. 363.
55. Helen Hacker, "Women as a Minority Group," in *Social Forces* 30 (October 1951): 67.
56. Erving Goffman, *Stigma* (Englewood Cliffs, N.J.: Prentice-Hall, 1963), pp. 131–34.
57. Sheila McVey, "Departmental Clashes," in *Academic Supermarkets,* Philip Altbach, et al., eds. (Berkeley: Jossey Bass, 1971), pp. 228–52.
58. Lawrence Simpson, "A Myth Is Better Than a Miss: Men Get the Edge in Academic Employment," in *Sex Differences and Discrimination in Education,* p. 94.
59. Ibid.
60. Bayer, *Teaching Faculty in Academe,* p. 30.
61. Lora H. Robinson, "Institutional Variation in the Status of Academic Women," in Rossi and Calderwood, eds., *Academic Women on the Move.*
62. Statistics from the National Center for Education Statistics, which were reported in *Chronicle of Higher Education,* September 27, 1976, p. 1.
63. Helen Astin and Alan E. Bayer, "Sex Discrimination in Academe," in Rossie and Calderwood, eds., *Academic Women on the Move,* p. 21.
64. Bonnie Cook Freeman, *New Political Woman,* chap. 3.
65. Bernard, *Academic Women,* p. 130.
66. Ibid., 199; Epstein, *Woman's Place,* p. 176.
67. Freeman, *New Political Woman,* chap. 3.
68. Beatrice Dinerman, "Sex Discrimination in Academia," in *Journal of Higher Education* 42 (April 1971): 253–64.
69. Theodore Caplow and Reece McGee, *The Academic Marketplace* (New York: Basic Books, 1958), p. 226.
70. Bernard, *Academic Women,* p. 178.

Education, Colonialism, and the American Working Class

Gene Grabiner

While the bulk of this volume is concerned with the education of colonized peoples at the hand of the colonizer, there is also a place for discussion of the education of the working classes in the home countries of the colonizers. One reason for this is that the organization and ideology of both colonial education and working-class education within imperialist powers are very similar and, in fact, have identical origins. Particular elements vary according to the concrete conditions under which such education occurs. Ultimately, however, both colonial education and working-class education derive from the capitalist system of production and serve the functions of capital accumulation (or concentration of capital for further capitalist expansion or production) and of reproducing workers, intellectuals, and the unemployed to fill positions in that system. Likewise, colonial education and working-class education serve to legitimate the relations of domination and subjection characteristic of capitalism.

Inequalities and uneven development in schooling, evident both between colonial and metropolitan education and within education in the metropole, are institutional, social, and ideological expressions of capitalist production. It is this mode of production in its historical establishment of the world market that sets up, likewise, the city-country, metropole-satellite relation typical of imperialism. Such uneven development is typical of the period of capitalism.

Capitalism has a historical development that differentiates it from previous forms of exploitative class society. On one side are the colonies and neocolonies—two "outward" aspects of capitalism's highest stage of development. On the other side, for a period of time, is the imperialist power, or metropole, with its "aristocracy of labor," its larger working class, and its own internal relative surplus populations. These latter populations move in and out of industry and vary in size over time, with a general tendency for both their relative and absolute numbers to increase.

This essay centers on the ideology and organization of schooling in the United States. Public schooling for working people has historically been organized around training in skills, grading in quality, and internalization of ideology and discipline required by American capitalism. To highlight the historical continuity of this thrust in schooling, I will briefly review arguments made for the organization of state-supported schooling in this country. Having established this historical trend, I will then briefly outline the role of education in the production and reproduction of differentiated varieties of the commodity, labor-power, as exemplified in higher education.

While established public schooling in the United States emanated from a set of dominant ideologies, these ideologies were not the only ones historically extant. There were others that never materialized in public education. Throughout American history there has been a tension between education organized from the "top down," on behalf of capital, and education organized from the "bottom up" for and by working people. These "bottom up" pressures still persist, and what schools offer in education for the working class does not in any way represent the sum total of education of the working class for itself. Alternative conceptions of "bottom up" education never gained ascendance within the public schools. Instead, ruling-class ideologies, so evident in the writings of Jefferson, Mann, Boutwell, Bagley, Cubberly, Dewey, and Conant, have dominated the organization and content of public schools precisely because of the development of the American political economy and the bourgeois state apparatus.

This essay concludes that the historical aims of public education to insure the concentration and expansion of capital and secure legitimation are the same today as when similar desires were expressed by Thomas Jefferson in 1779. The concrete expression of these aims varies in specific historical periods. The dominant ideology of education for the working class in America is, as I will show, similar to that articulated for colonized peoples, both within the United States and in what is termed the "Third World."

HISTORICAL CONTINUITIES

As far back as 1779 Thomas Jefferson attempted to get a "Bill for the More General Diffusion of Knowledge" passed in the Virginia legislature, but his bill was defeated. However, it is noteworthy because it was an expression of support for a desired system of tracked and public education. Such a system, of course, came into general use only much later on in the United States. Jefferson argued for a three-tiered system of education. The first level contained elementary schools offering three years of schooling at state expense. Jefferson also proposed secondary schools that he called "grammar schools." Some scholarships to these grammar schools were to be given to "boys who shall have been two years at least at one of the elementary schools in the ward and whose parents are too poor to give them further education." [1] These boys, one from each elementary school per ward, were to be "some of the best and most promising genius and disposition" and would "proceed to the grammar school of his district," there to be supported at state expense.[2] This filtration would be repeated when one of the seniors in each grammar school was to be chosen to go to William and Mary College, there to be "educated, boarded, and clothed, three years; the expense of which annually shall be paid by the treasury on warrant from the Auditors." [3]

Clearly the author of the Declaration of Independence was not opting for a very egalitarian system of schools, since only a few *male* children of poor but free *white* folk were to be supported at state expense. The outcome of his proposed three-tiered system was the crystallization and maintenance of schools with two tracks that would prepare young people for one of two groups in society, the "laboring and the learned." [4] Some members of the laboring classes would experience "upward social mobility" according to this scheme. But state support for these boys would be only to "those persons whom nature hath endowed with reason and virtue" to be "rendered by liberal education worthy to receive and able to guard the sacred deposit of rights and liberties of their fellow citizens." [5] Such a school system would, according to Jefferson, engage in "raking a few geniuses from the rubbish." [6]

Similar conceptions of tracked schooling providing education differentially to different social groups were echoed by persons who followed Jefferson and who were instrumental in setting up the American common school. The advocates of the common school, in addition to proposing selective schooling, also saw education as a means of capitalist social control. For example, Reverend George Washington Hosmer, who fought in Buffalo in the 1840s to establish free public schools, argued that, despite the expense, the common schools, as proposed by Jefferson, were necessary to maintain the dominant order. Said the good reverend:

> Thousands among us have not dreamed of the effects of popular education; they have complained of its expensiveness, not foreseeing that it will diminish vagrancy and pauperism and crime, that it will be an antidote to mobs; and prevent the necessity of a standing army to keep our own people in order; every people may make their own choice "To pay teachers or recruiting sergeants," to support schools or constables and watchmen.[7]

Reverend Hosmer foresaw the common schools as a means by which the poor could become socially mobile but only after they had appropriately internalized capitalist morality and so "might acquire intelligence and virtue enough to perceive and abhor the fawning, hypercritical arts of corrupt ambition." [8] The school, according to Hosmer, was one of the pillars of the state, and he noted that "the school then stands paramount to the halls of legislation; the district school-house has a vast significance; it is a main prop to the republic." [9]

Between Jefferson's and Hosmer's times the United States had changed. In 1779 no city in the country had a population over 100,000. By the 1840s the urban population was increasing by a third per decade. Urbanization was but one change. In the same period the United States began to industrialize. More and more Americans (including recent immigrants to America) became employed in mills and factories, and with employment in mills and factories came labor struggles. The first factory strikes occurred in 1824 and became common from that time on. In the context of this increasing industrialization, urbanization, labor unrest, and immigration, concentrated in the northeastern United States, emerged the common school, replete with the ideological underpinnings earlier expressed by Buffalo's Reverend Hosmer. Horace Mann, secretary of the Massachusetts State Board of Education, expanded on Hosmer when he declared:

> Education, then beyond all devices of human origin, is the great equalizer of the conditions of men—the balance wheel of social machinery. . . . It does better than to disarm the poor of their hostility toward the rich; it prevents being poor.[10]

With Mann, as early as 1848, those two ideological chestnuts of American public schooling, "equality of educational opportunity" and "upward social mobility," became articulated.

The instituted form of education, the system of public schools, has, since Mann's time, been presented as an intervening variable, a supposed corrective to class antecedents, family conditions, and parents' position within the stratified work force. Mann not only saw common schooling as a means of capitalist social control but also (like Hosmer) as a cheaper means of social control than armies or police. For him universal education would put an end to immorality, a euphemism for social unrest such as class struggle.

Mann's major support in establishing common schooling came from factory owners in Massachusetts whose interests in universal education were similar to Mann's and who at the same time saw education as a means of increasing worker productivity (and, as a result, owners' profits). Homer Bartlett, an agent of the Massachusetts Cotton Mills and a contemporary of Horace Mann, wrote:

> From my observations and experience, I am perfectly satisfied that the owners of manufacturing property have a deep pecuniary interest in the education and morals of their help, and I believe that the time is not distant when the truth of this will appear more and more clear. And as competition becomes more close, and small circumstances of more importance in turning the scale in favor of one establishment over another, I believe it will be seen that the establishment, other things being equal, which has the best educated and most moral help will give the greatest production at the least cost per pound.[11]

Bartlett did not share Mann's sophisticated rhetoric about "reforming mankind"; rather he emphasized moral values for workers only (the mill owners presumably already being quite moral). This stress on education as fostering moral behavior appears not only among supporters of the common school in America but also among administrators of British and French colonies.[12]

The ideology of school as inculcator of proper virtues to the unvirtuous, as a substitute for or parallel with police and armies, and as the means to train productive and docile workers for emerging industrial capitalist production was most clearly enunciated by Horace Mann's successor in the Massachusetts State Board of Education, George Boutwell. Boutwell boasted that

> In Lowell, and in many other places, the proprietors find the training of the schools admirably adapted to prepare the children for the labors of the mills.[13]

Schooling, he argued, had already shown its value, for it "prevents labor unrest." He explained this in the following way:

> The owners of factories are more concerned than other classes and interests in the intelligence of their laborers. When the latter are well educated and the former are disposed to deal justly, controversies and strikes can never occur, nor can the minds of the masses be prejudiced by

demagogues and controlled by temporary and factious considerations.[14]

By the 1840s the common school was firmly entrenched in America. By 1842 some 80,000 such schools had been established. They were, as the preceding discussion has indicated, built on an ideology that implicitly or explicitly used terms like "equality of educational opportunity," "upward social mobility," "morality," and "intelligence." At the same time this ideology emphasized the school's role in maintaining the capitalist social order and increasing worker productivity while proposing differential education for differential strata of the working class.

Later developments in education paralleled the expansion of American capitalism and its movement to monopoly from its pre-1860 laissez-faire base. As capitalism put increasing stress on "efficiency," that conception also became a tenet of public schooling and public-school ideology. This was clear in the work of Ellwood P. Cubberley, Dean of the School of Education at Stanford University, who promoted the corporate concept of efficiency in the schools, even constructing a teacher efficiency score card [15] to help principals check teachers out, and in books like William Bagley's *Classroom Management*, which, as Joel Spring has noted, underwent thirty editions between 1907 and 1927.[16] In *Classroom Management*, Bagley argued for routinized and authoritarian classroom instruction because it would produce "efficient and productive assembly-line workers for industry." Such an organization of the classroom, he said, would change the "child from a little savage into a creature of law and order, fit for the life of civilized society."

With the "cult of efficiency" in the schools came also the concept of the technocratic "expert" in education who would see that the educational enterprise ran smoothly. Although not generally known as such, one of the most prominent advocates of efficient school management by experts was John Dewey, who in his 1900 work *Moral Principles in Education* said:

School mastering has its own special mysteries, its own knowledge and skill into which the untrained layman cannot

> penetrate. We are just beginning to recognize that the school and the government have a common problem in this respect. Education and politics are two functions fundamentally controlled by public opinion. . . . But just where shall public opinion justly express itself and what shall be left to expert judgement . . . the selection and the prosecution of the detailed ways and means by which the public will is to be executed efficiently must remain largely a matter of specialized and expert service. To the superior knowledge and technique required here, the public may well defer.[17]

Dewey, in short, proposed that "efficiency" could be operationalized only by experts, who could (and would) decide for students and families what education should consist of and what it should be for.

The dominant ideologies behind American public schooling in the nineteenth and early twentieth centuries are still evident today. They are perhaps best illustrated in the 1959 Carnegie Commission Report, written by James Bryant Conant and published by Conant under the title *The American High School Today*.[18] This report essentially blends the cult of efficiency and the worker education laid out earlier, for in it Conant emphasizes two things: "career education" and "individualized" instruction. Much before the current focus on career education he urged that career education begin in the elementary school based on aptitude and achievement tests, school records, and teacher evaluation to guide students into an education, "individualized" for each, in order to give the student skills that were marketable within the American economy. Individualization was supposed to make such preparation more efficient and would not make students feel they were being tracked, regardless of whether the school was in fact tracking them. Individualization, in Conant's terms, was not tailor-made programming; rather, it was the ability-grouping of students. Students would be fed directly into the job market by ability groups. Conant proposed making students' records readily available to their prospective employers. He went so far as to suggest that students be given a mini-transcript card for such purposes that they were to carry in their wallets.

Conant suggested that schools prepare students specifically for the local job market. In a nutshell, he proposed that:

> Programs should be available for girls interested in developing skills in typing, stenography, clerical machines, home economics, or a specialized branch of home economics which, through further work in college, might lead to the profession of dietician. Distributive education should be available if the retail shops in the community can be persuaded to provide suitable openings. If the community is rural, vocational agriculture should be included. For boys, depending on the community, trade and industrial programs should be available. Half a day is required in the eleventh and twelfth grades for this vocational work. In each specialized trade, there should be an advisory committee composed of representatives of management and labor. Federal money is available for these programs. The school administration should constantly assess the employment situation in these trades included in the vocational programs. When opportunities for employment in a given trade no longer exist within the community, the training program in the field should be dropped. The administration should be ready to introduce new vocational programs as opportunities open in the community or area.[19]

The above clearly indicates that the schools respond to the interests of the capitalist order and its needs for labor-power and only incidentally to the interests of the student. Interestingly enough, by Conant's time there was less talk about education and "social mobility." The emphasis instead was on slotting children into their proper places efficiently. And, as Samuel Bowles and Herbert Gintis have pointed out, capitalist education has allocated children into positions generally equivalent to those of their parents and their work places and has not been (nor could it ever be) an intervening variable in terms of upward mobility or an equalizer of class.[20]

We have now looked at dominant views of the ideology and organization of education within the United States. We have seen through many examples that the aims of education were set in terms of controlling the masses of people for the goals of capital. Such goals were by no stretch of the imagination set by the working people. The goals of education set by working people were quite different, as the next section indicates.

ALTERNATIVE CONCEPTIONS: THE WORKERS' EDUCATION MOVEMENT

Compulsory education, when made a reality in the United States, emerged from the ruling class's requirements and was supported by bourgeois ideology. However, free compulsory education was first demanded by organizations of workingmen. In 1828, for example, the New York Working Men's Party agitated for free public education and secured that demand by 1832. In Pennsylvania the Working Men's Party had success in 1836.[21]

While workingmen fought for public schools, they never controlled them. The American Federation of Labor (A F of L) supported public education and did not generally present any alternatives to the public schools. At the 1894 convention of the A F of L one speaker did criticize the public schools for their failure to "put poverty underground," but still the A F of L did not initiate an educational program of its own. In 1900 it turned down an appeal by Walter Vroman, co-founder of Ruskin College (a labor college at Oxford University), for funds to open a labor college in Trenton, Missouri.[22]

Despite the A F of L hesitancy to promote alternative education, there already was a long history of workers developing education for themselves. American women and male immigrant mill workers in New England in the 1820s organized classes on their own time.[23] The most significant movement for workers' education outside the public schools, however, was the National Women's Trade Union League (NWTUL). Its 1907 convention asked its local leagues to establish classes on the struggle between workers and employers. In 1911 the New York league developed pamphlets for its classes on the history of industry, rents, wages, profits, and the history of the labor movement. In 1914 the league opened a school for organizers in Chicago.[24]

The National Women's Trade Union League was clearly aware of the contradictions of education under capitalism. It criticized the sexist practices of the vocational education movement[25] as well as the vocational education movement's attitudes toward labor and their general use of the public schools as indoctrinational and simple training mechanisms.

These self-organized educational activities, whether taking place within the formal units of workers' education, such as the NWTUL or any of the labor colleges, from Work People's College (the Finnish Socialist College in Duluth, Minnesota) to Brookwood (the liberal-socialist labor college founded by the Fellowship of Reconciliation in Westchester, New York) and the bilingual Hungarian Free Lyceum, were all workers' education insomuch as elements of America's urban proletariat were participants and it was organized apart from the public schools.[26] Many of these programs, such as the Work People's College and the NWTUL programs, emphasized class struggle and socialism.

The Eastern European Jewish immigration to the United States in the late nineteenth and early twentieth centuries added still another current to the Workers' Education Movement. An example of the schools started by these immigrants was Drs. Peskin, Stone, and Ingeman's Workers' School, begun in 1899. The school, later to become the Workers' Educational League, taught courses in the sciences, economics, and socialism.[27] Despite public education and the A F of L's lack of interest, workers' education developed staying power. By 1925 over 25,000 workers from coast to coast were enrolled in such programs.[28]

As noted before, the A F of L, dominant in the American labor movement, did not support workers' education, although it supported public education. Rather, in the 1920s it sought to contain workers' education. This was clearest in its attacks on Brookwood Labor College in 1928[29] in which the conservative A F of L leadership accused the college of being communist and radical and withdrew its support from the college.[30]

In short, while workers themselves did devise alternatives to the public schools in the United States, those alternatives were never able to flourish as did the public schools. Partly this was because of the lack of funding for such enterprises and because of the antipathy toward these alternatives shown by the conservative leadership of the largest labor organization in the United States, the A F of L, who saw workers' education correctly as something meant *for* workers' rather than capitalists' control.

WORKING-CLASS EDUCATION: EDUCATION FOR WORKERS—BUT NOT WORKERS' EDUCATION

Limits within Bourgeois-Democratic Political Forms: Working-Class Control of Boards of Education

In his classic 1917 study "Who's Who on Our Boards of Education," Scott Nearing demonstrated that out of a total of 104 large American cities reporting, "nine tenths of the school board members of the large American cities are selected from one sixth of the gainfully occupied population, which is above the rank of wage earner or clerk." To put it more specifically:

> [M]ore than three fourths of all the board members of the cities reporting were business or professional men. The businessmen constitute the largest single group, comprising more than half the total number of board members . . . 144 of the businessmen were merchants, 78 were manufacturers, and 104 were bankers, brokers, real estate and insurance men. . . . Of the 333 professional men 118 or more than one third were doctors and dentists, 144 or about two fifths were lawyers. The total number of teachers was 18. These were for the most part college professors.[31]

Nearing's results were confirmed in a 1927 replication of his study by George Counts.[32] And, according to a comment from John Dewey, penned in 1900, this lack of real democratic control of schooling was exactly as it should be:

> The administration of the schools, the making of the course of study, the selection of texts, the prescription of methods

of teaching, these are matters with which the people and their representatives upon boards of education cannot deal save with danger of becoming mere meddlers.[33]

These data suggest that the belief in the "public school system" and its possibility of "democratic school control" was a sham, for the proletariat never has gained full and democratic representation and participation on boards of education commensurate with its majority position in the society. In 1940 it was clear that workers had only 3 percent representation on boards of education countrywide.[34] The same held true in 1953.[35] As late as 1970 the situation had not changed much. An article entitled "Local School Governance" demonstrates this. It shows that for school boards either appointed or elected (most large-size cities have elected boards as of this writing and have had them since at least 1962), in districts serving 25,000 or more pupils, 72.6 percent of the board members had graduated from college.[36] Further, as in all previous studies of this sort, it was found that business and professional people dominate school boards in numbers way out of proportion to their numbers in the general population. They comprise more than three-fifths of the board members. Housewives account for 7.2 percent. Workers, skilled and unskilled, comprise 9.4 percent of all board memberships in this national survey. However, "the highest proportion of business and professional membership (75.2 percent) was found in larger school systems."[37] Of course, given industrialization, urbanization, and proletarianization, the greatest concentration of the American working class also happens to be in the largest cities—those having the largest school systems. Consequently, the disproportionate number of business and professional people as school-board members in just such districts serves only to emphasize the underrepresentation of working people on boards of education. Accordingly, either the skilled and unskilled component and/or the "housewife" component of school-board membership would be altered in those large districts to reflect this greater disproportion. Furthermore, even considering the national data, the responsibilities of school-board membership, the hours of meetings, etc., tend to suggest that the "housewife" component is one largely drawn from among the wives of business and professional people. As for the group "skilled and unskilled workers," without analysis of the "labor aristocracy" element among skilled workers it is difficult to tell what portion of the 9.4 percent worker membership of school boards nationwide represents the greatest mass of workers today.

In 1962 Marilyn Gittell did a similar study in six major urban centers: Detroit, Chicago, Philadelphia, New York, Baltimore, and St. Louis. Each board reflected an apparent attempt to represent varying ethnic groups in its city. Yet, for example, "the typical Negro member" was usually some kind of professional person with no connections to the civil rights movement or struggles. Gittell's findings confirmed a suggestion made above regarding the "housewives" who were school-board members. On each of the six boards she found that "women board members are representatives of established women's civic groups." Usually, such activities are not closely associated with the social life of working-class women. About 75 percent of all school-board members were college educated, and about half had advanced or professional degrees. "The most common advanced degree of board members was the law degree. In each of the cities, at least one and usually more of the board were lawyers." The business community was represented on five of the six boards.[38] No teachers were represented on any of the boards, while organized labor was represented in Chicago, New York, and Detroit. Gittell attributed this labor representation to the strength of unions in those cities. And, while that's true, we must keep in mind the disjuncture between more conservative labor bureaucrats and the rank-and-file as well as other contradictions within labor that, because of a history of economistic relations, mitigate against straightforward proletarian democratic participation in the life of that class.

It's clear that from 1917–1967 very little has changed with regard to working-class control of boards of education.

SOCIAL MOBILITY VIA EDUCATION: HAS THE WORKING CLASS "MOVED UP"?

Dominant conceptions of upward mobility via education, as noted in the first section of this essay, varied from Jefferson's elitist "raking a few geniuses from among the rubbish" to Mann's more democratic notion of the total elimination of poverty. What has been the case for the working class in the twentieth century?

Although educationists generally speak of both upward and downward social mobility of groups, the focus is generally on individual, as opposed to group, ascendance. In a very real sense, the conception of "upward social mobility" is nothing more than a shorthand expression for the persistence of inequality. For, in order to "move up" and in order for this motion to be a continuous, historical, and social process, it is clear that the limits of "top" and "bottom" must persist. Here I am not even talking about the elimination of relations of domination and subjection that arise from the social relations of production in societies typified by exploitative and antagonistic class relations. My discussion of mobility centers around much more parsimonious conceptions—namely, the simple, directionless, and hierarchical ranking typical of stratification theory, not class analysis of societies. Given that bourgeois scholars look at and conceptualize inequality in terms of market analogies (i.e., inequality in the sphere of distribution of commodities), when they speak of "upward social mobility" or "strata" in capitalist society, let's see if capitalism has "delivered the goods."

Robert J. Havighurst, writing in 1958, concluded that (using occupational status as an indicator) education would be the key to any further upward mobility for the working class. He saw this as a trend and spoke of the "industrial and democratic society of the year 2000," which "will be even more open and fluid than the most highly industrialized societies today, so that education will be the main instrument for upward mobility, and lack of education or failure to do well in one's education will be the principal cause of downward mobility." [39]

In 1975 Robert J. Havighurst and Bernice L. Neugarten stated that "[e]ducation has become the principal avenue of opportunity in twentieth century America: college education for upper-middle-class occupations, and high school education for such lower-middle-class occupations such [sic] as clerical work, sales work, and skilled technical work." [40]

As of 1919–20, 16.8 persons per 100, aged seventeen years, had graduated from secondary schools in the United States. As of

1972–73, that figure had risen to 78 per 100.[41] Now, Havighurst has argued that education, generally, is the route to upward mobility and the "avenue of opportunity." What gains did high-school graduates make in the twentieth century? Because of lack of consistent data it is extremely difficult to graph jobs available to high-school graduates in 1919–20 or, for that matter, 1929–30 and make an accurate comparison to the jobs and types of jobs available to high-school graduates presently. This kind of work, however, is necessary and should be done. It is possible, though, to examine America's college attendance from 1929–30 to 1972–73 in terms of possible advance in occupational status and upward social mobility in general.

Martin Trow has held that the United States has experienced a shift from elite to mass to universal post-secondary education.[42] A glance at United States census data would tend to confirm this notion. For example, as of 1889–90, only 3 persons per 100 of the age cohort eighteen to twenty-one had gained some undergraduate-degree credit in an institution of higher education. This figure almost doubled every twenty years until 1969–70, when the increase over 1949–50 was not 100 percent but only 63 percent. This doesn't indicate any decline, because the figures for 1972–73 show a 78 percent increase over 1949–50. As of 1972–73, fifty persons per 100 of the age cohort eighteen to twenty-one had gained some undergraduate-degree credit at an institution of higher learning.[43]

In the face of this apparent democratization of higher education, however, there is a serious structural differentiation. In going "behind" these data, the picture is anything but democratic.

The City University of New York (CUNY) exemplifies such differentiation, for within the city university there are three tracks: the preprofessional track, which is the elite education given in that system at Queens, Brooklyn, and Hunter colleges; the social-services track, which offers programs at six senior colleges and three community colleges; and the clerical-vocational track, emphasizing subprofessional and career programs at two of the senior colleges within the system.[44] The population composition of colleges within the CUNY system betrays its stratified and racist character. Table 1[45] demonstrates this. The clerical and vocational track is attended almost exclusively by blacks and

Table 1
Projected Profile of the New CUNY

Elite Track	Social-Services Track	Clerical and Vocational Track
Three senior colleges	Five senior colleges Transfer program in three community colleges	Five community colleges Career programs in three community colleges
High average in high school (over 82.5)	High-school average from 75–82	Any high-school average, most under 75, many under 70
Academic diploma in high school	Mainly academic diplomas	General and vocational degrees
Mainly white	Ethnically mixed in the senior colleges; white in the transfer programs	Higher percent of blacks and Puerto Ricans but still many whites
High percent Jewish students	High percent Catholic students	Mixed
Mainly middle class	Middle, lower-middle and working class	Mainly working and lower class
Most students aimed for graduate or professional schools	Most students aimed for careers in teaching; social work, health and public administration, or engineering	Most students geared toward lower-level technical, clerical, or paraprofessional jobs

Source: Ellen Kay Trimberger, "Open Admissions: A New Form of Tracking?" in *The Insurgent Sociologist* 4 (Fall 1973): 29–43.

Puerto Ricans, the poorest people in New York City, while the elite preprofessional track is predominantly white. Equally significant as the population composition is the lack of mobility within tracks. The clerical-vocational track increasingly offers terminal degrees that do not allow students to enter the four-year colleges. Selection into each track is based on grades citywide, which means that "poor achievers" (usually those who are poor) have little chance of entering anything but the clerical-vocational track despite the open-admission policy that was in effect at CUNY until spring 1976.

Table 1 is based on 1972 statistics. Since 1972 the situation at CUNY has changed. The City University has ended open admission, raised "standards," and begun charging tuition. The imposition of tuition will ultimately cut back on the enrollments of poor and minorities who do not do well in high school and who are unable to pay tuition. This is clear in the retrenchment at CUNY in 1975–76. In that year the City University closed Evers College and attempted to close Hostos College. The former was a four-year senior college that first opened in 1971 and had an 84 percent black student body.[46] Evers was a unit within the social-sciences track of CUNY. Hostos College is a two-year community college in the clerical-vocational track of CUNY composed predominantly of Puerto Rican students, and *all* instruction is bilingual.

The differentiation explicit in the CUNY system is not confined to New York City. It is a nationwide phenomenon wherever states have developed an extensive three-tiered system of higher education. Statistics show this clearly. Between 1958 and 1972 students enrolled in higher education increased more than two and a half times, from 3,420,000 to 9,204,000. The greatest growth was clustered in the junior colleges, where enrollment jumped from 525,000 to 2,625,000 (an increase of about 500 percent). In the fall of 1972, 28 percent of all students attending college were enrolled in junior colleges; by 1980, 40 percent are projected to attend them. The Carnegie Commission has suggested that junior colleges have become the major selective device in determining who will really go to college and has urged that, by 1980, 70 percent of college-bound people should begin their education at junior college in order to test their ability to handle college work.[47]

The above statistics can be interpreted in several ways. Most have chosen to see them as indicating greater democratization in higher education and allowing for more equitable educational and therefore social opportunity. On the surface this might be plausible: More people go to college than ever before. However, such an interpretation is based on the assumption that going to college, any college, yields the same opportunity within the American political economy. Clearly, the differentiation documented above indicates that there are colleges and colleges. As Martin Carnoy points out, the apparent democratization of higher education has been accompanied by the firming up of the elite character of certain institutions:

> Twenty years ago a degree from any university assured someone of a high status job in the United States. Now a degree has to come from an elite university, such as Harvard, MIT, or Stanford, to assure the same status. These are the very same universities which are open primarily to children of the ruling class, either through connections or through a selection system which favors their success.[48]

Today, a two-year college degree is required for jobs that twenty years ago were open to high-school drop-outs.

CONCLUSION

I have shown in the previous section that the dominant conceptions spoken of earlier have held organizational and ideological sway for the greatest mass of working people going to school in the United States in the twentieth century. Yet, as should be noted from the fact that there even were alternative conceptions, capitalist concepts of schooling and education have not represented a monolithic organization of ideas, nor have they been located in a total institution. The dominant conceptions have been dominant because of the relationship of forces between the working class and the ruling class in the United States. As it becomes more apparent that amount of schooling doesn't necessarily equate with degree or quality of education, nor even with the capitalist promise of "upward social mobility," the contradiction of schooling under capitalism will become more apparent to more and more working people. As Christopher Jencks et al.[49] have shown, the group rate of social mobility within the United States has been stable since the end of World War I. This means that the expansion in both secondary and tertiary education attendance hasn't made for mass "upward social mobility."

Such data should not be construed to make an argument for massive school closings based on the scarcity of group "upward social mobility." Nor is it necessary to support the Jencks et al. type of conclusion that schools may as well keep children occupied or provide somewhere for them to go, even if they don't deliver equality. I would argue the contrary—that many more teachers than are presently working in the public elementary, secondary, and postsecondary institutions *should be hired.* Class size in all schools should be diminished, not just in "experimental programs." All the necessary ancillary services should likewise be increased. Surely it is a contradiction for the federal government to contemplate building the B-1 bomber at a cost of $87 million per plane when that same figure is the total education budget of the city of Cincinnati for one year. There is a need for increased educational support on a mass basis in the United States.

Although the dominant conceptions were, and are, the ones that characterize the public schools ideologically and organizationally, the forces that fought for workers' education have never thoroughly disappeared. Nor, for that matter, has the objective basis for workers' education, the working class, been fully and completely integrated into capitalist production relations and social relations.

Given the material conditions, the forms of struggle on the educational front have changed. There is no longer an independent workers' education movement. There have been, however, massive and increasing numbers of strikes among public schoolteachers. Likewise, resistance among students has never been fully submerged.

While all ideologies have a material base, the material base for ideology in capitalist society (as in all antagonistic class societies) is two-sided, contradictory. While, on the one hand, following rigid hierarchy in a factory or plant is a rule of thumb for workers so as not to get fired, it is not at the same time true that such workers do not consciously foul up assembly lines, slow them down, sabotage production, or go on strike. Many contemporary authors have reduced these properties to a mechanical materialism, resulting in a one-sided conception of ideology. This conception argues that workers (and necessarily working-class children) reproduce authoritarian ideology because it has a payoff at work in terms of keeping their jobs. A subjective element enters here as well. The presumption is that if workers are "clean" and not "political" and keep their "noses to the grindstone," they will keep their jobs. However, capitalist crises occur independent of human will. Such crises result in the firings of even the most loyal employees.

Even though there is not presently a broad workers' education movement, resistance to capitalist education is not dead. It takes many forms and is expressed in varying ways in the schools. It may be expressed by students in the manner of individual and inverted, incomplete and distorted acts of isolated rebellion. For example, depending on causal factors, it might be very reasonable to conduct a study of school suspensions, expulsions, detentions, cut slips, etc., as administrative responses to acts of rebellion of the sort referred to above. Such a study would involve devising indicators of students' class background within the stratified working class and/or within the middle class and correlating those data with the students' track in high school, their ethnic background, and the frequency and type of disciplinary actions received. A reasonable suspicion is that those high schoolers who are in the academic track are seldom suspended and, if they are, the measures taken in enforcement of sanctions vary widely and are less punitive than parallel sanctions and suspensions applied to those students in vocational and general tracks (whether black, white, Puerto Rican, etc.). This is not to imply that students in the academic track are from the bourgeoisie. On the contrary, there is labor-market segmentation and a stratified proletariat that are treated differentially by capital according to its requirements for the differentiated commodity, labor power. This includes highly trained and less trained labor power.

I have argued in this essay that great similarities exist in the organization and ideology of schooling for colonized peoples and the working class of the colonizer within the metropole. The bulk of the article has been devoted to demonstrating the historical and present tension between dominant ideologies and what workers want and have wanted in terms of education as materialized in the public schools.

The ideological elements that comprise dominant views of education for the working class include elitism, equality of opportunity, upward social mobility, "intelligence," morality, efficiency, and technocratic expertise. Some of these ideological foundations can be located in the context of education for the colonized. As such, these elements are expressions of dominant conceptions reproduced in the colonial setting. For example, there was a colonial necessity to indoctrinate the colonized with "moral" ideologies. In 1847 Earl Grey, England's Secretary of State for the Colonies, requested a report from the Committee of Council on Education. This report was to deal with the means of conducting industrial schools in the colonies with an eye toward combining intellectual and industrial education. With regard to England's black, agrarian colonies, Philip Curtin has noted that the committee planned education for "social and racial inferiors."

> Religious instruction was to form the backbone of the curriculum, with agricultural training for the boys and domestic science education for the girls making up the only other outstanding part of the school program. Like social inferiors, black children were to be taught "the habits of self-control and moral discipline." Like racial inferiors, they were to be taught "the domestic and social duties of the colored races" with respect to the European mother country.[50]

The above sentiments were not much different from John Dewey's later promulgations about the completely black segregated and vocationally oriented "Mr. Valentine's School" (P.S. 26 in Cincinnati), which he celebrated as "a real step forward in solving the 'race question' and peculiar problems of any immigrant district as well." [51] Similar conceptions are pointed to by Robert Havighurst in relating the statements of a white public-school principal addressing a group of black ghetto parents in Brooklyn, New York, in 1966:

> Through our PTA we are going to try to instill a greater sense of responsibility in some of our parents. We will try to understand the importance of: 1. Cleanliness, 2. Proper dress, 3. Punctuality, 4. Attendance—unless ill, 5. Care of school property, 6. Neat, clean, complete accurate notebooks, 7. Academic achievement.[52]

The parallels are clear. While much discussion has not been devoted to the unity of structural origins for both working-class education within the metropole and within the colony in this essay, significant data have been presented regarding the metropolitan working class. Replication of such research among colonies and neocolonies is a task taken on by other scholars, both within this volume and in future research. I suspect, however, that the outcome will validate the hypothesis suggested herein.

Notes

1. Julian P. Boyd, et al., eds., *The Papers of Thomas Jefferson* (Princeton, N.J.: Princeton University Press, 1950, et seq.), quoted in Henry J. Perkinson, *Two Hundred Years of American Educational Thought* (New York: McKay, 1976), p. 55.
2. Ibid., p. 56.
3. Ibid., p. 57.
4. David Tyack, *Turning Points in American Educational History* (Waltham, Mass.: Blaisdell, 1967), p. 89.
5. Ibid., p. 109.
6. Ibid., p. 89.
7. Erie County Common School Education Society, *Minutes* (Buffalo, 1840), p. 7. I am indebted to Jo Blatti of radio station WBFO for making this document available to me.
8. Ibid., p. 8.
9. Ibid., p. 4.
10. Michael Katz, *School Reform Past and Present* (Boston: Little, Brown, 1971), p. 141.
11. Samuel Bowles and Herbert Gintis, *Schooling in Capitalist America* (New York: Basic Books, 1976), p. 162.
12. Eric Stokes, *English Utilitarians in India* (Oxford: Oxford University Press, 1959).
13. Bowles and Gintis, *Schooling in Capitalist America.*
14. Ibid.
15. Ellwood P. Cubberley, *An Introduction to the Study of Education and to Teaching* (Boston: Houghton Mifflin, 1925); *Public School Administration* (Boston: Houghton Mifflin, 1929).
16. Joel Spring, *Education and the Rise of the Corporate State* (Boston: Beacon Press, 1972).
17. John Dewey, *Moral Principles in Education* (Boston: Houghton Mifflin, 1900), pp. vi–vii.
18. James Bryant Conant, *The American High School Today*

(New York: McGraw-Hill, 1959). The first work looking at the significance of Conant's post-World War II policy recommendations for secondary education is Joel Spring's recent book, *The Sorting Machine* (New York: McKay, 1976).

19. Ibid., pp. 51–52.
20. Bowles and Gintis, *Schooling in Capitalist America.*
21. Margaret T. Hodgen, *Workers' Education in England and the United States* (New York: Dutton, 1925), p. 167.
22. A F of L, *Proceedings* (Washington, 1894), p. 65.
23. Charles Dickens, *American Notes* (New York: Sheldon & Co.), quoted in Hodgen, *Workers' Education,* p. 201.
24. Ibid., p. 206.
25. Maxine Seller, "The Education of the Immigrant Woman: 1890–1935" (Paper delivered at Berkshire Conference on Women's History, June 1976).
26. Ibid.
27. Hodgen, *Workers' Education,* p. 211.
28. Ibid., p. 214.
29. Nat Hentoff, ed., *The Essays of A. J. Muste* (New York: Bobbs-Merrill, 1967), p. 84.
30. For example, Matthew Woll, the A F of L vice-president who condemned Brookwood as communist, was simultaneously acting president of the National Civic Federation (NCF), a class collaborationist organization of the leaders of big capital and conservative labor executives and bureaucrats. Its goals were not workers' control of society, education, and industry but capitalist control of labor. For further discussion of labor leaders' early sellouts to capital via the NCF, see Gabriel Kolko, *The Triumph of Conservatism* (Chicago: Quadrangle, 1967), and James Weinstein, *The Corporate Ideal in the Liberal State: 1900–1918* (Boston: Beacon Press, 1968).
31. Scott Nearing, "Who's Who on Our Boards of Education," in *School and Society* 5 (January 20, 1917): 89–90.
32. George Counts, *The Social Composition of Boards of Education: A Study in the Social Control of Public Education* (Chicago: University of Chicago Press, 1927).
33. John Dewey, *Moral Principles in Education,* p. vii.
34. Mark Starr, Educational Director of the International La-

dies' Garment Workers' Union, cited in T. R. Adam, *The Workers' Road to Learning* (New York: American Association for Adult Education, 1940), p. 16.

35. W. W. Charters, Jr., "Social Class Analysis and the Control of Public Education," in *Harvard Educational Review* 23 (Fall 1953); idem, in Elizabeth L. Useem and Michael Useem, eds., *The Education Establishment* (Englewood Cliffs, N.J.: Prentice-Hall, 1974), p. 101.
36. Mario Fantini, Marilyn Gittell, and Richard Magat, "Local School Governance," in Useem and Useem, eds., ibid., p. 89.
37. Ibid.
38. Ibid., p. 90.
39. Robert J. Havighurst, "Education and Social Mobility in Four Societies," in A. H. Halsey, Jean Flood, and C. Arnold Anderson, eds., *Education, Economy and Society* (New York: The Free Press, 1961), pp. 119–20.
40. Robert J. Havighurst and Bernice L. Neugarten, *Society and Education* (Boston: Allyn and Bacon, 1975), p. 62.
41. Ibid., p. 295.
42. Martin Trow, "Reflections on the Transition from Mass to Universal Higher Education," in *Daedalus* 99, no. 1 (1970): 1–42. I am indebted to Andy Trusz for some important discussions centering about this topic. His unpublished Ed. D. thesis, The Activities of Governmental Education Bodies in Defining the Role of Post-Secondary Education since 1945: A Comparative Case Study of the State of New York and the Province of Ontario, 1945–1972 (State University of New York at Buffalo, 1976), is a significant work in this area.
43. U.S. Office of Education, *Digest of Educational Statistics*, 1972. U.S. Bureau of the Census, series P. 23, no. 44 (March 1973).
44. Ellen Kay Trimberger, "Open Admissions: A New Form of Tracking?" in *The Insurgent Sociologist* 4 (Fall 1973): 29–43.
45. Ibid., p. 32.
46. Ibid., p. 42.
47. Fred Pincus, "Tracking in the Community Colleges," in *The Insurgent Sociologist* 4 (Spring 1974): 19, 21.

48. Martin Carnoy, "Schooling and Income," in *Pacific Research and World Empire Telegram* 2 (July–August 1971): 5.
49. Christopher Jencks, et al., *Inequality: A Reassessment of the Effect of Family and Schooling in America* (New York: Harper & Row, 1973).
50. Charles Lyons, *To Wash an Aethiop White* (New York: Teachers College Press, 1975), p. 81.
51. John Dewey and Evelyn Dewey, *Schools of Tomorrow* (New York: E. P. Dutton, 1924), pp. 207–8, 209, 215–16.
52. Robert J. Havighurst, "Overcoming Value Differences," in *The Inner-City Classroom: Teacher Behaviors*, Robert D. Strom, ed. (Columbus, Ohio: Charles E. Merrill, 1966), p. 44.

Education, Class, and Ethnicity in Southern Peru: Revolutionary Colonialism

Pierre L. van den Berghe

The purpose of this essay is to examine the impact of the formal educational system on the ethnic and class structure of southern Peru, especially in the Department of Cuzco, where I conducted extensive research.[1] Before turning to the educational system, however, I shall briefly 1) define the concept of colonialism and its derivatives; 2) sketch the class and ethnic divisions in Peruvian society, as well as the patterns of regional inequality and dependency within the country.

Since the nineteenth century, colonialism has meant the political rule and economic exploitation by one nation over others. More specifically, colonialism generally meant overseas imperialism of Western nations over non-Western nations. By extension, then, the term "internal colonialism" appeared some twenty years ago in the social-science literature to refer to such relationships as existed between the government of South Africa and its indigenous subjects in the "Native Reserves."[2]

Internal colonialism was simply a form of government that showed all the characteristics of colonialism but within the confines of a single contiguous land mass. In the last few years the meaning of "internal colonialism" has been extended to what I would consider the point of meaninglessness. All kinds of groups or regions of countries that have ranked below national averages on any number of statistical indices of education, urbanization, industrialization, per capita income, or whatever, have been described as internal colonies. Women, blacks, and Appalachian whites in the United States,[3] the Scots and Welch in the British Isles,[4] southern Italy in relation to the north, and countless other regions or groups are now said to be "internal colonies." The phrase, like "racism" and many other currently fashionable epithets of the political lexicon, is catchy and contains within it an indictment. These heterogeneous "internal colonies" are then said to share with the former classical colonies membership in that extraordinary amalgam of strange bedfellows, "Third World Peoples."

In my opinion, the concept of internal colonialism, when so diluted, loses all of its use for purposes of social-science analysis. I shall therefore propose to treat internal colonialism as an ideal type with the following characteristics:

1) Rule of one ethnic group (or coalition of such groups) over other such groups living within the continuous boundaries of a single state.

2) Territorial separation of the subordinate ethnic groups into "homelands," "native reserves," and the like, with land-tenure rights distinct from those applicable to members of the dominant group.

3) Presence of an internal government within a government especially created to rule the subject peoples, with a special legal status ascribed to the subordinate groups. Typically, members of the dominant group are incorporated into the state as *individuals*, while members of the subordinate groups have a corporate, *group* status that takes precedence over their individual status.

4) Relations of economic inequality in which subject peoples are relegated to positions of dependency and inferiority in the division of labor and the relations of production.

Such a definition of internal colonialism excludes mere regional differences in economic development, mere class differences in the system of production, and, *a fortiori*, differences based on age, sex, slave status, caste, sexual behavior (e.g., homosexuality), physical handicaps, and countless others. The usefulness of the concept to understand the situation of a group is a function of that group's approximation to the characteristics of the ideal type. For instance, in the United States, internal colonialism describes the position of Amerindians quite well, of Chicanos somewhat, of blacks poorly, of Appalachian whites hardly at all, and of women, old people, homosexuals, and convicts only by the most fanciful stretch of the academic imagination. This is not to say that some of the groups excluded from my definition of internal colonialism may not be as badly or worse off than the denizens of the internal colonies. Their position is fundamentally *different*, however, and, hence, the internal colonial model is a poor one to understand their predicament. Internal colonialism is but one of many ways of getting the short end of the stick.

There remains to define the term "revolutionary colonialism," which I coined for the purposes of this article. By revolutionary colonialism I mean the peculiar brand of internal colonialism that is perpetuated, often with the best of intentions, by reformist governments that utter revolutionary rhetoric but practice authoritarian paternalism. The Peruvian government since the 1968 revolution is a case in point. It repeatedly proclaimed its intention to abolish the conditions of dependence existing between Peru and the advanced industrial countries, between the various regions of Peru itself, and between the social classes within the country. It diagnoses the bases of these forms of dependence in Marxist terms: Inequality lies in differential relations of production. Ethnic differences do not fit into this interpretation of the situation, and, therefore, Indians are simply redefined as peasants (*campesinos*), the most oppressed of all social classes. Expropriate the landowners, and the peasants will be liberated, argues the government.

Now, the land reform is an accomplished fact, but the subordination of Indians vis-à-vis mestizos is as great as ever. The government remains a mestizo monopoly as much as before the revolution, and the agents of government (including the teachers) cannot conceive of a different relationship to the Indians than one of benevolent paternalism at best, new forms of exploitation at worst. The continuity between the pre- and post-1968 period is especially striking in the field of education, where the cultural and linguistic aspects of mestizo domination are especially evident. The culture-bound premises of the educational philosophy are treated as axiomatic by nearly all agents of the system who, irrespective of their ideology, see themselves as the carriers of a superior culture entrusted with a civilizing mission in regard to the Indians. Thus, the ethnic differences between Indians and mestizos make the dependence of Indians qualitatively different from that of working-class mestizos relative to middle-

and upper-class ones. Indians are collectively subjected to a system of internal colonialism in a way in which working-class mestizos are not.

Before turning to the Peruvian educational system in the heavily Indian areas, however, I will discuss inequality in Peruvian society as a whole and its relationship to internal colonialism. Inequality in Peru has three main interrelated components: sharply marked *class* differences, glaring *regional* disparities in economic development, and persisting *ethnic* (i.e., cultural, especially linguistic) differences between Indians and mestizos. Peru, in short, is not only a class-differentiated society but one characterized by a large degree of internal colonialism.

There are, broadly, three Perus: 53 percent of the 1.3 million square kilometers and 7.5 percent of the country's 14 million people are in the eastern Amazonian lowlands, a vast and still largely undeveloped area; the remainder of the population is divided nearly equally between a highly urbanized and developed coastal strip (50.1 percent) where Spanish is the dominant language and the Andean valleys and high plateaus where Quechua (and, in parts, Aymara) are the main mother tongues of the inhabitants (41.4 percent of the total). By contrast to the coast, the Andean area, generally known as *sierra*, has an archaic agricultural economy, virtually no manufacturing industries, a low level of urbanization, literacy, education, fluency in Spanish, and a per capita income of only a little more than half that of the coast. In 1961, for instance, the coast was 70 percent literate and 69 percent urban, while the sierra was 41 percent literate and 26 percent urban.

The contrast between coast and sierra is even greater if one restricts the latter to the heavily "Indian" departments of southern Peru, the *mancha india*,[5] where at least two-thirds of the population are nonliterate, Quechua-monolingual peasants, dominated by Spanish-speaking, largely literate, urban middle- and upper-class mestizos. The relationship between coast and sierra and the ethnic and class relations both within and between these regions have been described by a number of social scientists as relations of dependence or internal colonialism.[6]

Patterns of dependency and centralized control that exist between the capital and the provinces and between regions are replicated at the regional and local levels. Each of Peru's twenty-three departmental capitals is a regional center of political and economic control, with its government bureaucracy, its urban commercial bourgeoisie, its army and police headquarters, its secondary schools and universities, and, until the land reform of the 1960s and early 1970s, its landowning elite.[7] Each department is divided into provinces and the latter into districts. The small towns that serve as provincial and district capitals all have a petty bourgeoisie of shopkeepers, landowners, craftsmen, teachers, and civil servants who constitute local oligarchies. At the bottom of this pyramid of control are the peasant masses who still make up some three-fourths of the sierra population and who live either on their own communal lands or on recently expropriated haciendas that the revolutionary government of Juan Velasco converted into "cooperatives" under central government control.

To complicate matters further, this regional class structure overlaps in good part with ethnic differences between Indians and mestizos. A detailed description of ethnic relations would take us well beyond the scope of this essay, but, in gross terms, sierra peasants are overwhelmingly classified as Indians, while the population of the towns are referred to as mestizos. Sometimes the term *cholo* is used to designate a transitional category of small-town petty bourgeois of Indian origin who are not yet accepted as mestizos. Indians are defined as people who are nonliterate and monolingual in Quechua (or Aymara), who till the soil and who dress in homespun clothing. Mestizos are overwhelmingly nonpeasants (who may, however, own land and even cultivate it on a part-time basis) who exhibit various degrees of bilingualism in Quechua and Spanish, are mostly literate (at least the men), and live principally in the urban centers. Among mestizos there is a wide range in class status from working class to the regional and national elites. The distinction between Indians and mestizos is not based on "race" or physical appearance, and tens of thousands of Indians are in the process of "passing" into the mestizo group every year, although a complete transition from Indian peasant to mestizo urbanite typically takes two or even three generations.

The two main processes through which an Indian can change

his status to that of a mestizo and thus move up in the class order as well are migration and education. By leaving his village and rural household an Indian is in effect taking the first steps on a road that frequently will, over a period of years, lead to his absorption into the mestizo group. The change is by no means inevitable or irreversible, and a number of persons remain ambiguously poised on the margin of both groups; but the social, political, and economic incentives for "passing" are sufficiently strong to insure that the great majority of those who have the opportunity will in fact do so. Migration to the non-Indian urban settlements may be more or less permanent. Many people return periodically to their rural homes or alternate between periods of urban and rural residence, but the overall movement of population is from farm and rural areas to towns, from small towns to larger ones, and from the sierra to the coast (and to the *selva,* or jungle). Young Indian girls become maids in mestizo households; young men get drafted into the army or go to towns and to coastal or jungle plantations in search of cash wages. Some Indians who manage to accumulate savings or who lack land try their luck at itinerant trade and become "penny capitalists," buying up wool or agricultural produce and selling manufactured goods. The necessary condition for all of these nonpeasant activities is migration to urban centers or to the coast, areas that are culturally mestizo and where the Spanish language is the dominant medium of public life. Changes in clothing, life-style, occupation, and linguistic behavior (increasing fluency in Spanish) all lead to a gradual ethnic redefinition of people by themselves and by others: They become less Indian and more mestizo.

This complex process of social mobility, in both class and ethnic terms, is also greatly influenced by the system of formal education. This we will now proceed to examine in greater detail, concentrating on the Department of Cuzco, one of the heavily Indian departments of the southern sierra. What I say about Cuzco, is, however, applicable to the entire *mancha india* of Peru.

The Department of Cuzco, with an area of 76,329 square kilometers, had a population of 713,000 in 1972, 76.1 percent of which lived at elevations of between 3,000 and 4,000 meters. The city of Cuzco, with a population of 121,000, is the regional metropolis and the only real city in the department. It is an important center of both commerce and administration but has virtually no large-scale industry. In all, 36.0 percent of the departmental population are classified as urban, but this figure is deceptively high, since the population of all provincial and district capitals is so defined. Of the eighty-nine district capitals, none exceeded 5,000 inhabitants, some had fewer than 100, and only thirty-three exceeded 1,000. By a generous estimate, 32.9 percent of the department's population was literate in 1961, but a more realistic test put functional literacy at 16 percent. Agriculture was the occupation of 61.8 percent of the economically active population. Before the recent land reform, land ownership was extremely polarized between small farms and large estates: 85.3 percent of the farming units were smaller than five hectares, but these small holdings accounted for only 4.3 percent of the land; conversely, the 0.7 percent of the estates over 500 hectares made up 81.3 percent of the land.

Linguistically, only 9.8 percent of the population were native speakers of Spanish, and only 39.5 percent (by a generous estimate) spoke any Spanish beyond a few greeting forms. This is to say that virtually all Cuzqueños, both mestizos and Indians, speak Quechua; but whereas the mestizos are bilingual in Quechua and Spanish, the Indians are Quechua monolinguals. If one excludes from these statistics the overwhelmingly mestizo city of Cuzco, the percentage of illiterate Quechua monolinguals—i.e., of Indians—rises to some three-fourths of the population. If one excludes all the "urban areas," illiteracy and Quechua monolingualism ranges between 80 and 90 percent in the highland provinces of the department. The overall rate of rural literacy for Cuzco in 1961 was 21.7 percent for both sexes over fifteen years of age and 7.6 percent for women, but these figures, even today, overstate reality in terms of functional literacy.[8]

The close linkages between education, class, and ethnicity, as well as the highly pyramidal nature of the educational system, are starkly apparent in the statistics of tables 1 and 2, derived from the 1961 census.[9] Those are the most recent figures that are available, and while the level of education has increased since, especially in the lower primary levels, the inequalities have not appreciably diminished. Categories one to three in the two tables

Table 1
Use of Spanish by Occupational Category, Department of Cuzco, 1961

	Occupation	Percent of category knowing Spanish	Percent of category who are native speakers of Spanish	Number of workers in thousands
1.	Professional and technical	100.0	61.9	4.4
2.	Managers and administrators	94.3	51.9	1.3
3.	Office workers	99.2	53.1	3.3
4.	Sales personnel	71.0	17.2	16.3
5.	Drivers	98.2	38.0	1.4
6.	Artisans	58.4	12.2	27.0
7.	Unskilled workers	77.1	13.1	3.3
8.	Domestic servants	61.4	13.9	15.9
9.	Mining and quarrying	78.6	9.0	1.2
10.	Agriculture, livestock breeding, fishing	32.0	3.1	125.6
11.	Others	—	—	5.8
	Total population	39.5	9.8	205.5

make up less than 5 percent of the labor force and represent the urban managerial, professional, and technical elite. They are all mestizos who not only speak Spanish but who, unlike over 90 percent of all Cuzqueños, are mostly *native* speakers of Spanish. At the other end of the occupational spectrum are the six-tenths of the labor force who are farmers (category 10) and who are 97 percent native speakers of Quechua. (The 3 percent who speak Spanish as their mother tongue are mestizo landowners, not peasants.) The intermediate categories (4 to 9) constitute the urban petty bourgeoisie and working class and make up about a third of the labor force. For the most part they speak some Spanish, at least the men, but they are mostly native speakers of Quechua and thus often of recent Indian origin, though they are considered mestizos or at least *cholos*.

Table 2
Percent of Given Occupational Group at Various Levels of Education, Economically Active Population, Department of Cuzco, 1961

Occupational Group	Level of Education							
	No Schooling	Primary	Secondary	Higher	Unspecified	Total %	Number of workers in thousands	Percentage of labor force in each occupation group
1. Professional and technical	3.7	11.2	32.6	50.8	1.7	100.0	4.4	2.1
2. Managers and administrators	12.1	31.9	41.8	13.7	0.5	100.0	1.3	0.6
3. Office workers	3.5	24.6	58.1	13.0	0.8	100.0	3.3	1.6
4. Sales	39.8	47.7	11.0	0.7	0.8	100.0	16.3	7.9
5. Drivers	3.7	65.7	29.4	0.6	0.6	100.0	1.4	0.7
6. Artisans	48.5	44.8	6.0	0.1	0.6	100.0	27.0	13.1
7. Unskilled workers	37.1	57.9	4.3	0.1	0.6	100.0	3.3	1.6
8. Domestic servants	63.1	28.0	4.3	0.3	4.3	100.0	15.9	7.7
9. Mining	36.1	59.5	3.2	0.2	1.0	100.0	1.2	0.6
10. Agriculture and herding	70.4	27.1	1.5	0.1	0.9	100.0	125.6	61.3

It must again be stressed here that Indians are socially defined by their ignorance of Spanish rather than by their knowledge of Quechua. Nearly all mestizos born in the sierra (i.e., those who are not recent immigrants from the coast) are bilingual in Quechua and Spanish, even in the upper crust of urban society. Only Quechua monolinguals are socially defined as Indians. The figure of 39.5 percent of the labor force who know Spanish is thus very close to that for Spanish-Quechua bilingualism. Perhaps 5 percent of them would be Spanish-speaking monolinguals, but at least two-thirds of them would be more fluent in Quechua than in Spanish.

Table 2 shows the close relationship between occupation and education. The top three categories generally require secondary or even higher education and thus fluency in Spanish. In the agricultural category, made up almost entirely of Indian peasants, seven-tenths have had no formal education at all, and nearly all the rest have gone only to primary school (and then usually for no more than three or four years). To all intents and purposes, the overwhelming majority of this group are functional illiterates (roughly 90 percent of the men and practically all women). The 1.6 percent of that category who have gone beyond primary school are mestizo landowners. In the intermediate categories (4 to 9)—that is, in the one-third of the labor force who make up the urban petty bourgeoisie and the working class—people divided roughly equally between those who have had no education at all and those who have gone only to primary school. In practical terms, this translates into a functional literacy rate of about 50 percent for men and perhaps 25 percent for women. Among these intermediate categories 4 to 9, the educational level is much higher in the all-male category 5 (drivers of motor vehicles) and much below average among the predominantly female domestic servants.

Sex differentials in access to education (and, thus, in opportunity to learn Spanish) are an important feature of the system, as is indeed characteristic of all developing countries. This bias is the result not so much of sex discrimination in the school system itself as of parental attitudes. Most parents want to keep their daughters at home more than their sons, especially after the onset of puberty. Indian girls are more drastically affected than mestizo girls, because the average age of Indian pupils is some two or three years older than that of mestizo pupils in the same grade. While most mestizo girls can complete primary school before they become pubescent, many Indian girls see their school careers interrupted in the third or fourth grade, assuming they were lucky enough to get any schooling at all. In addition to reasons of parental control over sexual behavior, poor parents, whether Indian or mestizos, often make the realistic assessment that the economic return on educational investment is greater for boys than for girls. Anticipating sex discrimination in the labor market, parents systematically choose to educate boys longer than girls, if it comes to a choice. For all intents and purposes, only the daughters of urban middle-class parents have a chance to attend secondary school. The few educated Peruvian women, however, probably encounter less sex discrimination in employment than is true in the United States. (For one thing, they can generally afford maids to liberate themselves of household work! A high-school-educated woman working in a clerical job or as a teacher can earn $75 to $100 a month and hire a maid for $10 to $15 a month plus food.)

It is against this ethnic, class, economic, and political structure that the formal educational system must be studied. This system is, at the same time, a major determinant of the class and ethnic order and a main source of change therein. On the one hand, the formal educational system entrenches the cultural domination of the mestizos and discriminates grossly against Indians and working-class mestizos in terms of access to schools, quality of education, attrition rates, and expenditure per pupil. On the other hand, education is probably the most important single factor making social mobility possible. At any rate, it is the necessary (and often the sufficient) condition for entry into the "modern" sector of the urban middle class—that is, the civil service, the police, clerical and sales occupations, trade beyond the smallest retail level, and, of course, professional and managerial occupations. Education can thus be said to *perpetuate and consolidate the class and ethnic structure and to provide the main mechanism for individual upward mobility within it.*

Like nearly all key social resources in Peru, education is centrally and hierarchically controlled, according to a formal structure patterned after the French Napoleonic model in the early nineteenth century and substantially unchanged since, except for its ever-growing size. The educational hierarchy can be looked at from three distinct perspectives, which we shall take up in turn.

THE ADMINISTRATIVE AND LEGAL STRUCTURE

In theory, education in Peru is compulsory at the primary level, free at the primary and secondary level, and secular in the public schools. There are also private schools, where religion can and often is taught, but even private schools are partially state-supported and state-supervised. At all three levels of education, state schools outnumber private ones by a wide margin, though private schools are often more prestigious, if not intellectually, at least socially. Universities, which are overwhelmingly state-supported, enjoy a modicum of academic autonomy and have been frequent foci of antigovernment activity and agitation, but when the government decides that they have exceeded the limits of tolerable opposition, it does not hesitate to close them down, reorganize them, and arrest, deport and expel both students and professors. Cuzco has one university, founded as a religious seminary in 1692 and secularized since independence in the 1820s. Its student population is around 5,000, and its political history, especially since the 1950s, has been stormy. Students often taken an extra two or three years to complete their degrees because of periodic closures.

State primary and secondary schools are all firmly under the control of the Ministry of Education, which directs all matters of appointment of teachers, construction of schools, allocation of instructional budget, curriculum, and so on. The Ministry has regional offices, and the city of Cuzco is the headquarters for the Fifth Educational Region, which comprises three departments. The ministerial bureaucracy extends down to the provincial and the district levels, and the entire system is a single hierarchy run from Lima, the national capital. Directions go down the chain of command; information and statistics flow up the hierarchy. Teachers are salaried civil servants, and they too are organized at the national level into two main trade unions. The larger one is also the more radical one; it stands considerably to the left of the

Revolutionary Government and has been extensively repressed.[10]

Despite the government's high-sounding rhetoric of grass-roots "participation," of idealization of the "peasant masses" and of "consciousness-raising" (*concientización*), the educational system is, if anything, more bureaucratic and more authoritarian than it was before the "revolution." Now the Ministry of Education is not only a vast bureaucracy but one that has to toe an official ideological line or, at any rate, pretend to do so. Also, under the elective civilian regime, oligarchical, capitalist, and elitist though that regime was, the bureaucrats were at least restrained by legislation. Now, the revolutionary military government and its bureaucratic agents rule by decree. In terms of educational policy, this has meant the deliberate introduction of political indoctrination in school textbooks, semicompulsory "re-education" seminars for teachers, and the like. Students and their parents have virtually no voice at all in educational policy, and even the teachers are more than ever subordinated to bureaucrats.

THE STUDENTS

From the point of view of its accessibility to and retentivity of students, the Peruvian educational system is glaringly biased on the basis of both class and ethnicity. Although ostensibly selective on the basis of merit, the system is strongly biased against the lower classes, the rural population, and the Indians. Indian peasants, being both a subordinate ethnic group and the bottom of the class pyramid, bear the brunt of that double bias. To be sure, the system also selects students on the basis of ability and motivation, increasingly so in the higher levels, and members of the lower strata who successfully run the gauntlet of attrition and enter universities tend to be far above average in intelligence, perseverance, ambition, and diligence. There is no question that such a fiercely competitive school system is partially meritocratic and rewards the very qualities required for upward social mobility. Indeed, education in Peru is first and foremost a school for success in which most pupils are programmed to fail. It provides an important enough avenue of upward mobility for appreciable numbers of the peasantry and working class to enter the middle class, but the lower one descends in the class and the ethnic pyramid, the lesser the chances of success. Let us now document these biases in greater detail.

The most glaring fact that appears from enrollment statistics is the high rate of attrition from grade to grade but especially between primary and secondary education and between secondary schools and universities. In 1972, for example, over three quarters (77.0 percent) of all students enrolled in the Fifth Educational Region (which includes Cuzco) were in primary education, compared to only 13.0 percent in secondary education, 7.0 percent in adult education, and 0.5 percent at the tertiary level. Approximately 40 percent of the Department of Cuzco population under fifteen years of age is not enrolled in school, and this means virtually the entire *rural* population of *secondary* school age. In fact, the situation is even worse than these statistics suggest, for enrollment figures are grossly inflated in the rural areas.

Teachers are the ones who report these statistics to the Ministry of Education, and they manage to make a good showing by getting parents to enroll their children when the school year opens. Actual attendance on any given day in a rural school seldom exceeds half of the official enrollment. Teachers are generally indifferent to absenteeism, and in the remote rural areas they are pretty much their own masters. Indeed the absenteeism rate among teachers is also quite high. Rural teachers seize on any pretext not to hold classes or even to leave their posts with or without official leave: sickness, family problems, transportation breakdowns, bridging weekends and national holidays, village and town fiestas, anniversaries, weddings, deaths, baptisms, even union elections. Many rural schools in the Indian areas are in actual operation fewer than 100 days a year, with perhaps 25 or 30 percent of the children of school age in attendance (and mostly boys at that).

The high rate of attrition has two major causes: economic constraints and inaccessibility of schools. Education is free in theory, but among peasants, and even in the urban working class and mercantile petty bourgeoisie, the labor of a child cannot be easily spared after age ten or eleven. Children baby-sit for younger siblings, spin wool, tend to flocks, or work in the family workshop or store. Also, pupils are supposed to provide their own books and uniforms. There is a single school uniform throughout Peru, which from the perspective of an urban mestizo is a democratic measure minimizing class differences. However, the uniform is a heavy financial drain on poor urban families and is totally beyond the reach of Indians. It includes such expensive items as shoes, which are never worn by Indians. (Luckily, the uniform regulations are not enforced in the rural Indian schools, where children come in their traditional homespun clothing.) As for books and even paper and pencils, rural children cannot afford any, and many poor urban mestizo children go without them as well.

Inaccessibility of schools is another problem, especially in the mountainous topography of Peru. Most Indian villages are accessible only on foot or horseback. District and provincial capitals are generally accessible by dirt roads, but even teachers cannot afford private cars, and, in many cases, the only motor connection with the outside world is a truck that comes to the weekly market to pick up produce. Not only the level of schools locally available but also their quality deteriorates as one goes down from Lima to the departmental capitals, to the provincial capitals, to the district capitals, and finally to the Indian villages.

Let us start at the bottom. The government, with the help of the local peasants, has made a serious effort to extend *lower* primary education to virtually all Indian villages. Even remote hamlets now have a one- or two-room adobe brick building that serves as lower primary school and offers the first three or four years of instruction in the six-year primary school curriculum. These schools are built by the unpaid voluntary labor of the Indian communities. The Ministry of Education may provide such luxuries as corrugated iron for the roof, window panes, a couple of doors, and perhaps some cement for the floor, but the adobe bricks, the rafters, and other building materials are often furnished by the community. The latter may even build a house for the teacher and provide it free of rent. In the urban areas schools are built directly by the Ministry, without any direct cost to the community. Thus, the Indian peasants who are the poorest pay in the form of labor taxation, the heaviest burden for their education.[11]

These lower primary schools in the Indian villages are Spartan in the extreme. Furniture is typically limited to a blackboard, a small table and a chair for the teacher, and a few rough benches for the pupils. (Pupils sit on them while listening to the teacher. When they have to write, they squat on the floor and use the bench as a desk.) Books are a rare luxury. Only the teacher has copies of the required texts. The Ministry may, from time to time, hand out a meager supply of pencils and paper for the students, but even these are scarce and are distributed only rarely and parsimoniously. In the name of practical education and teaching the dignity of manual labor, schoolchildren spend a portion of their school time doing chores for the teacher, such as cultivating and watering a vegetable garden, cleaning the school and the teacher's house, and the like. Both teacher and pupil absenteeism make learning at best a sporadic activity in these lower primary schools.

Added to all these material impediments, Indian children also have to face an overwhelming cultural barrier that mestizo children do not encounter. Ever since formal education existed in Peru, it has always been considered axiomatic that Spanish should be the exclusive medium of instruction. Despite evidence of the benefits of teaching literacy through the child's mother tongue, literacy continues to be taught in a language alien to Indian children. Teachers, to be sure, are bilingual, but they are mestizos who regard Spanish culture as superior to Quechua culture, who speak fluent Quechua but use Spanish exclusively as a written language, and who generally take a superior, condescending attitude vis-à-vis their Indian pupils.

Teachers in these village schools speak almost exclusively Quechua to their pupils, except when they attempt to teach the "three r's." There, the child is suddenly confronted with what to him is gibberish. As a result, even the few pupils who attend school regularly for three or four years learn little Spanish and do not achieve a functional standard of literacy. They have learned by rote a few greeting forms, recitations and songs in Spanish (which they perform with great gusto for visiting school inspectors, anthropologists, and other mestizos); they can sign their name, count to a hundred, and recognize the letters of the alphabet: Those are the fruits of three or four years of effort.

Not only the linguistic medium of education is alien to the

Indian child, but so is the content. The curriculum is almost entirely academic in orientation. That is, primary school is intended to lead to an academic secondary school, which in turn gives access to the university. School subjects are totally unrelated to the rural child's life experience. For instance, the Indian child whose previous experiences are almost totally bound by his local community is suddenly told that he is a Peruvian, that Simón Bolívar liberated him, that the Chileans are his enemies because they invaded and devastated his country in 1879–83, and so on. I remember a geography lesson about three natural regions of Peru: the coast, the sierra, and the jungle. When a pupil was asked in Quechua how he understood the lesson, it was clear that he had reinterpreted it in terms of three ecological zones in his own immediate habitat: the high-altitude pastures, the potato fields in the valley, and the banana and coca fields in the lowlands.

Perhaps a couple of star pupils in these lower primary schools who, through close association with the teacher (who is typically the sole Spanish speaker in the village) learned a little more Spanish, leave their village every year to complete their last two or three years of primary school in the neighboring district capital. The latter typically has a complete six-grade primary school, with half a dozen teachers. The district capital is generally located within a day's walk from its satellite Indian communities but is often too far away for daily commuting. The school building, though still typically built in adobe bricks, begins to resemble a real Western-style school. It consists of several larger classrooms with often a cement floor, regular glass windows, desks for the pupils, larger blackboards, wall maps, a couple of anatomical charts, color lithographs of national heroes, and the like. Instruction is somewhat more formal and regular; Spanish becomes the main language in the classroom, though Quechua still predominates on the playground. Teachers are more closely supervised by their principal and by the higher school authorities who pay occasional visits in a Ministry vehicle.

Pupils are both children of small-town mestizos who are fluently bilingual in Spanish and Quechua and a sprinkling of Indian children who still speak limited Spanish and who have just come from their home villages. Obviously, the school environment strongly favors the mestizo child, but a bright, adaptable Indian child who attracts the favor of a teacher has a fair chance of graduating from the sixth grade with enough literacy and knowledge of Spanish to escape his status as peasant and as Indian. The crucial factor here is that upward mobility in the class system, made possible by education, almost inevitably entails a *shift in cultural identity* from Indian to mestizo. By definition, there can be no such thing as an educated Indian. As a consequence, education does indeed provide some possibility for an Indian to improve his condition. Peru does not have a racial caste system like the United States, for instance. However, such mobility is individual and does not improve the condition of those who remain Indians. Indeed, the opposite is the case, for the process of social mobility, by automatically absorbing the upwardly mobile into the mestizo group, deprives the Indian communities of their youngest, most enterprising, and often most intelligent members. Here again we see how individual mobility contributes to systemic stability.

When the Indian child finishes primary school in the mestizo small town, he typically lives with a mestizo family who are often his godparents or the landowners of his parents or sometimes his teacher or even an older relative who has already made the transition from Indian to mestizo. In return for room and board and permission to attend school, he performs household duties as a kind of unsalaried servant, family retainer, or poor relative. If he completes primary school and spends two or three years in the town, he will, in all likelihood, cease to be regarded as an Indian. It may take several more years before he will be fully accepted as a mestizo, and he may be called a *cholo*. Very few children of Indian origin, and indeed only a minority of the mestizo children of these district capitals, continue their education beyond the sixth grade. With basic literacy, primary-school graduates typically become small traders and shopkeepers, apprentice themselves to a craftsman, or secure a minor clerical or supervisory job such as hacienda overseer, town clerk, or municipal policeman.

The next big step on the educational ladder is entry into secondary school, where another six years of an academically oriented curriculum gives access to university. After a couple of years of secondary school, a pupil may enter one of the lower grades of "normal schools," or teachers' training schools. Teachers' training is the only form of vocational schooling offered on a wide scale in the sierra and the only one that offers decent prospects of secure employment. As the statistics given earlier indicate, the attrition rate between primary and secondary school is quite large, and less than half of those who begin secondary school complete it.

Secondary schools are few and far between. Many of the provincial capitals have one, but very few of the district capitals do. The city of Cuzco has two large public high schools and half a dozen private, Catholic ones. Going to secondary school thus almost inevitably entails residence in a bigger town, farther away from home, in a more mestizo environment; all these conditions discriminate against Indians and poorer mestizos. Secondary schools, especially the ones in the city of Cuzco, are large modern buildings of brick or concrete, housing up to a couple of thousand students and scores of teachers. They are run quite formally, with quasi-military discipline, and teaching conforms closely to the official curriculum. At this stage, students must wear strict uniforms and buy their own books, a severe economic burden on the lower classes. There is a hierarchy of prestige between the secondary schools of Cuzco city, and the private, Catholic schools charge fees that are beyond the reach of the working class or even the lower middle class.

The universities, too, are clearly hierarchized. That of Cuzco has some reputation because of its venerable age, but several universities in Lima are more prestigious. Consequently, the Cuzco upper class usually sends its children to Lima or even to European and North American universities, largely leaving the local university to the upwardly mobile middle class.

It might be asked what the Revolutionary Government is doing to democratize the educational structure. It passed a "Law of Educational Reform" inspired by the most enlightened social-science thinking and full of laudable precepts.[12] The law recognizes the handicap suffered by the Indian child on entering a school system where Spanish is the official medium of instruction. It condemns elitism, ethnic prejudice against Indian cultures, scholastic education unrelated to the child's experiences, and all the numerous factors that have retarded the spread of literacy in the rural areas. Yet, it also wishes to retain the benefits of learning Spanish for the Indian and to develop a genuine national culture, while at the same time not deprecating Quechua, Aymara, and the other "vernacular" languages.

In short, the Educational Reform Law is a compendium of pious wishes that bear only coincidental resemblance to what goes on in classrooms and to what is likely to go on for the foreseeable future. Most of the teachers and administrators of the Ministry of Education of whom we asked what the educational reform meant could either give no coherent answer at all or else saw it purely as a reshuffling of offices and renaming of administrative structures.

In order to understand resistance of the system to change, we must examine the situation of teachers, to whom we shall now turn our attention.

THE TEACHERS

In most underdeveloped countries teachers play a more important role and enjoy more power and privileges relative to the mass of their countrymen than they do in developed countries. Peru is no exception. The approximately 80,000 Peruvian teachers are the largest and one of the best organized and most vocal professional groups in the country. They largely control the vast educational apparatus; they create the demand for their services; they produce their own replacements; and they are themselves among the most successful products of the system. In short, through their professional monopoly, they perpetuate both themselves and the system of which they are both creatures and masters. One could scarcely conceive of a more closed system.

Peruvian teachers exhibit the seemingly paradoxical characteristics of great political radicalism at the rhetorical level and authoritarianism, ethnocentrism, intellectual elitism, educational conservatism, and general bourgeois conformism in their day-to-day behavior. The radical teachers' union, SUTEP, espouses a radical ideology, far to the left of the Revolutionary Government, and receives overwhelming support from teachers against its more conservative government-sponsored rival. Yet, those supposedly radical teachers either fail to comprehend the spirit of the Law of Educational Reform or oppose it if they do understand it.

Instead, their educational ideology is unreconstructedly conservative. With few exceptions they cannot conceive of an educational system based on a language other than Spanish or on values other than those of the dominant mestizo group to which they belong by definition. This is true even though sierra-born teachers are virtually all fluently bilingual in Quechua and Spanish and despite the fact that a substantial number of primary-school teachers are themselves children of Indian peasants. They enthusiastically espouse a rigidly authoritarian and disciplinarian role in the classroom, complete with quasi-military drill and corporal punishment and an archaic pedagogy based on uncomprehending rote memorization. They often share other mestizos' stereotypes of Indians as backward, dirty, rendered stupid by alcohol and coca —in a word, *bruto*.[13] Conversely, they have a flattering Leninist conception of themselves as the vanguard of the masses and the pioneers of progress and enlightenment.

These paradoxes are readily explained through the life experiences of teachers. Most teachers, especially primary-school teachers (who are the product of normal schools, not of universities), are upwardly mobile small-town mestizos of working-class or, at most, petty-bourgeois status; indeed, quite a few primary-school teachers are only one generation removed from Indian villages, and many more are only two generations away from their peasant origins. They became teachers because they were successful in the educational system, often against long odds and at the cost of great effort and deprivation. Thus, they readily sustain a conception of themselves as a self-made elite, a meritocracy. They naturally support the values of the system that consecrated their success, and they espouse a moralistic mission to inflict on their pupils the vexations to which they once were subjected: If discipline was good for them, it must be good for their pupils.

The system also rewarded them to the extent that they became urban mestizos and rejected everything Indian. To be sure, Peruvian schoolbooks extol the grandeur of the Inca empire and romanticize the Indians to some extent. In practice, however, pupils are told that to become acceptable to their teachers they must wear shoes, discard their homespun clothes, and wear neatly ironed school uniforms, keep their hair neatly combed, their fingernails clean, and their hands and feet free of "dirt." The more their Spanish approximates the "grammatical" standard of urban upper-class mestizos, the better and the more correct it is said to be. They are told that manual labor, though noble in theory, is in fact to be avoided at all costs and only good enough for Indians. Calloused hands are a stigma of inferiority; long manicured fingernails, especially on the little finger, are a badge of high status. In short, the process of getting an education for the upwardly mobile has been one of cleansing oneself of Indian and lower-class traits. The rewards for success have been a life free of the drudgery of manual work and replete with the comforts of urban residence.

Let us look more closely at the rural primary-school teacher who represents the broad basis of this self-perpetuating educational system. The teacher in the Indian village is in a unique position. He is often of a very modest social origin, but he sees himself as having escaped it.[14] He could not afford to go to university, so he got his training at a normal school. This means that he is at the bottom of the teaching profession, with little prospect of rising to the much more prestigious secondary-school level, where a university degree is the usual qualification. His starting salary of $50 to $75 a month is meager by urban standards, being comparable to that of a journeyman or minor clerical employee, but it makes him rich by the standards of the Indian village. (Besides, he is usually housed free of rent, often receives food from the peasants as gifts for minor favors, and can draw on free labor from children and even adults for his garden and household chores, so his expenses are minimal.)

Even among primary-school teachers, it is the least qualified and the youngest (and preferably unmarried) who get assigned to Indian villages. Those so posted thus see their assignment as a term of purgatory from which they expect to be relieved in two to five years for good behavior. A few are conscientious. Most serve their time with great reluctance, while applying for transfer to a more urban area. Often they are the only mestizo in the village, or they have only one or two colleagues. Since they are brought up not to consider Indians as company, they complain of loneliness and take very little part in the community's life.[15] Yet, they wield considerable power, for they represent in the eyes of the peasants "the authorities." For example, the central government often appoints them to supervise village council elections or to take the census.

In short, they generally feel superior to the Indians. They typically resent having to live among them. They despair of their ability to be effective teachers with *bruto* Indian children. They absent themselves on trips to the neighboring town as much as they can get away with, and they impatiently wait for that official envelope from the Ministry of Education announcing their transfer to an urban area. When they get transferred to an urban primary school, they have half a dozen colleagues with whom to discuss revolutionary politics around a couple of bottles of Cerveza Cuzqueña. They commiserate with one another on how difficult it is to lift such ignorant, backward peasants out of their poverty and degradation. They attack the government for being in league with the CIA, and they wait for their transfer to the city of Cuzco.

CONCLUSION: THE DYNAMICS OF REVOLUTIONARY COLONIALISM

Three illustrative vignettes of revolutionary colonialism may help us understand the apparent paradox between ideology and practice:

Exhibit A. Graduating high-school and university classes are in the habit of naming themselves (usually by choice of the students with some ideological input from the teachers) after some notable figure. Of late, saints of the revolutionary pantheon, such as Che Guevara, Fidel Castro, Mao Tse-tung, Ho Chi Minh, et al., have been quite popular. The front page of a Cuzco newspaper published in 1972 the photograph of the graduating class of a fashionable, upper-middle-class, private, Catholic girls' school under the caption: *"La promoción Vladimir Illich Lenin del Colegio de Señoritas Virgen del Rosario."*

Exhibit B. The scene is a ceremony at a secondary school. The army general who was the regional representative of the central military government was visiting the school and was one of half a dozen speakers haranguing the students for approximately two and a half hours on the wonders of the revolution. He was comfortably sitting on a platform at a large table, flanked by a couple of his officers, plainclothes policemen, and the high-school teachers in their Sunday best. The students faced the platform, standing in military formation, while a couple of the junior teachers walked between the ranks to make the pupils keep neat rows. One of the young teachers, a vocal Maoist, nattily dressed in a gray suit and tie and who treated his students like a military martinet, was privately telling me in bitterly critical terms how the general and the government were "bourgeois reformists" and was proudly describing how he was developing "revolutionary consciousness" among his pupils. When I suggested that there was, perhaps, an inconsistency between his egalitarian politics and his authoritarian pedagogy, he was genuinely surprised and uncomprehending. Likewise, he found it quite natural that his students should stand in the sun for over two hours, listening to someone of whom he disapproved and about whom they probably could not care less.

Exhibit C. The University of Cuzco had organized one of its many protest meetings against government policies, and a few hundred people were marching from the campus to the central square of Cuzco, the traditional destination of most political manifestations of this type. The marchers were carrying placards and shouting slogans in rhythmic unison, the main slogan being "*Campesinos, obreros, estudiantes, unidos*" ("Peasants, workers, and students, unite"). A closer look at the cortege revealed a glaring incongruity, however. Not only did the marching order show a quasi-military discipline, but it was rigidly segregated into class-based contingents: First came a platoon of impeccable professors in coats and ties; then, a few steps behind, a fashionable group of secretaries and other members of the university's clerical staff; then a large group of students, also in middle-class urban dress; finally, a group of Indian laborers from the university's experimental farm dressed in shabby ponchos and work clothes.

Peru is, of course, not unique in this seemingly paradoxical role of education as a source of both structural stability and individual change. Indeed, the popularity of education at virtually all class levels in all countries that have adopted the Western model is easily understandable in terms of this apparent paradox. The technocratic and bureaucratic ruling class supports a meritocratic educational system because the system gives it a head start and legitimates and consolidates its rule. The underprivileged masses support the system because it offers them a tangible avenue of escape, even though the dice are heavily loaded against them. Education for the masses is a kind of national lottery in which there is a small but real chance of winning. Insofar as an educational system based at least in part on meritocracy detracts the masses from revolutionary solutions to their predicament, legitimates inequality, and permits individual movement without threatening the class and ethnic order, formal education, in both capitalist and socialist countries, has been a conservative force.

In a fundamental way, conservatism is always built into the age structure of formal education systems. Education is almost invariably older people's notions about what the young should learn. However, this conservative influence is even stronger in countries that, like Peru, are at a relatively early stage of their industrial development. Such countries still have considerable scope for upward mobility, and the rewards of education are relatively much greater than in advanced industrial countries. Education, by itself, is a more important determinant of class differentials, and the differentials themselves are much larger in developing than in developed countries. The case of Andean Peru that we have examined clearly illustrates the phenomenon I have called "revolutionary colonialism." Notwithstanding the present government's intention to effect a radical transformation in the class and ethnic structure of Peru, and despite the fact that the ideology of many (if not most) teachers is even farther to the left than that of the government, the educational system remains unreconstructedly conservative. While the system increases its scope, it continues to support the present ethnic and class order, because the bureaucrats and teachers who are its guardians are at the same time its most successful products. The marriage between radical politics, however sincere, and intellectual arrogance, ethnocentrism, authoritarianism, and the most unimaginative kind of educational conservatism is, thus, an easy one, incongruous though it appears at first glance.

The class biases of the educational system are obvious enough, but, for Indians, the burden of ethnic bias is added to that of class bias. It is one thing to be taught skills of dubious relevance by middle-class-oriented teachers. It is much worse to be taught these things by strangers in a foreign language. The very processes of upward social and ethnic mobility that formal education encourages insure that Indians cannot develop within their own group an alternative school system rooted in their own traditions. Formal education skims off its successful Indian products, absorbs them into the dominant mestizo group, and thereby perpetuates the ethnic cleavages and prejudices between mestizo teacher and Indian pupil.

The problem is intrinsically insoluble because educational reform among Indians, if it is to become anything more than a new brand of mestizo paternalism, would have to come from among the Indians themselves. This, in turn, implies political and economic liberation. Unfortunately, the prognosis for internal colonies is even worse than for external ones.

Notes

1. The project was sponsored by the National Institute of Mental Health, and the research, on changes in class and ethnic status, was conducted between July 1972 and November 1973. I was ably assisted in the field by George Primov and Gladys Becerra de Valencia, and I am also grateful to Jorge Flores Ochoa, Sean Conlin, and Benjamin Orlove, with whom I exchanged data and ideas throughout the period of field work. Some of the findings were published in Pierre van den Berghe, ed., *Class and Ethnicity in Peru* (Leiden: E. J. Brill, 1974), and in George P. Primov, *Ethnicity in Highland Peru* (unpublished Ph.D. dissertation, University of Washington, 1975). The main monograph is Pierre van den Berghe and George P. Primov, *Inequality in the Peruvian Andes, Class and Ethnicity in Cuzco* (Columbia, Mo.: University of Missouri Press, 1977). Data on Peruvian rural education can be found in G. Alberti and J. Cotler, eds., *Aspectos Sociales de la Educación Rural en el Perú* (Lima: Instituto de Estudios Peruanos, 1972); Erwin Epstein, "Education and Peruanidad: 'Internal' Colonialism in the Peruvian Highlands," in *Comparative Education Review* 15 (June 1971): 188–201; and George Primov, "The Political Role of Mestizo Schoolteachers in Indian Communities" (Paper presented at the annual meeting of the American Anthropological Association, Mexico City, 1974). My main conclusions regarding the nature and effect of the educational system in the rural areas are in agreement with those of Alberti and Cotler even though their interpretation stresses class factors more, and ethnic factors less, than mine. I am also in nearly complete agreement with Epstein, who emphasizes ethnic and linguistic factors.
2. Leo Marquard, *South Africa's Colonial Policy* (Johannesburg: South African Institute of Race Relations, 1957), and

Pierre van den Berghe, *South Africa: A Study in Conflict* (Berkeley, Calif.: University of California Press, 1967).

3. Robert Blauner, *Racial Oppression in America* (New York: Harper & Row, 1972).
4. Michael Hechter, *Internal Colonialism: The Celtic Fringe in British National Development, 1536–1966* (London: Routledge and Kegan Paul, 1975).
5. The term means literally the "Indian stain" and is somewhat pejorative.
6. F. Fuenzalida Vollmer, et al., *El Indio y el Poder en el Perú* (Lima: Instituto de Estudios Peruanos, 1970); Robert G. Keith, et al., *La Hacienda, la Comunidad y el Campesino en el Perú* (Lima: Instituto de Estudios Peruanos, 1970); and Anibal Quijano, "Nationalism and Capitalism in Peru," in *Monthly Review* 23, no. 3 (1971): 1–28.
7. In 1968 the elected, civilian government of President Belaunde was overthrown by a military coup, which established a "Revolutionary Government of the Armed Forces" led until 1975 by General Velasco, who was in turn replaced by a bloodless mini-coup within the ruling junta. The Revolutionary Government adopted policies that are a complex blend of native APRA-style populism, Latin American nationalism, socialism, *indigenismo,* Mussolini-style corporate-state fascism, and a strong dash of plain old military authoritarianism. In a series of reforms it broke the power of the old capitalist and landowning oligarchy of Peru and instituted an even more highly centralized and authoritarian regime of army officers, technocrats, and bureaucrats. While it did introduce many progressive and long-overdue reforms, especially the abolition of large haciendas, and the expropriation of certain key industries, it also suspended elections, suppressed political parties, undermined trade unions, destroyed the freedom of the press, and persecuted political opposition of both right and left with decreasing restraint over the years. Even before 1968, however, the functioning of democratic institutions in Peru has always been sporadic at best and replete with class and ethnic biases.
8. *Censos Nacionales, Población, Vivienda y Agropecuario,*

1961, vol. 7 (Lima: Oficina Nacional de Estadística y Censos, 1970).

9. Ibid.
10. Hundreds of its leaders were arrested and detained without trial in 1973, for example, and, though the government's repressive measures are relatively restrained by the standards of a military dictatorship, civil liberties are best described as in a state of indefinite suspension.
11. *Corvée* labor for peasants is not limited to schools. Indians are also traditionally made to keep up the roads and bridges and even to perform unpaid work of street cleaning and building construction in the mestizo-dominated district capitals. The system of corvée goes back to Inca times, was extended under Spanish rule, continued after independence, and is now perpetuated by the Revolutionary Government under the banner of national development and "social mobilization." It should be added, however, that peasants work willingly on projects they consider beneficial to their community, such as schools, though they naturally resent working on urban projects from which they derive no tangible benefits.
12. Ministerio de Educación, *Reforma de la Educación Peruana. Informa General* (Lima: Ministerio de Educación, 1970).
13. A sierra saying states: *El indio es el animal que mas se parece al hombre,* which translates: "The Indian is the animal that most closely resembles man."
14. For illustrative purposes, I use the masculine pronoun to refer to both sexes. Actually, roughly half of the primary-school teachers are women; so are perhaps a fifth of the secondary-school teachers and no more than 5 percent of the university professors. The teaching profession is thus stratified by sex as well as by level.
15. George P. Primov, "The Political Role. . . ."

Neocolonialism

The Distribution of Knowledge in the Third World: A Case Study in Neocolonialism

Philip G. Altbach

No nation or culture is truly independent in terms of its intellectual life, and all depend to some extent on an exchange of knowledge. The more "modern" a nation is in terms of involvement with technology, industrialization, and current political and social thought, the more dependent it tends to be on an international network of creation and distribution of knowledge. This international network operates in many ways. Books and journals are circulated across international boundaries, films are exported from one country to another, educational advice is given, experts circulate knowledge on a wide range of topics, students travel beyond their countries, and translations of publications from one language to another are commissioned.

Many institutions participate in this network. Publishing firms, the major focus of this essay, are often multinational corporations that participate in the global distribution of knowledge. International agencies such as UNESCO, the United Nations, and the Organization of American States stimulate and often assist international intellectual exchange. The foreign-aid programs of many industrialized nations foster various kinds of interdependence. Journals, from the *Reader's Digest* to the *British Journal of Sociology,* are circulated internationally. Radio and television programs are widely exported and imported, either as a result of governmental policy or through the operation of private enterprise.

This essay presents in broad outline the ways in which global patterns of knowledge dissemination affect that distribution of knowledge in the Third World. At the core of my interpretation there are several assumptions that should be clearly articulated. The Third World suffers from an "unfavorable balance of intellectual payments." It imports many more knowledge-products than it exports. The Third World is beholden to the industrialized nations for books and journals and also for knowledge in most scientific and technical fields, for applied-research findings, and often for the results of research about the Third World itself. Further, knowledge and information are generally channeled through the industrialized nations and therefore filtered through their publishing houses, journals, and academic institutions before reaching audiences in the Third World. In short, the Third World finds itself in a classic position of dependency vis-à-vis the industrialized nations.

The Third World, then, has escaped colonial bondage only to enter into an era of neocolonial dependency.[1] Neocolonialism as used in this essay means the continuing domination, direct or indirect, of the industrialized nations over the Third World. The postcolonial situation is, of course, very much more complicated than traditional colonialism, since Third World countries technically have the freedom to shape their own destinies. But it is clear that for a variety of economic and political reasons the Third World is still in many ways under the influence of former colonial powers and other industrialized nations.[2]

In addition to the neocolonial aspects of relations between industrialized and Third World countries, there is another element of the equation of dependency. This might be called the "metropolis-province" dichotomy.[3] In a sense, the industrialized nations are the metropolitan centers containing the key elements of intellectual life, such as universities, publishing houses, research institutes, and the like. Their languages are used in the international network of communications to a large degree. It is not surprising that most Third World nations are in a sense "provinces" of these centers as a result of the sheer inequality of resources and the weight of tradition. The provincial status of the Third World countries puts them at a disadvantage in terms of the creation and distribution of knowledge.[4]

It is my conviction that the development of independent means for the creation and distribution of knowledge by Third

World countries is an important goal. As one observer put it in discussing publishing:

> To establish an indigenous publishing house is an act of liberation, and therefore, a necessity because it breaks the control, indeed the monopoly, which the white races have had over world literature, for which reason they have controlled the mind of the African.[5]

The establishment of independent centers of creativity and distribution is a difficult process, but it is one of considerable importance to the Third World, since without such indigenous centers the control of intellectual life will remain in the hands of forces that at best are unconcerned with the development of the Third World and at worst interested in reinforcing patterns of dependency.

Knowledge is a critically important commodity in any society. It contributes to economic growth, technological development, cultural transmission and advancement, and political communication. Knowledge is created by many agencies, such as universities, research institutes, and private policymaking groups. Knowledge is distributed through many means: books, the mass media, educational institutions, religious agencies, and in some societies through oral tradition. Knowledge is preserved by libraries, schools, universities, and other institutions. Unless individual intellectuals in the Third World have established paths of access to the multiple institutions that dominate knowledge production they are barred from free participation in the international intellectual community.

This essay focuses on the distribution of knowledge in the Third World by concentrating on publishing as a key element in the distribution apparatus. More specifically, I am concerned with the type of publishing that contributes directly to the advancement and communication of scientific information and cultural and political commentary—with "serious" and scholarly publishing. While publishing is by no means the only means of knowledge distribution, the book remains one of the key means for distribution of the conceptual knowledge so important to technological and social development in the Third World.

THE ROLE OF PUBLISHING[6]

The printed word is a key to creating and diffusing knowledge, to having active intellectual life, and to developing advanced technology. Further, books, periodicals, and other reading materials are central to the educational system, to research, and to the creation of an independent national culture in the modern sense of the term. Regardless of what advances have been made in the diffusion of information, scholars, policymakers, and the intellectual community depend, for the most part, on the printed word to communicate. Books are not the sole artifacts of a culture; however, they are among the prerequisites of a modern society.

Publishers control the process of book production and distribution. They are a crucial, although usually ignored, element in the intellectual equation.[7] Publishers not only make ideas available to a broad public but in many ways decide which ideas will emerge in the arena of public discourse. They are, in a sense, "gatekeepers" of knowledge and culture.[8] The publishing industry, then, has special significance in the Third World, where books are urgently needed for both education and for broader intellectual and technological purposes and where books and journals have a major role in part because of the relatively underdeveloped state of other mass media.

The nature of the Third World's "book hunger" is complex.[9] It is, in part, a simple shortage of books particularly for schools and literacy programs.[10] But the shortage of books is also linked to a limited market for indigenously produced books because of low purchasing power, a small library system, reliance on oral tradition for certain kinds of communications, and other infrastructural factors. Low literacy rates naturally limit the numbers of potential readers, and a linguistically bifurcated market, as exists in many Third World countries, is also a severe problem.[11] The control of a considerable share of the book industry by foreigners and the orientation of even indigenous publishers to foreign models also plays a role in inhibiting book development.[12]

The most basic challenge for the Third World's knowledge-distribution network is one of shortage. There is a shortage of books for 70 percent of the globe.[13] The thirty-four industrialized nations, which have only 30 percent of the population, produce 81 percent of the world's book titles.[14] Although literacy rates in these nations are higher than in the Third World, the rates alone do not begin to account for the disparity in book production. Figures for Asia dramatically illustrate the book gap. In 1967 the eighteen developing countries of the region, with 28 percent of the world's population, accounted for only 7.3 percent of the total number of book titles and 2.6 percent of the total number of copies produced per year, and half of these were textbooks.[15] This represents only thirty-two book titles per million population; in Europe the average was 417 per million. Not only are too few books produced in the Third World, but the kinds of books published may not meet national priorities. For example, only 10 percent of all book titles published in India are concerned with pure or applied sciences. By comparison, 54 percent of the books published in the Soviet Union and 25 percent in the United States are on scientific subjects.

The Third World, then, has a need for a great many more books to attain a competitive intellectual standing with industrialized nations, but the demand for books in developing nations remains limited because of low literacy levels and other reasons. Strong, indigenous publishing houses suffer and often fail. It becomes easier to import books than to produce them, and Third World nations are trapped in a cycle of dependency.

THE HERITAGE OF COLONIALISM

The colonial past remains a major influence on the intellectual and educational life of many Third World nations and has had considerable impact on publishing as well. Indigenous intellectual institutions atrophied under colonialism. Employment in the modern sector was linked to knowledge of the colonial language and to European-style education. Gradually, the colonial language became the medium for commerce, politics, science, and government. Publishers are clearly part of the colonial heritage. With some exceptions, modern publishing originated in missionary and/or colonial government activities. The influential publishers up to independence were generally firms based in the metropole, and most of their books were issued in the colonial language.[16]

Colonial authorities often controlled the kinds of materials that could be published. They placed major stress on the production of textbooks for use in the developing school systems. These texts were usually adapted from books used in the metropole at the time. At the college and university level, virtually all books were imported. The colonial authorities, not surprisingly, favored the European firms, and it was very difficult for indigenous publishers to emerge. As a result of colonial policy and the very limited market for books in the colonies, there was very little indigenous publishing at the time of independence in any of the Third World nations.

Publishing firms tended to develop along Western lines in the early days of independence. The continuing impact of the metropolitan firms—such as Oxford University Press, Macmillan, and others in such ex-British areas as India, Nigeria, Tanzania, and Kenya—remained strong, as these publishers continued to operate and in many cases to dominate publishing. Further, the dominant model of publishing was Western; efforts were made to design books along Western lines and up to prevailing metropolitan standards even where less expensive and less lavish books would better serve local needs. Inevitably, Western ideas of the very concept of the book—in terms of production standards, language, content, and methods of distribution—dominated publishing at this early stage and still do to a considerable extent. It is only recently that publishers in some Third World countries have been shifting gradually to indigenous languages and have been concerned with producing basic literacy materials, inexpensive mass-market paperbacks, and the like. It is fair to state that the heritage of colonialism remains with the Third World publishing industry.

LANGUAGE

Language is a key to the intellectual situation in many Third World nations. Language also plays a role in the distribution of knowledge, since the medium through which material is communicated determines accessibility.[17] Many Third World nations are multilingual states in which questions of language policy are often politically volatile. With some exceptions, most books published in the Third World are issued in the language of former European masters. Slightly under half of the books published in India are issued in English, although less than 2 percent of the Indian population is literate in English. More than half of Indian newspaper circulation is in English, and an even higher proportion of intellectual journals appear in that language. A large proportion of debate on national social and political issues takes place in English, and virtually all scientific research is communicated in the English language. In anglophone Africa, the situation is even more dramatic, with upward of 90 percent of indigenous publishing taking place in English. Several anglophone African countries have been slowly moving toward a publishing enterprise in indigenous languages, with Nigeria and Tanzania taking the lead. Francophone Africa remains firmly linked to French as the language of all elements of the "modern" culture and economy.

The use of a European language as the central medium for intellectual exchange blocks access to knowledge for large portions of the populations of many of the multilingual Third World nations. Language becomes a mechanism of social stratification. Those who command a European language are able to enter the professional sector and the modern business world; those who lack a European language are barred from many positions with the potential of upward mobility. As a result, language policy has become a politically volatile question in many multilingual Third World nations.

The persistence of Western languages in the Third World has many causes. The weight of the colonial tradition is important. Third World nations find it difficult to displace Western languages because the colonial medium permeates the modern social structure, from the legal system and administration to the operation of the military and the writing of poetry. Ruling elites also find it useful to continue to use European languages in part because these languages help to maintain their monopoly over power. In multilingual societies the choice of an indigenous language as a national language is often a politically difficult decision, and the continued use of a European language has been an easy way out for policymakers.[18] The technical and intellectual problems of linguistic change are considerable, and many Third World nations have placed emphasis on other, more obvious, development-related issues rather than tackle the language question. The dominance of the major "international" languages in commerce, politics, and in intellectual life also makes a shift difficult. Even smaller European countries seem to rely increasingly on the use of English or in some cases French for growing segments of their commercial and academic life.[19] And the major Western nations have attempted, through foreign-aid programs and other means, to maintain the influence of European languages in the Third World.[20]

The colonial language has been the medium for scholarship and for the dissemination of "high level" materials. The continued domination of the highest levels of the educational system by Western languages has resulted in a paucity of technical and scholarly books in indigenous languages. English or French continues to be a key to graduate education and to research studies in the Third World, even in countries with some commitment to indigenous languages. Furthermore, libraries and institutions, which comprise the bulk of the market for scholarly and nonfiction books and journals, are accustomed to buying books in European languages. Even where classes in universities are conducted in indigenous languages, a Western language is usually necessary for library research. Thus, authors wishing to write for a national audience and to reach their intellectual peers generally write in a European language.

Even in Indonesia, one of the few former colonies that has made a concentrated and fairly successful effort to promote the use of an indigenous language, *Bahasa Indonesia,* indigenous scholarly books and advanced textbooks do not yet exist, and materials in English are widely used. In anglophone and francophone Africa, where virtually all books, except certain kinds of popular fiction and some primary textbooks, are published in the metropolitan language, the 80 to 95 percent of the population who do not know English or French are barred from the higher levels of education and hence from the elite. The diffusion of technological information in fields such as agriculture is made more difficult because most farmers are unable to read materials in European languages.[21]

The role of translations in the international network of knowledge diffusion indicates how unbalanced the situation is and how the Third World languages are essentially in an intellectual backwater. Most of the world's translations are from the major European languages into other, more "local" languages. Fully three-fourths of the 40,000 titles translated in 1970 were from English (which itself accounted for 16,471 translations), French, German, and Russian. In fact, none of the top fifteen languages from which translations were made were Third World languages.[22] Of the top fifty authors whose works were translated, only two were from Third World nations, Mao Tse-tung and Swami Vivekananda.

A similar picture can be seen for book exports. The vast majority of book exports are from the industrialized nations. The role of Third World nations in the export-import trade is relatively modest, but it is very clear that the Third World nations are large net importers of books, with the majority of books coming from foreign sources. This is especially true for many African nations, which have started indigenous publishing very recently. Even India, which has a large and flourishing publishing industry—and indeed ranks eighth among the world's nations in book-title output—imports a large number of books, the vast majority of which are in English.

The kind of books imported indicates something of the book trade and of national priorities. Elementary-school textbooks are by far the largest source of book imports, with English grammar and dictionaries following in importance. Popular American and British novels are imported in large numbers, as is Tarzan and other light fiction. Some of these volumes are imported in numbers up to 40,000 copies per title.[23] The influence of Western language and culture, then, is not confined to the Third World's intellectual elite but also pervades the elementary education and leisure time of the literate population.

The international traffic in translations and book imports and exports indicates that the Third World is directly taking knowledge from the industrialized nations and using it for its own purposes. Direct import of books from the industrialized world also has implications. Not only do books cost valuable foreign-exchange earnings, but imported books necessarily limit the potential for growth of a domestic publishing industry in Third World nations. Indian publishers, who recognize the barrier mass imports create for local growth, have argued that it is entirely appropriate to import books that will have a small sale and would therefore be uneconomic to reprint locally but that it is wasteful to import thousands of copies of single titles.

Developing nations are not the only countries affected by this inequality of translations and imports. Smaller European nations, such as Holland, Czechoslovakia, Denmark, Israel, and others, translate large numbers of books from the "major" international languages and import many books as well. Experts in these smaller industrialized nations as well as in the Third World have speculated about the long-term implications for indigenous intellectual life, publishing, and for the health of local languages in an international system of dissemination of books that is so heavily weighted toward the major industrial powers.[24] While a few "small language" nations subsidize local literature and local publishing, there is at present no clear solution to the problem.

THE EDUCATIONAL SYSTEM AND INTELLECTUAL LIFE

In most countries, the home for intellectual activity is the university. Even in industrialized nations, intellectual journals probably would not survive were it not for the academic market of university libraries and individual scholars. In the West, scholarly books are often published by nonprofit university presses and universities, especially those in the United States, where research and publication are emphasized as the main criteria for promotion and academic success. Faculty members are allowed time for research activities, and funding is sometimes available for research. The milieu of the academic community and the nature, organization, and size of the university system contribute considerably to knowledge creation and distribution in a nation.

Universities in the Third World are colonial institutions in that they are almost without exception based on a foreign model and reflect many of the values and organizational patterns of foreign institutions.[25] In many instances the language of instruction remains a foreign language, and many of the faculty have been trained outside the country. Foreign models brought to the Third World did not emphasize research or creative intellectual endeavor, since colonial powers created universities largely to provide training for the middle levels of the colonial bureaucracy. Thus, much of higher education in the Third World reflects European models and academic norms but is not up to modern Western standards of quality.

The academic "infrastructure" of the Third World cannot support the network of intellectual communications that is necessary to stimulate a full range of scholarly activity. For example, university systems tend to be smaller and there are fewer libraries to purchase books, fewer professors to write them, and fewer students to read and purchase textbooks. Universities seldom have adequate funds for research, and governments usually must spend first on immediate development needs rather than on less tangible research work. There are few university presses, partly because they are expensive and require trained manpower that is often in short supply. The conditions for research are often poor—laboratories and computer facilities are scarce, libraries are inadequate for modern advanced scholarship, and funding is short. In the Third World, research is not always a fundamental part of the academic enterprise, and scholarly publishing is not always seen as a key to professional advancement, largely because the nineteenth-century British and French institutions—models for many Third World universities—did not emphasize research. In addition, many faculty members are too busy with heavy teaching loads or with such responsibilities as advising government agencies or holding outside jobs to pursue research interests.

Faculty salaries are seldom high enough to cover the price of books and journals, and, what is perhaps more important, colleagues and students provide little impetus for research within the university. Without the material resources and the academic subculture to stimulate research and writing, Third

World universities contribute less than they might to the production of research and knowledge. They are not even active as consumers of locally produced knowledge, as might be expected.

The intellectual system, both academic and nonuniversity, does not encourage the emergence of an active publishing establishment or a viable means for the distribution of knowledge. In general, intellectuals in the Third World lack adequate working conditions and can obtain little public financial support for their work. It is almost impossible to earn an adequate living by writing, and the academic system can absorb only a limited number of intellectuals. Few journals and publishing houses exist to provide indigenous outlets for scholarly and critical writing. Due to low literacy levels, there is only a small audience for either scholarly or nonscholarly work. With neither public support nor a large book-buying public, very few intellectuals can support themselves solely from their writing or research.[26]

In part because of the weak domestic infrastructure and in part because of orientations toward the West, many Third World intellectuals and scholars try hard to communicate with a Western audience and publish in the West. If there is prestige in publishing, it lies in writing for such Western journals as *Encounter* or *Les Temps Modernes.* Publication abroad may bring money and the opportunity to communicate with other Third World intellectuals, since communication seldom runs directly between one developing country and another but is mediated through industrialized nations. Many Third World intellectuals feel most at home writing in a Western language, and they are cut off from most of their countrymen. There has been very little effort to develop needed vocabulary so that the indigenous languages can be used for all kinds of scientific communication.

There is, in a sense, a vicious circle of circumstances that works against the emergence of a viable intellectual community and a means of communication within that community and with other segments of the population. The orientation and training of many intellectuals impel them to continue to use a European language and to keep a European reference group in mind when doing research or writing. This, then, means that indigenous languages are ignored. Domestic journals and publishers are subordinated to foreign outlets for written work, and local publishers suffer as a result. The very limited market for local printed materials and the generally inadequate quality of writing complete the circle and contribute to the continuation of a situation of dependence on books, journals, and ideas from the industrialized nations. The lack of journals means that an important channel for publicity about books is missing, and book reviews, which help to maintain standards of writing through criticism, are usually missing.

THE ECONOMICS OF PUBLISHING

The economics of publishing concerns much more than the cost of producing and distributing a book in a particular country. Rates of literacy, reading habits of the population, government policy toward books, copyright regulations, and the nature of libraries are all part of the economic equation.[27] For example, low literacy rates, low per capita purchasing power, and a diversity of languages—all common in Third World nations—contribute to a limited market for books. Many of the smaller Third World countries find it economically impossible to publish most kinds of books because the internal market is simply too small. Even in such large nations as Nigeria, India, and Indonesia, only some textbooks, certain kinds of popular fiction, and religious books are profitable to publish. Little effort has been made to develop regional markets, which might assist the smaller nations in establishing networks for the dissemination of books and journals. Although labor costs are lower than in the West, total costs remain high in relation to purchasing power since print runs are small and distribution is expensive and difficult.

Publishing firms find their work quite difficult in Third World nations. Paper costs tend to be high, and well-trained personnel for editorial work are rare. Printing equipment is often in short supply, and the quality of printing is indifferent. The process of seeing a book from the manuscript stage to the printed product tends to be complicated by delays and chronic shortages. Capital is often in very short supply, and this means that publishers must often turn down good manuscripts because they cannot afford to publish them. Because of small print runs, profits are limited, and it usually takes a long time to recover investment. Publishing is not seen as a viable industry either by government or private entrepreneurs, and as a result publishers find it difficult to borrow money.

Book distribution may be the single most difficult dilemma of publishing in the Third World. Dan Lacy divides the problem into three elements: (a) the actual demand for books as distinguished from the need; (b) the network of distribution—for example, booksellers, wholesalers, book clubs, etc.; c) the means of conveying information about books, such as reviews, advertising and book trade journals.[28] Low reader density, great distances between settlements, and poor transportation facilities make book distribution in the Third World particularly difficult. Just as Third World countries themselves are at the periphery of the world's knowledge system, regions outside the major cities, especially rural areas, which are often completely without access to books, periodicals, or newspapers, are at the periphery of knowledge systems *within* the Third World nations.[29]

SCHOLARLY PUBLISHING AND JOURNALS

The publication of specialized books, monographs, and journals aimed at an academic audience or intended to further the technology or culture of a society constitutes a special publishing problem.[30] Even in the most advanced nations, scholarly publishing is usually not an economic proposition. Books tend to be expensive to print, sell in small numbers, and are difficult to sell because of the dispersion of the market. Library sales account for a high proportion of total income. In the Third World, the problems of scholarly publishing are magnified since the general conditions of intellectual life are more difficult. Yet, scholarly publishing is particularly important for Third World nations, as it is a crucial element of an independent intellectual culture.

Scholarly publishing almost inevitably requires subsidy, even in industrialized nations. In the United States, for example, the return on investment in scholarly books is negligible compared to other high-profit industries in the private sector, and, as a result, scholarly publishing has increasingly become a province of the university press. Both direct and indirect subsidies are channeled through university presses. Direct subsidy is provided by the university itself as well as by foundations and learned societies. Indirect subsidy is made available through federal-government grants to libraries, which are the primary purchasers of the scholarly books put out by university presses.

The university press provides a useful model for scholarly publishing in the Third World because it can channel subsidies for publishing through an agency that can have considerable autonomy and maintain a high standard of quality. These presses carry the prestige of their sponsoring institution and have easy access to the academic community for distribution. The university press is a new phenomenon in the Third World, and its growth has been limited. However, several countries, such as Nigeria, Singapore, and Malaysia, have recently established active university presses, and there is substantial interest in other areas.

The university press is not the only means of disseminating scholarly materials. Research institutes, government agencies, and some private agencies are engaged in scholarly publishing in many Third World nations.[31] Indeed, the government is probably one of the largest publishers of specialized scholarly materials in Third World nations. Private publishers are also active in scholarly publishing, although the economics of this type of publishing necessarily limits the role of the private sector. In India, a significant proportion of the scholarly books are published by private firms, which are able to find a market for editions of 1,000 or fewer copies and are able to recoup their investment. These publishers engage in scholarly publishing more as a matter of prestige than as a profitable enterprise.

Scholarly publishing may seem a very small matter for nations faced with massive problems of development. Yet, despite the very limited investment needed, the small audiences for specialized books, and the difficulties of distribution, scholarly publishing is of considerable importance. It is the way Third World scholars can communicate new knowledge that is directly relevant to their own situations. It is a means of stimulating indigenous scholarship that otherwise may not be done or may be oriented toward foreign publishers. It is a means of communicating debates in scientific and technical fields among Third World nations that would not occur if scholarly books were published only in the industrialized nations. Scholarly publishing helps to bring a research-mindedness to the universities and can stimulate more writing and publication. It will help to lower the dependence on the impact of foreign books.

Along with scholarly books, academic and "highbrow" journals play an active role in the dissemination of knowledge. In many ways they are admirably suited to the situation of the Third World, as journals are relatively inexpensive to produce, fairly easy to distribute, and often within the purchasing power of academics to buy. They permit the quick transmission of knowledge and are easily accessible to specific scholarly or other communities. Journals can provide a sense of unity to an emerging academic discipline, intellectual current, or other trend. They are particularly useful in providing applications of more "basic" research, and they have the considerable advantage of speed of publication. Journals cannot, of course, provide the depth of analysis that a book can, but shorter articles are often sufficient to communicate ideas and innovations. Journals also communicate current development in a field, print letters to the editor that can give a sense of participation in academic and intellectual affairs and book reviews that are crucial to maintaining academic standards and to publicizing new books.[32] Journals can stimulate an intellectual dialogue and a continuing debate in a way that books cannot. Journals are also in a position to update and revise scholarly fields.

Journals are important to intellectual life in the industrialized nations; they are even more crucial in the Third World. Virtually all of the academic journals are published in the West, and they dominate the mainstream of intellectual discourse in their respective fields. The prestige of Western journals and magazines, from *Time* and the *Economist* to the *American Sociological Review* and *Race,* is unchallenged and is also a problem for the Third World. As in the case of imported books, the orientation of these journals and the content of their articles reflect the concerns, interests, and ideologies of the West. Further, distributing Western journals presents problems, and their cost is high and beyond the reach of most Third World intellectuals. Thus, the present international network of scholarly and intellectual journals, which is strongly dominated by the West, does not serve the interests of the Third World. As in all aspects of this analysis, it is unlikely that the monopoly of power of the industrialized nations can be broken since most of the key scholars are located in the West, and most theoretical contributions to fields of science are made in the West. Nevertheless, it would seem useful for journals to be expanded in the Third World as part of the construction of a network of intellectual institutions that can help in the dissemination of knowledge.

Journals do exist in Third World nations, and some countries such as India support a large number of general and specialized magazines. At least fifty academic journals are published in India in a large variety of fields. There are, however, relatively few advanced-level scholarly, intellectual, and professional journals in most Third World countries, and virtually none that are published in the Third World have an international circulation. Many of the existing journals are sponsored by individual universities and have only a small circulation outside their home institutions. Most journals are published in the former colonial language.

THE FOREIGN IMPACT ON PUBLISHING

An important part of the Third World's cultural dependency stems from political, trade, and intellectual relationships with industrialized nations. Industrialized nations export their products—in this case, books, journals, and expertise—to the developing countries. Foreign-aid programs, while seeking to provide help to the Third World, often deepen existing patterns of dependence.[33] The international arrangements controlling the flow of knowledge, such as copyright agreements, commercial publishing practices, etc., are dominated by the industrialized nations and reflect their interests.

The International Network

Commercial arrangements built up over years of colonialism persist in many developing countries.[34] Branches of British or French publishers continue to operate in the Third World and in some places dominate the publishing scene. The advantages held by foreign firms operating in the Third World are considerable. They have considerable expertise in terms of the local market as well as technical know-how concerning book production. They have the backing of foreign capital and a worldwide distribution network. They are able to print in larger editions because some of the books can be exported and can draw on the financial reserves of the parent company. Perhaps most important, the foreign firms have considerable prestige and a backlist of books that makes them well known in the local book trade and among intellectuals. Foreign publishers also act as importers of books from abroad, and here too they have an advantage over local firms. It seems clear that the foreign firms have made it even more difficult than normal for indigenous publishers to emerge in the Third World.

In general, British and French firms have dealt in commercially successful and uncontroversial textbooks, which constitute the overwhelming proportion of the market in most Third World countries. In addition to textbooks, these firms also deal with book imports. They have published relatively few original works by local authors, although this situation is changing as the foreign firms are under increasing pressure to "indigenize" their operations. In recent years, American publishers have followed the same pattern. For the most part they have established themselves in developing areas where United States foreign-aid programs have been active. The American firms have largely been engaged in importing American books and participating in publishing programs related to foreign-aid projects. They have not participated substantially in indigenous publishing efforts. The balance, however, is not entirely negative. Foreign firms provided an early base for publishing and have increasingly taken responsibility for training indigenous personnel for editorial and other functions.

In addition to the foreign publishers functioning within Third World nations, the international network of the book trade has worked against the developing countries. The traditional network has divided the world between the British publishers, who have exported to the formerly British colonies, and the Americans, who had the Latin American market. Some areas are "open" to both nations. While this informal system has broken down in recent years, it has made it difficult for Third World countries to obtain books quickly and at the cheapest prices. The market, in a sense, was dominated by trade agreements among the sellers. Industrialized-nation publishers often refused to grant permission to Third World publishers to reprint books locally, preferring to make more money by exporting their own editions. This too works against indigenous publishers and in the long run against the reading public as well.

The copyright system has traditionally worked against the Third World. The major international copyright agreements—the American-sponsored Universal Copyright Convention and the European-backed "Berne Agreements"—both have made it difficult for Third World nations to reprint books that are needed in these areas and do not take into account special needs of the Third World. This situation is in the process of changing with the gradual introduction of liberalized policies, but the international agreements still are dominated by the industrialized nations.[35]

While copyright has protected authors and has contributed to the protection of intellectual property, it has also served to keep knowledge from the "have not" nations, to make translations from one language to another difficult, and to work in the interests of the industrialized nations, which dominate the international agreements and publish the bulk of the world's books. It might be pointed out that the United States, when it was in the process of developing its own publishing industry and declaring its intellectual independence from Britain, regularly flouted copyright agreements, which were seen as limiting the development of an indigenous book trade.[36]

"Foreign Aid" and Publishing

Foreign-aid programs have had an impact on publishing in the Third World and on the distribution of knowledge in general. While "intellectual" aid is only a small part of the total aid program of any industrialized nation, this kind of aid has entailed technical assistance to educational systems, the sponsorship of Western-style institutions such as technical universities, the provision of books for libraries, and assistance to publishing enterprises and to book-related activities. While the United States has sponsored the largest aid efforts, other countries have also engaged in aid programs. For example, the English Language Book Scheme (ELBS), sponsored by Britain, each year sells more than one million copies comprising several hundred titles, intended mainly for use as college and university textbooks. These books are standard British books and are printed in England, thus depriving either Third World academics or publishers of any benefit. On a considerably smaller scale, West Germany and the Soviet Union have also sponsored intellectual assistance, including aid to publishing firms. The various kinds of intellectual aid programs have cost millions of dollars over the past two decades and have included a large variety of programs in many different Third World countries.

Foreign aid, particularly intellectual assistance, cannot be separated from the policy goals of the donor country or, for that matter, from the policies and orientations of the recipient nation's government. The American rationale for book-related aid programs has involved both the technical importance of books in development and the ideological elements of anticommunism.[37] Between 1950 and 1964 the United States Information Agency assisted in the production of 9,000 editions and printed 80 million copies in fifty-one languages.[38] U.S. programs have provided assistance for book exports to Third World countries, funds to purchase American printing equipment, and technical advisers to help with book-related activity.

The Indo-American Textbook Program was one of the largest American efforts. Under the PL480 program more than 1,000 different textbooks were reprinted in English for use by Indian college and university students, and more than 4 million copies were distributed at subsidized prices. Although the titles were predominantly in the natural sciences, the reprints included many topics in the social sciences and humanities. The Indian government gave full approval to the program, and a joint Indo-American committee selected the textbooks. With the recent cooling in Indo-American relations and changing U.S. foreign-aid priorities, textbook aid has virtually ended in India.

Like similar programs in other countries, the Indo-American Textbook Program had certain negative results. In some fields, particularly the social sciences, American books were not relevant to the Indian situation, and the orientations of American social scientists reflected their own ideological biases. Yet the subsidized books tended to drive their more expensive unsubsidized domestic counterparts off the market. The artificially low prices for American books gave buyers a distorted sense of the real cost of books. Finally, several subsidiaries of U.S. publishers were able to establish themselves in the Indian market through the aid programs, and their growth may have retarded the development of indigenous Indian publishing.

Yet not all aspects of foreign book programs are pernicious. Aid programs place inexpensive books in the hands of students and can make textbooks in a range of disciplines quickly available. Such programs often provide technical assistance, printing, or other equipment to local publishers and sponsor translations into indigenous languages. It is necessary, however, to evaluate such programs carefully. Do aid programs help Third World publishers to establish strong roots and to bring out relevant locally written books? Or do they circulate materials the industrialized countries think will win them influence at the cost of discouraging the development of local publishing? The answers to such questions are complicated but certainly require more attention at the planning and implementation stages of aid programs than they have been given to date.

Another aspect of intellectual neocolonialism is the impact of Western research on the developing countries. Most research, particularly in technology and the natural sciences, is done in the West. Despite some efforts at research in the Third World, it is likely that this monopoly will persist—if anything, the developing countries will lag farther and farther behind. It is not that scholars in the Third World do not have the ability to do research; in India, such individuals as M. N. Srinivas and André Bétille in sociology have done outstanding work. But, as we noted earlier, the universities do not stress research, and funds are seldom available to finance it.

In fact, Western scholars have done much of the research on the Third World, and indigenous scholars often must learn about their own political system or agricultural situation through the writings of their Western counterparts. Certainly much of the

Western scholarship has been useful and reasonably accurate; but as long as knowledge about the nature of society in developing countries is mediated through Western sources, it is suspect for all the possible methodological and ideological biases, misperceptions, and other problems such mediation may entail.[39] In addition, much scholarship and interpretation concerning the Third World is published in the West and accessible only with difficulty in the developing countries themselves.

The range of foreign influences on Third World publishing in particular and intellectual activity generally is considerable and has had a varying impact. Some of this impact is an element of the normal set of relationships between the industrialized nations and the Third World that can be discerned in trade relations of all kinds. Other elements, particularly the foreign-aid programs, are a result of deliberate policies of the industrialized countries.

CONCLUSION

Knowledge is not a commodity like oil or wheat; yet it is traded in the international marketplace. Like other commodities, knowledge is subject to various pressures of supply and demand and political or economic power. The dissemination of knowledge is a highly complex matter, involving the mass media, publishing firms, educational institutions, and other elements. Third World nations find themselves in a situation of scarcity when it comes to knowledge, as is also true in other areas of the economy. The means of dissemination tend to be controlled by the industrialized nations for a variety of reasons, and it is not surprising that those who are in control use their power over ideas and technology for their own interests in many cases. The international network of knowledge distribution is based in the industrialized nations, who are at the center of the world's intellectual, research, and technological currents. The Third World finds itself at the periphery and finds it difficult to catch up. Publishing can be seen as a case study in the dissemination of knowledge, as it is one of the key means of providing access to information. It has been seen in this analysis that publishing in the Third World faces difficult problems, some due to the colonial heritage, some to the policies of the Third World nations themselves and to the very real internal problems facing such nations, and some to the policies of the industrialized countries. The nature of the international network also works against the Third World.

This analysis has indicated that the problems of knowledge distribution in the Third World are systemic and related to a very complex series of relationships. In this situation of drastic inequality there is a limited amount that the Third World can do to establish independence immediately. Yet there are a number of strategies Third World nations can use to increase their independence and the viability of their publishing enterprises.

A few Third World nations have attempted radical solutions to the problem of dependency. The best known examples, China and Tanzania, have stressed an ideology of self-sufficiency to redirect the educational system and intellectuals toward a completely indigenous orientation. These efforts have been strengthened by severing many intellectual and cultural ties with industrialized nations, by forcing intellectuals to become involved with the day-to-day problems of the peasantry through work in villages, and by stressing practical technology in schools and colleges. While it would seem from available reports that both China and Tanzania have achieved some success in reorienting intellectual life, it remains to be seen how effective these experiments will be in the long run.[40]

Other Third World nations have used more modest means to achieve some degree of intellectual independence and indigenous cultural development. Some countries have stressed the use of a national language as a means of cultural unification. Others have severely limited the importation of Western films and, in some cases, books in order to stress indigenous values. A few countries have allocated funds to projects, such as the National Book Trust in India, which promote local authorship, cultural development, and publishing. Finally, many Third World countries have nationalized textbook publishing to insure that these books reflect values and orientations appropriate for national development. But with few exceptions these efforts have been piecemeal. There has been little cooperation among Third World nations in joint cultural programs or even in sharing information and publications.

The following suggestions are intended to provide some ideas that can be easily implemented and may help to ameliorate the existing inequalities in the world of books and publishing. These suggestions are realistic in the sense that no major changes in the relationships between industrialized nations and Third World nations are required to implement them. Clearly, more radical solutions to the problems of inequality are needed to effect basic change. But to suggest modest reforms is not to deny the need to restructure radically the relationship between the rich and poor nations.

As a first step, communications between Third World nations should be improved so that common problems and issues can be discussed directly without being mediated through institutions and publications in the industrialized nations. This is particularly important on a regional basis—for example, among the nations of francophone Africa and of Southeast Asia. As a part of communications development, Third World countries must also create viable means of book distribution among themselves and between themselves and industrialized nations.

With the strengthening of indigenous publishing and internal distribution facilities in the Third World, intellectuals need not publish their work abroad. Such an effort should include financial and technical assistance from the public sector when necessary. Foreign scholars working in developing nations should publish their findings in the countries where they conduct their research. In this way local publishing will be strengthened and relevant research will be available to local audiences. The intellectual infrastructure in many Third World countries needs to be strengthened in other ways. Libraries, journals that review books, and bibliographical and publicity tools for publishing should be supported.

In addition, major national policy questions that relate directly to books, including the language of instruction in the educational system, levels of literacy, and the ownership of the publishing apparatus, must be solved by Third World governments with an understanding of their implications for the balance of intellectual production. Part of any language reform effort should be assistance to publishing in indigenous languages. Finally, Third World leaders must carefully evaluate foreign-aid programs to insure that their nations benefit without local publishing industries or intellectual autonomy being undermined.

These are but a few suggestions for the solution of a complex problem. While publishing is a small part of the relationship between industrialized and developing countries, Third World nations can institute reforms in the publishing process because massive financial investments are not required and power politics are not involved. Through understanding the complexities of the issue, individuals in both industrialized and developing countries may be able to begin exploring constructive solutions.

Notes

1. For further discussion of neocolonialism, see Philip G. Altbach, "Neocolonialism and Education," in *Teachers College Record* 72 (May 1971): 543–58. I am indebted to Gail Kelly and Sheila McVey for their comments on an earlier draft of this essay.
2. See Tibor Mende, *From Aid to Colonialism: Lessons of a Failure* (New York: Pantheon, 1973); Gunnar Myrdal, *Asian Drama* (New York: Pantheon, 1968); and J. D. Cockcroft, et al., eds., *Dependence and Underdevelopment* (Garden City, N.Y.: Anchor Books, 1972).
3. This theme is more completely elaborated in Edward Shils, "Metropolis and Province in the Intellectual Community," in E. Shils, *The Intellectuals and the Powers and Other Essays* (Chicago: University of Chicago Press, 1972), pp. 355–71.
4. It is not just Third World nations that find themselves "provinces" of the major industrial centers. Such nations as Canada, Belgium, Holland, and others are faced with similar problems vis-à-vis such metropolitan centers as the United States, Britain, France, or West Germany.
5. Dan and Barbara Dodson, "Publishing Progress in Nigeria," in *Scholarly Publishing* 4 (October 1972): 62.
6. For a general analysis of the role of publishing, see Philip G. Altbach, "Publishing and the Intellectual System," in *Annals of the American Academy of Political and Social Science* 421 (September 1975): 1–13.
7. Much of this analysis is taken from Philip G. Altbach, *Publishing in India: An Analysis* (Delhi: Oxford University Press, 1975), and from Philip G. Altbach, "Literary Colonialism: Books in the Third World," in *Harvard Educational Review* 45 (May 1975): 226–36. See also E. Oluwasanmi, E. McLean, and H. Zell, eds., *Publishing in Africa*

in the Seventies (Ile-Ife: University of Ife Press, 1975), and S. Minowa and A. Arboleda, eds., *Scholarly Publishing in Asia* (Tokyo: University of Tokyo Press, 1973).

8. The "gatekeeper" notion is best elaborated by Lewis Coser in his article "Publishers as Gatekeepers of Ideas," in *Annals of the American Academy of Political and Social Science* 421 (September 1975): 14–22.
9. For an excellent general discussion of the problems of books and publishing in the Third World, see Ronald Barker and Robert Escarpit, *The Book Hunger* (Paris: UNESCO, 1973).
10. Recent UNESCO statistics indicate that a major international effort to reduce illiteracy has not been successful and that the number of illiterates in the world increased from 735 million in 1965 to 800 million in 1975. Part of the blame was placed on a shortage of books and problems with producing books in appropriate languages. A. Freund, "Illiteracy Rises Despite UNESCO Efforts," in *New York Times* (February 4, 1976), p. 21.
11. Dan Lacy, "Practical Considerations, Including Financial, in the Creation, Production, and Distribution of Books and Other Educational Materials," in F. Keppel, ed., *The Mohonk Conference* (New York: National Book Committee, 1973), pp. 55–66.
12. See Keith Smith, "Who Controls Book Publishing in Anglophone Middle Africa?," in *Annals of the American Academy of Political and Social Science* 421 (September 1976): 140–50.
13. Barker and Escarpit, *Book Hunger*, p. 16.
14. Ibid., p. 16.
15. *Book Development in Asia: Report on the Production and Distribution of Books in the Region* (Paris: UNESCO, 1967), p. 25.
16. There are some notable exceptions to this generalization. For example, indigenous Vietnamese publishers were active under French rule. Countries such as Thailand and China, which were not under direct colonial rule, developed fledgling publishing enterprises in local languages. But these efforts were the exceptions rather than the rule.
17. For a broader consideration of language problems in the

Third World, see Joshua Fishman, Charles Ferguson, and J. Das Gupta, eds., *Language Problems of Developing Nations* (New York: Wiley, 1968). See also R. B. LePage, *The National Language Question: Linguistic Problems of Newly Independent States* (London: Oxford University Press, 1964).

18. See J. Das Gupta, *Language Conflict and National Development: Group Politics and National Language Policy in India* (Berkeley, Calif.: University of California Press, 1970), for an excellent case study.
19. Ben Russak, "Scholarly Publishing in Western Europe and Great Britain: A Survey and Analysis," in *Annals of the American Academy of Political and Social Science* 421 (September 1975): 106–17.
20. See Steve Whitley, "English Language as a Tool of British Neo-Colonialism," in *East Africa Journal* (December 1971), pp. 4–6. See also Smith, "Who Controls Book Publishing . . ."
21. Latin America is an exception in this regard since either Spanish or Portuguese is the language of a great majority of the population, and a large regional market for books exists. The two publishing giants of the region, Mexico and Argentina, have fairly effectively used this linguistic unity to build thriving publishing industries.
22. These statistics are extracted from the *UNESCO Statistical Yearbook, 1972* (Paris: UNESCO, 1973).
23. Indian book import statistics were supplied by the Federation of Indian Publishers in a memorandum dated December 15, 1975.
24. The fact of much translating does not necessarily mean problems of intellectual dependency. Japan, for example, is one of the largest translators from Western languages, yet it also supports a flourishing indigenous publishing industry and considerable creative talent and scholarly enterprise in Japanese.
25. See Altbach, "Education and Neocolonialism," for an elaboration of this point.
26. For a sensitive portrait of the Indian scene, see Edward Shils, *The Intellectual between Tradition and Modernity: The Indian Situation* (The Hague: Mouton, 1963).

27. The most concise guide to the general problems, including economic, of Third World nations is Datus Smith, Jr., *A Guide to Book Publishing* (New York: Bowker, 1966).
28. Lacy, "Practical Considerations . . . ," p. 60.
29. The Third World is not alone in this situation, although it is much more serious in these countries. In the United States, for example, there are few good bookstores outside of the major metropolitan areas and university campuses.
30. See S. Minowa and A. Arboleda, eds., *Scholarly Publishing in Asia*, for an overview of the Asian situation.
31. For a short discussion of scholarly publishing in India, see Altbach, *Publishing in India*, pp. 77–82.
32. There is very little analysis available concerning the role and nature of scholarly and professional journals. For some discussion, see "Communicating and Diffusing Social Science," in *International Social Science Journal* 26, no. 3, (1974): 371–445.
33. Mende, *From Aid to Colonialism.*
34. See Smith, "Who Controls Publishing . . . ," for a thorough discussion of the continuing role of Western publishers in Africa.
35. For a discussion of copyright, see Irwin Olian, Jr., "International Copyright and the Needs of Developing Countries: The Awakening at Stockholm and Paris," in *Cornell International Law Journal* 7 (May 1974): 81–112. See also *International Copyright: Needs of Developing Countries* (New Delhi: Ministry of Education, Government of India, 1966).
36. See Sheila McVey, "Nineteenth-Century America: Publishing in a Developing Country," in *Annals of the American Academy of Political and Social Science* 421 (September 1975): 67–80.
37. Curtis Benjamin, *Books as Forces in National Development and International Relations* (New York: National Foreign Trade Council, 1964). See also Stanley Barnett and Roland Piggford, *Manual on Book and Library Activities in Developing Countries* (Washington, D.C.: Agency for International Development, 1969).
38. Benjamin, *Books as Forces*, p. 72.

39. An example of the possible effects of Western interpretation is the widespread notion of the key role of the middle classes in promoting stability and development in the Third World. Such a notion, while perhaps correct in some respects, fits neatly into the ideological predispositions and interests of American foreign policy and has become, over the years, the dominant interpretation of American social science. While some social scientists in both the United States and in the Third World disagree with the interpretation, it has had a great influence on thinking in developing countries.
40. For discussion of recent trends in Chinese education, see M. Bastid, "Economic Necessity and Political Ideals in Educational Reform during the Cultural Revolution," in *China Quarterly* 42 (1970): 16–45; and P. Seybolt, "China's Revolution in Education," in *Canadian and International Education* 1 (1972): 29–41.

The African University as a Multinational Corporation: Problems of Penetration and Dependency

Ali A. Mazrui

Many characteristics attributed to commercial multinational corporations in Africa may also apply to cultural multinational corporations, of which the university is a preeminent example. Almost all African universities started as overseas extensions of European metropolitan institutions, and decisions about priorities for educational development followed the dictates of parent cultural corporations in Britain, France, or Belgium. The cultural goods the universities sold were not necessarily relevant to the needs of the new African clientele.

In this essay I shall first briefly discuss the European motives for the cultural penetration of Africa, which resulted in the emergence of the university as the most sophisticated instrument of cultural dependency. I shall then examine the nature of this dependency, and finally I shall consider the slow but fundamental process of decolonization of the university. African universities and multinational businesses in Africa both face the same fundamental problem—*how to decolonize the process of modernization without ending it.* An examination of African universities, partly on the basis of the analogy with business enterprises, should illustrate the relationships between economic and cultural dependency, as well as between economic and cultural development.

Reprinted, with permission, from the *Harvard Educational Review* 45 (May 1975).

THE ROOTS OF DEPENDENCY

Each African country now celebrates a day of independence. But independence in this context is purely political. The heavy weight of foreign economic and cultural domination persists. African economies, for example, depend too much on foreign capital and capital-intensive projects and too little on the efficient use of surplus labor. They still rely excessively on export markets in determining what to produce. They still import foreign goods almost indiscriminately rather than developing schemes for substituting local products.

This economic aspect of domination was rooted in European imperialist expansion.[1] Europe needed to control Africa, in part, because of the rise of industrial capitalism, the need for raw materials for the new factories, the desire to create new overseas markets, the interest in the mineral wealth of distant countries, and the quest for new land for large-scale plantations growing tropical products. Industrial and commercial motives thus converged to create a compelling drive for expansion.

Most analysts of African development have emphasized economic dependency; little attention in the literature or in policy forums has been paid to issues of *cultural dependency*. This oversight is surprising in view of the struggles of some African nations to reduce European cultural influences. It becomes all the more startling if we recall how Europe originally regarded its African colonies. Imperial expansion was profoundly conditioned by ethnocentrism, and ethnocentrism is, in the final analysis, a cultural phenomenon. Images of ruling races and subordinate tribes and theories of Social Darwinism were powerful cultural motives underlying the rise of imperialism. Secular and religious evangelism were also important. Secular evangelism sought to spread Western civilization, to end ignorance and "barbarism" in Africa, and to bring the torch of European enlightenment to "dark and backward" societies. Religious evangelism, committed to the spread of the Gospel and the expansion of Christendom, was for a time the dominant of the two impulses. Christian missionaries were a major lobby in Europe urging continued imperialism. There was a time in England when the government was convinced that Her Majesty had enough black subjects, but English missionaries thought the Church did not have enough black followers. Uganda was annexed partly due to missionary pressure, and other parts of Africa might not have been colonized or settled as early, but for the pressure of religious groups.

With time, both economic and cultural motives for imperialism found expression through institutions established in Africa. Economic penetration manifested itself preeminently in the multinational company, which typically engaged in mining, in selling Western products, or in growing cash crops for export. The African university became the clearest manifestation of cultural domination. By the 1950s it had replaced primary schools and churches as the prime symbol of cultural penetration. The functions served by these two multinational institutions have been mutually reinforcing. The university is a cultural corporation with political and economic consequences, and the multinational commercial company is an economic corporation with political and cultural consequences.

Perhaps it is surprising to the reader that I indict African universities for perpetuating cultural dependency. From their birth, the African universities have been a potential force for liberation. They generated substantial political unrest that contributed to independence movements in many African colonies. In the words of British historian Sir Eric Ashby:

> From the graduates of the universities the currents of nationalism flowed into the press and the people. . . . Africa has stretched the word *nationalism* to cover new meanings. . . . It too was born in America and Britain: in the editorial room of the *African Interpreter* published by African students in the United States, at meetings of the West African Students' Union in London, in Paris cafés. Its sources of inspiration were Jefferson and Lincoln, J. A. Hobson and the Fabians. It grew into a popular movement in the newspapers and election platforms and goals of West Africa.[2]

After independence, university graduates were the hope for future development in these countries.

Even such an astute observer as Ashby assumed too readily that cultural liberation accompanied political liberation. African universities were capable of being at once mechanisms for political liberation and agencies of cultural dependency. University graduates in Africa, precisely because they were the most deeply Westernized Africans, were the most culturally dependent. They have neither been among the major cultural revivalists nor have they shown respect for indigenous belief systems, linguistic heritage, modes of entertainment, or aesthetic experience. The same educational institutions that have produced nationalists eager to end colonial rule and to establish African self-government have also perpetuated cultural colonialism.

UNIVERSITY STRUCTURE AND CULTURAL DEPENDENCY

The African university, like the multinational corporation, is not autonomous in Africa today, nor was it ever in the past. It relies on cultural exports from Europe and America. The basic assumption was that a university system appropriate for Europeans could still be made to serve Nigerians or Ugandans without major transformation. African universities were created as overseas colleges, or official extensions, of universities in Britian, France, and Belgium.

For example, Makerere College in Uganda, the University College at Ibadan in Nigeria, and the University College at Legon in Ghana were all originally branches of the University of London. They each admitted students on the basis of requirements specified by the University of London; they appointed lecturers and professors partly through the good services of the Inter-University Council for Higher Education in London. Although there was consultation between London and the African branches, London approval was needed even for syllabuses and examinations. Examination questions were first formulated in the colleges in Africa and then submitted to London for criticism and revision. Once the questions were approved in London, they were printed, put into envelopes, sealed, returned to the African campuses, and not opened until the actual taking of the examination. If changes had been made in London, they were discovered by the professor too late to do anything about it. Consequently, African faculty had little control over their courses.

When I was an assistant professor in the department of political science at Makerere, the faculty wanted to introduce Marx in a course on political philosophy. On receiving the recommendation, London questioned whether Karl Marx was a political philosopher at all but, in the end, permitted his works to be included in the syllabus.

I taught the political philosophy course and encouraged my students to pay particular attention to Marx and Lenin in preparing for the final examination. When I drafted the examination, I wrote three out of twelve questions on Marxism and, as required, submitted the examination to London for criticism and revision. On the day of the examinations, I was serving as invigilator (proctor) for my class. It was a solemn occasion. I broke the seal and distributed the papers to the nervous students. When I looked at the paper, it was much shorter than the one I had submitted. There was only one question on Marxism. I tried not to show the shock and anxiety I suddenly felt. But in the eyes of some of the students I thought I detected a charge of betrayal.

According to university rules, I could not explain to my students what had happened. I could only complain secretly to the chairman of my department. Much later we heard from London that the mistake was not really intended as an act of censorship but had taken place in the printing house. We were assured that the deletion of the additional questions on Marxism was a printing error rather than a deliberate policy decision. Perhaps it was.

After the examination was over I looked at the papers and then dispatched them for authoritative grading in London. A period of waiting ensued until London returned its verdict on the students at Makerere. A similar procedure was followed at the other overseas branches of the University of London and at Fourah Bay College in Sierra Leone, an extension of the University of Durham.

As closely governed as the British African universities were, French African institutions were even more intimately tied to their parent universities. For example, French students could attend the University of Dakar in Senegal as part of their program of study, and French professors often moved back and forth between universities in Paris or Bordeaux and Dakar. Indeed, the overwhelming number of professors at Dakar were Frenchmen.

Integration with the metropolitan system deeply affected the priorities of African scholars. In West Africa, Greek, Latin, and the history of Greece and Rome formed the core of the humanities. For many years no African language, not even Arabic, could be studied at the university level. As long as the University College at Ibadan in Nigeria maintained formal ties with the University of London, three of its seven one-subject honors schools were in the classics.[3] At Makerere University in Uganda, even after independence, English was the only language taught. Later the university added French and German, followed experimentally by Russian. All this occurred before any action was taken toward teaching an indigenous Ugandan language, or Swahili (which is widely understood in Uganda and throughout much of eastern Africa), or Arabic (the most important language of Uganda's neighbors in the Nile Valley).

Recently, African linguistics has been introduced as a subject at Makerere University. Students can study the technicalities of Bantu linguistic structure, but the teaching of African languages or African literature in indigenous languages is still, at best, an aspiration rather than an accomplished fact.

Louvanium University in Kinshasa, Zaire, originally affiliated with Louvain in Belgium, was an early exception to this pattern in that it incorporated courses in African languages and culture. Students at Louvanium were at least introduced to the history, literature, philosophy, and psychology of Africa. In addition, Louvanium offered a course of study in the Faculty of Philosophy and Letters, called *Philologies africaines,* based substantially on the study of African languages and cultures. Belgium's aspiration to make colonial education practical and relevant, and its missionaries' desire to produce African clergy versed in African cultural ways, contributed to cultural relevance at Louvanium. But Louvanium was by no means completely independent of metropolitan standards. The Faculty of Philosophy and Letters, for example, continued to require a *diplôme homologué d'humanités gréco-latines* as a university admissions requirement.

What is astonishing about this indifference to African languages is that so many black intellectuals and scholars continue to regard it as justified. Exhortations to pay more attention to African languages, to build systematically vocabularies for certain new areas of national life such as the law courts, parliament, and scientific research centers, and to integrate them more fully into educational systems, have often encountered either silent skepticism or outright derision among many black intellectuals and scholars.

Also strikingly absent from most African education systems is the study of African music. Because song and dance are domains of leisure in Europe, African educational institutions have treated African song and dance as if they were similarly divorced from work and productivity. But in fact these pursuits play an important social role in African societies.[4]

While industrialized countries worry about inflation and recession, agricultural communities worry about floods or drought. In times of famine there is always the danger of bitter jealousies and acrimony as families compete for meager resources. Songs foster economic solidarity where the need to share what is available is compelling. Communities need to reassert the importance of their collective identity, and they often turn to song and dance not merely in quest of cheerfulness or in pursuit of morale under trying circumstances but also to emphasize the constraints needed to remain a community.

Dance and song in a highly oral society also have significant functions in the socialization of the young. In all countries economic socialization involves teaching children values and skills necessary for their society's economic survival and emphasizes the need to serve the family. In Africa, proverbs and songs are the devices which enable the young to memorize lessons of social commitment and service and to remember with awe the hazards of disloyalty to kinsmen and ancestors.

Europe's colonization of Africa resulted in the partial demise of African dance patterns. Many schools were started by missionaries and others who regarded African dance as primitive and sexually suggestive, leading to sin and collective orgies. Schoolchildren were thus discouraged from experimenting with their own dance heritage. As adults, educated Africans moved away from traditional dance in favor of imported varieties of ballroom dancing and, later, rock and roll. Traditional dance lost the respect of Africans as they became Westernized.

In the universities, both social scientists and specialists in the arts have appeared to be supremely indifferent to this aspect of African experience. University systems in much of Africa have no provision at all for the study of African music. Even at universities in Ghana, Senegal, and Nigeria, where African dance has achieved new respectability, the sociology of African music has not yet been adequately integrated into an effective teaching program. This fundamental feature of African cultural life is taken seriously only by departments of theater arts at such universities as Ife in Nigeria and Dar es Salaam in Tanzania. Such departments are small and influence only a handful of the next generation of educated Africans.

What has happened in the study of music and languages, as in other areas of university content and structure, is that African systems of values have been distorted. Like commercial multinational corporations, universities have responded faithfully to decision-makers in Europe; they have used the metropole as the ultimate reference point. Like the multinationals, the universities have been engaged in a kind of commerce. They have sold cultural goods to a new African market—goods marked "made in Europe."

THE LINK BETWEEN CULTURAL AND ECONOMIC DEPENDENCY

During the colonial period the most immediate goal for Western education in Africa was to produce manpower suited to Western needs. But an equally important goal was to expand the market for Western consumer goods. The significance of an African university for commercial multinationals lay precisely in these two areas: producing appropriate manpower and redefining the market through acculturation. Let us take each of these in turn.

In the earlier stages of the history of Western education in Africa, colonial administration and expatriate companies needed lower-level manpower. By the 1930s in much of British Africa, young Africans with Cambridge School Certificates were in great demand for jobs as bank clerks, junior customs officials, assistant managers, government administrators, police cadets, teachers, and church novices.

By the 1940s some forward-looking companies were already seeking Africans for lower-level managerial roles, but the educational systems did not always keep pace with these demands. When I completed secondary school in Mombasa, Kenya, in 1948, my British headmaster found me a job with a Dutch multinational corporation. My Dutch employers wanted to train me to be a submanager, but at that time I had no more than a Cambridge School Certificate, Grade III. After experimenting for two months, my employers decided that I possessed neither sufficient Western education for rapid training as a submanager nor the maturity and experience to compensate for this deficiency. With apparent reluctance, the Dutch multinational sacked its young African protégé. My experience illustrates that as the more sensitive expatriate firms began to search for indigenous manpower, they wanted employees educated in the Western style. The higher the position, the higher the level of Western education required. Before long the highest managerial positions would require at minimum a bachelor's degree.

Ironically, the importance of Western education for Western investment in Africa grew with the development of African nationalism. Western education helped to stimulate local nationalism, and nationalists demanded the establishment of local plants. Once the plants were established, the need for manpower increased. Multinational companies in Africa, however, discovered early the advantages of employing indigenous managers who understood local markets and could buffer local hostilities. Nationalism demanded the Africanization of as many jobs as possible, and multinationals were compelled to appoint local people to higher and higher staff levels. Increasingly, faces behind managerial desks were African and members of boards of directors included coopted Africans who lent legitimacy to the companies' operations. Local, Westernized manpower, difficult to find in the 1940s, became abundant because of the success of African universities in socializing local personnel to Western ways. In successfully performing this task, the universities have served to consolidate economic dependence.

The second area linking cultural and commercial corporations was the expansion of the market for Western consumer goods. Canned foodstuffs, wristwatches, soap, cosmetics, cassettes and tape recorders, ready-made clothing, cigarettes, jam and marmalade, radio and television sets, detergents, lawnmowers, automobiles, and linens—some of these consumer goods were produced locally, but even many local products were linked to multinational companies. There were also African "middle countries" such as Kenya which attracted expatriate industries coveting regional markets in Africa. Goods produced in Kenya were exported to Tanzania, Uganda, and Zambia.

The growth of a market for Western consumer goods partly depended on the spread of Western values. Western tastes and lifestyles were disseminated through advertisements, magazines, films, television, and personal example. But central to the success of Westernization was the socialization of a solid core of educated and semieducated Africans, at once followers of the West and leaders of their own societies. Some aspects of African culture reinforced in local leaders the temptation to emulate the West. Because African culture has been traditionally collectivist and oriented around face-to-face encounters, prestige and the applause of kinsmen are exceptionally important to many Africans.[5] In an oral society where communication could not rely on mass-circulation newspapers or magazines, fame was established through a combination of ostentation, patronage, and hospitality. As a European life-style became part of the measure of social prestige, the market for Western consumer goods widened, with the more educated Africans setting the pace. While consumption of such excessive luxuries as Mercedes Benzes and imported mineral water may be declining, there are other aspects of the Western life-style that Africa's educated elite will not readily relinquish.

Irving Gershenberg, formerly of the department of economics at Makerere University in Uganda, has framed the situation aptly in a discussion of the impact of multinational firms on Uganda:

> A very impressive feature of the relationship between the expatriate multinational firm and the economically underdeveloped country is that the multinational has been able to socialize the indigenous to the norms and values of the metropolitan center. What this means in practice is that Black Ugandans are taught to accept the notion that they should act and behave like well-bred Englishmen—these become their significant reference-groups.[6]

As producers of Westernized manpower and markets for the multinationals, African universities have played an important role.

TOWARD CULTURAL IMPORT-SUBSTITUTION

In the face of all these aspects of dependency, hard new thinking is required. Clearly, the university is in Africa to stay. So is modernization. The process of modernization has been aided by the establishment of Western-type educational institutions, including the university. The question arises once again whether modernization can be decolonized without being destroyed.

To a large extent, this question is what development is all about. One could indeed define development in the Third World as modernization minus dependency. That is the challenging equation that African societies face. The changes that improve living standards, reduce infant mortality, curtail ignorance and disease, and enhance knowledge of human beings and their environments are ones imperialism helped to foster. These changes deserve to survive. But those aspects of modernization that reduce local autonomy, erode local self-confidence, and undermine the capacity of the Third World to contribute to a genuinely shared world culture should be eliminated. In time, the concept of modernization should become distinct from the concept of Westernization.

Like commercial multinational corporations, universities must reexamine what they import and determine the extent to which substitutions can reduce dependency. The university, a cultural corporation dealing in skills and values, must ask itself: Which skills need to be developed locally and which values should the educational system sustain? Two concepts of relevance are pertinent to this reexamination: practical relevance focusing on issues of skills and cultural relevance relating to issues of values. While the two dimensions are intertwined, they can be distinguished analytically.

Debates about practical relevance in African universities have been concerned with whether universities are producing appropriate personnel for the processes of economic and social development. Is there enough emphasis on training people skilled in modern agriculture? Are universities sensitive to the need for veterinarians in pastoral regions? Do they emphasize Shakespeare more than rural development?

Many African universities started as liberal-arts colleges, not as training centers for skilled manpower. Part of their prejudice against technical courses was inherited from the metropolitan powers themselves. In much of Europe, practical courses at the university level were latecomers and to the present day have often been placed in separate educational institutions. Universities were reserved for the study of high culture, for the pursuit of pure scholarship. In Africa, the University College of Ibadan in Nigeria offered courses in Latin, Greek, Christian Doctrine, and Medieval European History long before it recognized the need for courses in engineering, economics, geology, public administration, or even teacher training. Makerere in Uganda existed for more than forty years before it considered the idea of teaching engineering, forestry, or veterinary science.

In developing the University of Nigeria at Nsukka, Nnamdi Azikiwe used the land-grant college model, which encouraged the study of applied subjects. In Ghana, Kwame Nkrumah helped to promote Kumasi as a major center of technological training. But such advances have resulted much more often as a result of pressures from African governments than as a result of initiatives from within the ranks of academic communities. The problem of forging practically relevant education also involves the question of emphasis in the applied departments and faculties that already exist. What types of personnel should a medical school produce, for example? Graham Bull, a distinguished British professor of medicine, stated the problem in a West African medical journal in 1960, the year of Nigeria's independence:

> Expenditure should be mainly in the field of public health. Curative medicine is a luxury which must be dispensed very sparingly. . . . Public opinion is sufficiently ill-informed to prefer a hospital to a piped water supply, although the latter will probably save ten times as many lives. . . . British and American medical schools do not provide a suitable curriculum for doctors who are to work in Nigeria and other tropical countries. . . .[7]

Since 1960, medical schools in African universities have indeed developed departments of preventive medicine. But in each school, preventive medicine is only one of a dozen or more departments, each jealous of its separate identity. Some interdepartmental collaboration and much sound research on tropical diseases do take place, but the emphasis on preventive medicine remains weaker than African circumstances dictate.

A related question is whether African medical schools should only produce doctors who are traditionally trained and who can be employed anywhere in the world, or whether a more limited training program should be designed to produce large numbers of paramedical practitioners for rural clinics. Traditionally, most African universities have been reluctant to "dilute" their standards. Even the idea of different types of medical degrees meets considerable resistance from the University of Zambia in Lusaka to the University of Zaire in Kinshasa.

As for schools of engineering or faculties of technology, there is still a marked lack of interest in the phenomenon of intermediate technology. Such schools could profitably examine experiments in other developing countries using small-scale, labor-intensive technologies for their applicability in Africa. But once again, the compulsion to imitate the metropolitan model has prevented much progress in this area.

Performance has been even more deficient in the case of the humanities. We have referred to the insensitivity to African languages, music, dance, and, more generally, the oral tradition.

Changes are taking place in some areas. Most African historians now agree that oral traditions are proper material for historical reconstruction. Interpretations of the African past using linguistic evidence, oral tradition, and archaeological findings have introduced important breakthroughs in African historiography. While departments of literature have begun to follow historians in studying oral literature, their performance has been less impressive.

In the social sciences there have been changes in *what* is studied but not in *how* it is studied. More and more courses on Africa and on the economics of development have been initiated, but few methodological innovations comparable to the use of oral tradition in historiography have been introduced. Some academic reformers have substituted Marxian approaches to political science and economics for the standard Western analyses, yet Marxism, though radical, is also a Western tradition, and its uncritical invocation by African scholars reflects a form of residual intellectual dependence. Until African scholars drastically change foreign methodologies to fit the conditions of African societies, they cannot move much farther along the path of cultural import-substitution.[8]

Many continue to blame all African troubles on outside forces and at the same time they continue to seek solutions from the outside. As the Ugandan social philosopher, Okot p'Bitek, put it:

> We blame colonialists and imperialists and neo-colonialists; we blame Communists both from Moscow and Peking, and send their representatives packing. We blame the Americans and the CIA. . . . Another, but contradictory phenomenon is the belief that the solution to our social ills can be imported. Foreign "experts" and peace-corps swarm the country like white ants. Economic "advisers," military "advisers" and security "advisers" surround our leaders.[9]

Okot p'Bitek criticizes these attitudes and argues, in contrast, "that most of our social ills are indigenous, that the primary sources of our problems are native. They are rooted in the social set-up, and most effective solutions cannot be imported, but must be the result of deliberate reorganization of the resources available for tackling specific issues."[10]

My own view lies between p'Bitek's position and the attitudes he criticizes. The worst form of cultural dependency is indeed that dual dependency that blames all misfortunes on external forces and seeks all solutions from outside. Many African problems are indeed indigenous, but there are others that have been created by external forces. Some solutions to those African problems require external cooperation or changes in the total world environment, but many solutions can be found within.

The reluctance to transform educational systems to enable African societies to take greater part in solving their own problems has been one of the most obstinate aspects of cultural dependency.

THREE STRATEGIES FOR DEVELOPMENT

If true development for Africa requires the decolonization of modernization, then three major strategies are needed. The first strategy concerns the domestication of modernity, a bid to relate modernization more firmly to local cultural and economic needs. The second involves the diversification of the cultural content of modernity. Under this approach, the foreign reference group for an African institution expands beyond the West to include other non-African civilizations. The third strategy is perhaps the most ambitious: It involves an attempt by Africa to counterpenetrate Western civilization itself. The first two strategies can be implemented rapidly; the third requires more patient efforts.

The Strategy of Domestication

In the very process of producing educated manpower, creating new forms of stratification and accelerating Westernization and modernization, African educational institutions have been major instruments through which the Western world has affected and changed the African universe. Universities have been virtually defined as institutions for the promotion of Western civilization.

In order to change this definition, African societies must fundamentally influence their educational systems. It is not enough for an African university to send a traveling theater to villages to perform a play by Shakespeare or even one by the Nigerian playwright Wole Soyinka. Nor is it sufficient to establish extramural departments and extension services, however valuable these may be for increasing skills and expanding social awareness in rural communities. Like a number of professors at Makerere, I traveled many miles on hard roads to address students at rural schools and local gatherings on the implications of public policies in Uganda. But while such endeavors help expand the experiences of people in the villages, the social impact is still one-sided.

The first task toward decolonizing modernity is to enable the local society's influence on university policy to balance that of the West. In concrete terms, how can this be realized? To domesticate African educational systems, three major areas must be reexamined: university admissions requirements and their implications for primary and secondary curricula, criteria for faculty recruitment, and university organization.

University admissions requirements should be reformed to give new weight to indigenous subjects. Admissions should formally require demonstrated competence in an African language just as some faculties used to require Latin for entry. Some knowledge of African history, literature, and social and cultural anthropology should also be required for university entrance, and rigorous examinations in these subjects should promote their teaching at the primary and secondary levels. Similarly, African dance and music should be given a new legitimacy in pre-university education, regardless of the sensitivities of the missionaries in power.

Commitment to indigenous cultures will also affect criteria for faculty recruitment at the university. Must all teachers have formal degrees or should there be areas of expertise where faculty could be appointed on the basis of other criteria? For example, there are uncertified specialists in African languages who not only speak those languages but also understand their linguistic properties. I know one such specialist from Kenya who for many years taught Swahili in an American university with a sophistication unmatched by many who have degrees in that subject. In the United States he could never hope to receive tenure or even obtain a rank above instructor since he did not possess an advanced degree. When he returned to Kenya, the university there applied similar standards and would not consider him for appointment as a professor. Yet the same university would appoint a British Swahilist with a formal degree but less intimate knowledge of certain African languages than the Kenyan had already demonstrated over several decades.

What all this means is that there is a case for broadening the recruitment criteria to include both formal degrees and, where appropriate, demonstrable indigenous skills. Faculties of sociology could include indigenous specialists in oral traditions; departments of medicine could have courses in the uses of natural herbs in treating disease and, as part of the training of rural doctors, might even examine the medical implications of sorcery and witchcraft. Departments of history, literature, musicology, philosophy, and religious studies could consider recruiting faculty with skills other than those honored in Western institutions.

Furthermore, the structure and organization of the university should be examined in light of Africa's needs. In addition to the traditional Western disciplines, there is a case for having on the one hand a School of Rural Studies, encompassing agriculture, anthropology, and rural preventive medicine, and, on the other, a School of Urban Studies, sensitized to the link between city and country, labor migrations, ethnic associations, criminology, and urban preventive medicine. Other possibilities include schools of Oral Tradition and Historiography, Languages and Oral Literature, and Religion and Witchcraft.

More generally, the university's role in society should be examined. In Tanzania, Julius Nyerere has recognized the link between a country's educational system and its people's economic ambitions and therefore has sought to modify drastically the Tanzanian educational system. The University of Dar es Salaam is being reorganized to change the type of manpower it produces and to transform the type of values it transmits. Changes in admissions policies, such as assessing motivation as well as intellectual competence, are scheduled for trial during the 1975–76 academic year. Class sizes are already being determined on the basis of planned manpower projections. While it is too early to predict the final outcome of the experiments, Tanzania has clearly recognized the need to domesticate its cultural multinational corporation.

The Strategy of Diversification

The second strategy for decolonizing modernity involves diversifying the cultural content of modernity. This approach rests partly on the assumption that just as economically it is a greater risk to be dependent on one country than on many, so also culturally one foreign benefactor is more constraining than many. To be owned by one person is to be enslaved outright; to be owned by many masters, who can be played against one another, may be the beginning of freedom. In terms of culture, reliance on one external reference group is outright dependency; reliance on a diversity of external civilizations may be the beginning of autonomy.

It is not enough, however, for the universities to combine African traditions with those from the West. A dual process must occur: increased Africanization, as the society is permitted to reciprocate the impact of the university; and increased internationalization, as the foreign component in the university becomes less Eurocentric and more attentive to other aspects of the total human heritage.

It is more important than ever that African universities take seriously the cultures and experiments of other civilizations. The educational system should focus not only on Europe and Africa but also on Indian, Chinese, and, most important, Islamic civilizations. Although Arabic is the most widely spoken language on the African continent, it has received little attention in African curricula south of the Sahara, even in those countries that border Arabic-speaking areas or have large numbers of Muslim citizens.

As for Chinese studies, interest in Mao Tse-tung is evident in some political science departments these days, but Confucius is still ignored. The fact that Mao Tse-tung denounced Confucius does not mean Africans should not study Confucius, along with Thomas Jefferson and John Locke. A conscious effort to learn more about what is done in China and to understand its relevance to African needs could contribute important practical knowledge.

Mao's China has much to teach about intermediate technology, intermediate medicine, and new methods of agriculture, as well as about ideology and economic organization.

Cultural diversification will involve instituting new courses and requirements throughout the educational system. At the secondary level, classes should be introduced on the history of science: Dependency among young African school children arises, in part, from their awe of Western science. The prestige of the Western world, in a continent which is very conscious of prestige, derives disproportionately from Western leadership in science and technology. So great has that leadership been for the last three hundred years that Westernism and science are almost interchangeable in the perception of some young Africans.

In reaction to Western scientific preeminence, some Africans have sought refuge in negritude as a glorification of a nonscientific civilization. Leopold Senghor, leader of the negritude movement and president of Senegal, has emphasized, instead of science, Africans' spiritual and affective understanding of their environment, their "emotive attitude toward the world." [11] Other Africans, dazzled and lured by scientism, have sought answers in Marxism, partly because it seems to offer Africans the chance of rebelling against the West without ceasing to be scientific. The negritudist rebels against the scientific West by idealizing his own heritage; the African Marxist rebels against the West by embracing an alternative "scientism." Disagreements between these positions should be reflected in the curricula of African schools.

But at least as fundamental is the issue of how much Western science owes to other civilizations. From the Indus Valley to ancient Egypt, from imperial China to medieval Islam, the West has found intellectual and scientific benefactors. Very little of this history is communicated to young children in African schools. Their sense of awe about the West becomes a foundation for subsequent intellectual dependency. African secondary-school curricula should contain a compulsory paper which places science in its proper historical context, reveals the diversity of the human heritage, and breaks the dangerous myth of a Western scientific monopoly.

Another change that should be introduced into primary and secondary schools would require each African child to learn a minimum of three languages—one European, one Asian, and one African. The era of learning multiple European languages, some ancient and some modern, while other linguistic heritages are ignored, should come rapidly to an end.

At the university level a course on "Great Systems of Thought," with examples drawn from the range of human cultures, should be required of all undergraduates in the humanities and social sciences. All undergraduates, regardless of field, should take either an African or an Asian language at an advanced level. In addition, they should take a course on a Third World civilization, preferably but not necessarily linked to the language of their choice.

University reforms will require a fundamental change in attitude for all departments of African universities—away from excessive Eurocentrism and toward both increased Africanization and increased internationalization. This broader focus could change the African university into a truly multicultural corporation.

The Strategy of Counterpenetration

Domestication of modernity and diversification of Africa's cultural content will not be fully achieved until Africa itself can influence Western civilization. There are reformers in Africa who urge only domestication, some of those to the extent of espousing cultural autarky. But withdrawal from world culture would result in the continuing marginality of Africa in global affairs in a world that has shrunk to the point where many decisions can affect the entire human race. It would be futile for Africa to attempt a strategy of withdrawal or total disengagement. Modernity is here to stay; the task is to decolonize it. A world culture is evolving fast; the task is to save it from excessive Eurocentrism.[12]

Here the strategy of counterpenetration becomes vital. If African civilizations have been so permeated by Western culture, can they in turn affect Western thought and values?

The West has not completely escaped Africa's cultural influence. It has been asserted that the first piece of African carving to reach Europe arrived on a Portuguese trading ship in 1504.

African workmanship in leather and probably gold reached Europe much earlier.[13] Africa's impact on jazz and related forms of music through its sons and daughters exported to the New World as slaves has already been documented. So has the influence of African tales on the literature of other lands, particularly the southern United States and the Caribbean.[14]

But when all is said and done, Africa's cultural influence on the West has been far more modest than the West's influence on Africa. The asymmetry will continue for at least the rest of this century, but the balance of cultural trade can begin to be restored. Africa will need allies in its efforts at counterpenetration. The continent's most natural allies consist of the Arab world and the Black Diaspora. Arabs share a continent with black people. Indeed, the majority of Arabs and the bulk of Arab land are within Africa. The organization of African Unity includes both black and Arab states. It may be possible to exploit these circumstances to the advantage of both peoples.

Arab oil producers have already started economic counterpenetration of the West. Their activities range from buying real estate in England to controlling banks in the United States, from acquiring shares in West German industry to extending loans to Italy. As a result, the West, while eager for petroleum dollars, is anxious about their long-term consequences for Western economic independence.[15] There is some risk that the Arab oil producers might start playing an imperial role in Africa. They have begun to invest in multinational corporations operating in Africa. But with the risk of a new imperialism comes an opportunity for a Third World alliance. Once again economic power and cultural influence might be linked.

The rise of the Organization of Petroleum Exporting Countries (OPEC) in world affairs, however transient, may herald the political resurrection of Islam. Presently, two-thirds of the membership of OPEC—that portion which controls more than two-thirds of OPEC's oil reserves—is Muslim. Before the end of this century African Muslims may outnumber Arabs and will be making a strong bid for shared leadership of Islam. While money for Islamic counterpenetration would probably come from Arab oil producers, Islamic counterpenetration in the United States could be, in part, a process of transmitting African indigenous perspectives. It would not be surprising if, within the next decade, black African Muslims establish schools and hospitals in Harlem and preach Islam to black Americans.

Black Americans are at least as important as Arab money for African cultural entry into the West. As citizens of the richest and mightiest country in the twentieth century, they form, after Nigeria, the largest black nation in the world. As black Americans become more affluent, as they confront fewer social and political barriers, and as they participate more vigorously in the intellectual and creative world, their influence is bound to rise.

African universities can play a critical role in building the alliance with black Americans. Through black America they could reach the other Western nations. African universities would do well to encourage more black Americans to study in Africa. Here again, Arab money could be used for scholarships. South American and Caribbean blacks similarly could be encouraged to attend African universities. We should remember that counterpenetration will take longer than diversification. Counterpenetration would require that Africans possess the economic and technical resources to develop innovations that the rest of the world could use. If Africans can build a genuine partnership between indigenous cultures and educational systems, stimulated by the input of foreign cultural, intellectual, and technical skills, they may become leaders, not just followers, of academic trends.

The full maturity of African education will come only when Africa develops a capacity to innovate independently. That independence will require Africa to attempt three great tasks: balancing the weight of Western influence with its own culture, permitting non-Western civilizations to reveal their secrets to African researchers and teachers, and transforming its own educational and intellectual world to make genuine creativity possible. Only then will Africa be on its way toward meeting that elusive but compelling imperative—not only to decolonize modernity, nor even merely to participate in it, but also to help define modernity for future generations.

Notes

1. For a general discussion of imperialism, see George H. Nadel, ed., *Imperialism and Colonialism* (London: Macmillan, 1964); Harrison M. Wright, ed., *The "New Imperialism"* (Boston: D. C. Heath, 1961); Carlton J. H. Hayes, *A Generation of Materialism, 1871–1900* (New York: Harper and Brothers, 1941), pp. 218–28; Joseph A. Schumpeter, *Imperialism and Social Classes*, Heinz Norden, trans., and Paul Sweezy, ed. (New York: A. M. Kelley, 1951).
2. Eric Ashby, *African Universities and Western Tradition* (Cambridge: Harvard University Press, 1964), p. 3.
3. Ibid., p. 38.
4. Judith Lynn Hanna, "African Dance: The Continuity of Change," in *Yearbook of the International Folk Music Council* 5 (1974). I am grateful to Dr. Hanna for allowing me to read her article in typescript.
5. J. Clyde Mitchell and A. L. Epstein, "Occupational Prestige and Social Status among Urban Africans in North Rhodesia," in *Africa*, no. 29 (1959): 34–39. See also Ali A. Mazrui, "The Monarchical Tendency in African Political Culture," in *British Journal of Sociology* 18, no. 3 (1967): 231–50.
6. Irving Gershenberg, "The Impact of Multi-National Corporations on the Process of Development in Less Economically Developed Countries: Commercial Banking in Uganda" (Paper presented at the Conference on Dependence and Development in Africa, 16–18 February 1973). School of International Affairs (Ottawa: Carleton University, 1973), p. 3.
7. Graham M. Bull, "Impressions of a Medical Tour of the Eastern and Western Regions of Nigeria," in *West African Medical Journal*, NS 9 (1960): 139–44.
8. For examples of works that have creatively used Marxist categories, see Samir Amin, "Capitalism and Development in

the Ivory Coast" in *African Politics and Society*, Irving Leonard Markovitz, ed. (New York: Free Press, 1970), pp. 277–88; and Giovanni Arrighi and John S. Saul, *Essays on the Political Economy of Africa* (New York: Monthly Review Press, 1973); E. A. Brett, *Colonialism and Underdevelopment in East Africa* (London: Heinemann, 1972); and Colin Leys, *Underdevelopment in Kenya: The Political Economy of Neo-Colonialism* (London: Heinemann, 1975).

9. Okot p'Bitek, "Indigenous Ills," in *Transition* 7, no. 32 (1967): 47.
10. Ibid.
11. John Reed and Olive Wahe, trans. and ed., *Senghor: Prose and Poetry* (London: Oxford University Press, 1965), p. 34.
12. The Eurocentrism of world culture is discussed with passion and insight by Chinweizu, *The West and the Rest of Us: White Predators, Black Slavers and the African Elite* (New York: Random House, 1975); chaps. 14–16 are particularly relevant to this article. See also Ali A. Mazrui, *World Culture and the Black Experience* (Seattle: University of Washington Press, 1974).
13. Paul Bohannan and Philip Curtin, *Africa and Africans* (New York: Natural History Press, 1971), pp. 97–98.
14. Ibid., p. 82.
15. For a fuller discussion, see Ali A. Mazrui, "The New Interdependence: From Hierarchy to Symmetry," in *The U.S. and World Development: Agenda for Action, 1975*, James W. Howe, ed. (Washington, D.C.: Overseas Development Council, 1975).

Select Bibliography

This bibliography is by no means a complete listing of all available materials concerning education and colonialism. We have attempted to provide a judicious mix of references relating directly to education and the various aspects of colonialism and references relating to the underlying theoretical assumptions of many of the authors of essays in this volume. Our stress has been on current materials, although we have included some older references as well. Most of the references are in the English language. This bibliography is intended to provide a starting point for in-depth reading concerning colonialism and education.

General

BOOKS

Abernathy, David B. *The Political Dilemma of Popular Education: An African Case.* Stanford, Calif.: Stanford University Press, 1969.

Brown, Michael Barratt. *The Economics of Imperialism.* Baltimore, Md.: Penguin, 1974.

Carnoy, Martin. *Education as Cultural Imperialism.* New York: David McKay, 1974.

Chinweizu. *The West and the Rest of Us: White Predators, Black Slavers, and the African Elite.* New York: Random House, 1974.

Clignet, Remi, and Foster, Philip. *The Fortunate Few: A Study of Secondary School Students in the Ivory Coast.* Evanston, Ill:. Northwestern University Press, 1966.

Cockcroft, James; Frank, A. G.; and Johnson, D. *Dependence and Underdevelopment: Latin America's Political Economy.* Garden City, N.Y.: Anchor Books, 1972.

Foster, Philip J. *Education and Social Change in Ghana.* Chicago, Ill.: University of Chicago Press, 1965.

Freire, Paulo. *Pedagogy of the Oppressed.* New York: Herder and Herder, 1970.

Lenin, V. I. *Imperialism: The Highest Stage of Capitalism.* Moscow: Foreign Languages Publishing House, n. d.

Magdoff, Harry. *The Age of Imperialism: The Economics of U.S. Foreign Policy.* New York: Monthly Review Press, 1969.

Shils, Edward. *The Intellectuals and Power and Other Essays.* Chicago, Ill.: University of Chicago Press, 1972.

ARTICLES

Clignet, Remi. "Damned If You Do, Damned If You Don't: The Dilemmas of Colonizer-Colonized Relationships," in *Comparative Education Review* 15 (October 1971): 296–313.

———. "Colonialism and Education" (symposium), in *Comparative Education Review* 15 (June 1971): 113–259.

———. "Decolonization and Education" (symposium), in *Comparative Education Review* 15 (October 1971): 276–317.

Evans, David. "Decolonization: Does the Teacher Have a Role?," in *Comparative Education Review* 15 (October 1971): 276–87.

Galtung, Johan. "A Structural Theory of Imperialism," in *African Review* 1 (April 1972): 93–137.

Traditional Colonialism

BOOKS

Ashby, Eric. *Universities: British, Indian, African.* Cambridge, Mass.: Harvard University Press, 1966.

Basu, Aparna. *The Growth of Education and Political Development in India, 1898–1920.* Delhi: Oxford University Press, 1974.

Battle, Vincent J., and Lyons, Charles H. *Essays in the History of African Education.* New York: Teachers College Press, 1971.

Berman, Edward H. *African Reactions to Missionary Education.* New York: Teachers College Press, 1975.

Brunschwig, Henri. *French Colonialism, 1871–1914: Myths and Realities.* New York: Praeger, 1966.

Curtin, Philip D. *Images of Africa.* Madison, Wisc.: University of Wisconsin Press, 1964.

Fanon, Frantz. *Black Skins, White Masks: The Experiences of a Black Man in a White World.* New York: Grove Press, 1967.

———. *The Wretched of the Earth.* New York: Grove Press, 1968.

Furnivall, J. S. *Educational Progress in Southeast Asia.* New York: Institute for Pacific Affairs, 1943.

Girardet, Raoul. *L'Idée Coloniale en France, 1871–1962.* Paris: La Table Ronde, 1972.

Hardy, Georges. *Une Conquête Morale: L'Ênsignement en AOF.* Paris: Libraire Armand Colin, 1917.

Jones, Thomas Jesse. *Education in Africa.* New York: Phelps-Stokes Fund, 1922.

Lyons, Charles H. *To Wash an Aethiop White.* New York: Teachers College Press, 1975.

Mannoni, O. *Prospero and Caliban: The Psychology of Colonialism.* New York: Praeger, 1964.

Marr, David. *Vietnamese Anti-Colonialism, 1858–1925.* Berkeley, Calif.: University of California Press, 1971.

Memmi, Albert. *The Colonizer and the Colonized.* Boston, Mass.: Beacon Press, 1965.

Murray, A. Victor. *School in the Bush.* London: Longmans, Green, 1929.

Osborne, Milton E. *The French Presence in Cochinchina and Cambodia: Rule and Response (1859–1905).* Ithaca, N.Y.: Cornell University Press, 1969.

Roberts, Stephen. *The History of French Colonial Policy, 1870–1925.* 2 vols. London: P. S. King, 1929.

Robinson, Ronald; Gallagher, John; and Denny, Alice. *Africa and the Victorians: The Climax of Imperialism.* New York: St. Martin's Press, 1961.

Roff, William R. *The Origins of Malay Nationalism.* New Haven, Conn.: Yale University Press, 1967.

Tardits, Claude. *Porto-Novo: Les Nouvelles Générations Afri-*

caines entre leurs Traditions et L'Occident. Paris: Mouton, 1958.

Van Neil, Robert. *The Emergence of the Modern Indonesian Elite.* The Hague: W. Van Hoeve, 1960.

Wise, Colin G. *A History of Education in British West Africa.* London: Longmans, Green, 1956.

ARTICLES

Asiwagu, A. I. "Formal Education in Western Yourobaland, 1889–1960: A Comparison of French and British Colonial Systems," in *Comparative Education Review* 19 (October 1975): 434–50.

Benson, T. G. "The Jeanes Schools and the Education of the East African Native," in *Journal of the Royal African Society* 35 (October 1936): 418–31.

Berman, Edward H. "American Influence on African Education: The Role of the Phelps-Stokes Fund's Education Commissions," in *Comparative Education Review* 15 (June 1971): 132–45.

Bitek, Okot P. "African Culture in the Era of Foreign Rule," in *Thought Practice Journal* 2, no. 1 (1975): 53–66.

Botchwerk, Kwesi. "On Marx's Attitude to Colonialism—A Short Rejoinder," in *Africa Report* 4, no. 3 (1974): 473–80.

Bunche, Ralph J. "French Educational Policy in Togo and Dahomey," in *Journal of Negro Education* 3 (January 1934): 69–97.

Capelle, Jean. "Education in French West Africa," in *Overseas Education* 21 (October 1949): 956–72.

Clignet, R., and Foster, P. "French and British Colonial Education in Africa," in *Comparative Education Review* 8 (October 1964): 191–98.

Crouzet, P. "Education in the French Colonies," in International Institute of Teachers College, Columbia University, *Education Yearbook,* 1931, pp. 267–566.

D'Souza, D. Henry. "External Influences on the Development of Educational Policy in British Tropical Africa from 1923 to 1939," in *African Studies Report* 17 (September 1975): 35–44.

Gilbert, Irene. "The Indian Academic Profession: The Origins of a Tradition of Subordination," in *Minerva* 10 (July 1972): 384–411.

Jones, V. "The Content of History Syllabuses in Northern Nigeria in the Early Colonial Period," in *West African Journal of Education* 9 (October 1965): 145–48.

Kay, Stafford, and Nystrom, Bradley. "Education and Colonialism in Africa: An Annotated Bibliography," in *Comparative Education Review* 15 (June 1971): 240–59.

Kelly, Gail P. "Education and Participation in Nationalist Groups: An Exploratory Study of the Indochinese Communist Party and the VNQDD, 1929–31," in *Comparative Education Review* 15 (June 1971): 227–36.

Kinsey, David C. "Efforts for Educational Synthesis under Colonial Rule: Egypt and Tunisia," in *Comparative Education Review* 15 (June 1971): 172–87.

Labouret, Henri. "L'Education des indigènes: methods britanniques et françaises," in *L'Afrique Françaises* 38 (October 1928): 404–11.

McVey, Ruth T. "Taman Siswa and the Indonesian National Awakening," in *Indonesia* 4 (October 1967): 128–49.

Mumford, W. Bryant. "Malangali Schools," in *Africa* 3 (July 1930): 265–90.

Peshkin, Alan. "Educational Reform in Colonial and Independent Africa," in *African Affairs* 64 (July 1965): 210–16.

Radcliffe, David. "Ki Hadjar Dewantara and the Taman Siswa Schools: Notes on an Extra-Colonial Theory of Education," in *Comparative Education Review* 15 (June 1971): 202–18.

Schwartz, Karl. "Filipino Education and Spanish Colonialism: Toward an Autonomous Perspective," in *Comparative Education Review* 15 (June 1971): 202–18.

Vu Duc Bang. "The Dong Kinh Free School Movement, 1907–1908," in Walter F. Vella, *Aspects of Vietnamese History*. Honolulu: Asian Studies at Hawaii 8 (1973): 30–96.

Yates, Barbara. "African Reactions to Education: The Congolese Case," in *Comparative Education Review* 15 (June 1971): 158–71.

———. "The Triumph and Failure of Mission Vocational Education in Zaire, 1879–1908," in *Comparative Education Review* 20 (June 1976): 193–208.

Internal Colonialism

BOOKS

Fuchs, Estelle, and Havighurst, Robert J. *To Live on This Earth.* New York: Doubleday, 1972.

Szaz, Margaret. *Education and the American Indian: The Road to Self-Determination, 1928 to 1973.* Albuquerque, N.M.: University of New Mexico Press, 1974.

ARTICLES

Epstein, Erwin. "Education and Peruindad: Internal Colonialism in the Peruvian Highlands," in *Comparative Education Review* 15 (June 1971): 188–201.

Hurstfield, Jennifer. "The Educational Experiences of Mexican Americans: 'Cultural Pluralism' or 'Internal Colonialism'?," in *Oxford Review of Education* 1, no. 2 (1971): 137–49.

Peterson, Patti M. "Colonialism and Education: The Case of the Afro-American," in *Comparative Education Review* 15 (June 1971): 146–58.

Thomas, Robert. "Colonialism: Classic and Internal," in *New University Thought* 4 (Winter 1966–67): 37–44.

Neocolonialism

BOOKS

Altbach, Philip G. *Indian Publishing: An Analysis.* New York and Delhi: Oxford University Press, 1975.

Benveniste, Guy. *The Politics of Expertise.* Berkeley, Calif.: Glendessary, 1972.

Bodenheimer, S. J. *The Ideology of Developmentalism: The American Paradigm–Surrogate for Latin American Studies.* Beverly Hills, Calif.: Sage, 1971.

Cerych, L. *Problems of Aid to Education in Developing Countries.* New York: Praeger, 1965.

Dumont, René. *False Start in Africa*. New York: Praeger, 1966.

Hayter, T. *Aid as Imperialism*. Baltimore, Md.: Penguin, 1971.

Hensman, C. R. *Rich against Poor: The Reality of Aid*. Baltimore, Md.: Pelican Books, 1975.

Institute of the Black World. *Education and Black Struggle: Notes from the Colonized World*. Cambridge, Mass.: Harvard Educational Review, monograph no. 2, 1974.

Mende, Tibor. *From Aid to Recolonization: Lessons of a Failure*. New York: Pantheon, 1973.

Nairn, Ronald C. *International Aid to Thailand: The New Colonialism?* New Haven, Conn.: Yale University Press, 1966.

Nelson, Joan M. *Aid, Influence and Foreign Policy*. New York: Macmillan, 1968.

Nkrumah, Kwame. *Neo-Colonialism: The Last Stage of Imperialism*. New York: International Publishers, 1965.

Renner, Richard (ed.). *Universities in Transition: The U.S. Influence in Latin American Education*. Gainesville, Fla.: University of Florida, Center for Latin American Studies, 1973.

Saberwal, Satish (ed.). *Towards a Cultural Policy*. Delhi: Vikas, 1975.

Sandoval, R. P. *Dependency and Education in Colombian Underdevelopment*. Madison, Wisc.: Land Tenure Center, University of Wisconsin, 1973.

Schwab, Morton. *The Political Relationship between France and Her Former Colonies in the Sub-Saharan Regions since 1958*. Atlanta, Ga.: Emory University Press, 1968.

Stabler, Ernest. *Education since Uhuru: Kenya's Schools*. Middletown, Conn.: Wesleyan University Press, 1969.

Van den Berghe, Pierre. *Power and Privilege in an African University*. Cambridge, Mass.: Schenkman, 1973.

Ward, F. Champion (ed.). *Education and Development Reconsidered*. New York: Praeger, 1974.

ARTICLES

"Academic Colonialism: A Symposium on the Influences Which Destroy Intellectual Independence," in *Seminar* (New Delhi), no. 112 (December 1968): 10–43.

Adams, Bert N. "Africanization and Academic Imperialism: A

Study in Planned Change and Inertia," in *East African Journal* (May 1972), pp. 23–27.

Aknyemi, A. B. "The Organization of African Unity–Perception of Neo-Colonialism," in *Africa Quarterly* 14, nos. 1–2 (1974): 32–52.

Altbach, Philip G. "Neocolonialism and Education," in *Teachers College Record* 72 (May 1971): 543–58.

———. "Literary Colonialism: Books in the Third World," in *Harvard Educational Review* 45 (May 1975): 226–36.

Ankomah, Kori. "The Colonial Legacy and African Unrest," in *Science and Society* 34 (Summer 1970): 129–45.

Coussy, Jean. "Adjusting Economics Curricula to African Needs," in *International Social Science Journal* 21, no. 3 (1969): 393–405.

Elder, Joseph W. "The Decolonization of Educational Culture: The Case of India," in *Comparative Education Review* 15 (October 1971): 288–95.

Gillett, Margaret. "Western Academic Role Concepts in Ethiopian University," in *Comparative Education Reivew* 7 (October 1963): 149–62.

Goertzel, Ted. "American Imperialism and the Brazilian Student Movement," in *Youth and Society* 6 (December 1974): 123–50.

Kiven, Tuntung P. "Pseudo Politics and Pseudo Scholarship (in Africa)," in *Transition* 8, no. 4 (1972): 26–34.

Kunene, Daniel P. "African Vernacular Writing: An Essay on Self-Devaluation," in *African Social Research* 9 (June 1970): 639–59.

Lorimer, James. "Canadian Textbooks and the American 'Knowledge' Industry," in *This Magazine Is about Schools* 5 (Summer 1971): 47–63.

Newbry, Burton C. "AID Education Efforts: A Critique," in *Journal of Developing Areas* 3 (July 1969): 489–98.

Paulston, Rolland G. "United States Educational Intervention in Peru," in *Paedagogica Historica* 11, no. 2 (1971): 426–51.

Pieris, Ralph. "The Implantation of Sociology in Asia," in *International Social Science Journal* 21, no. 3 (1969): 433–44.

Scherz-Garcia, Luis. "Some Disfunctional Aspects of International Assistance and the Role of the University in Social Change," in *International Social Science Journal* 19, no. 3 (1967): 387–403.

Shils, Edward. "The Implantation of Universities: Reflections on a Theme of Ashby," in *Universities Quarterly* 22 (March 1968): 142–66.

Smith, Keith. "Who Controls Book Publishing in Anglophone Middle Africa?," in *Annals of the American Academy of Political and Social Science* 421 (September 1975): 140–50.

Sunkel, O. "Underdevelopment, the Transfer of Science and Technology and the Latin American University," in *Human Relations* 24 (February 1971): 1–18.

Van den Berghe, Pierre. "European Languages and Black Mandarins," in *Transition* 7 (December–January 1968): 19–23.

Ward, Jennifer C. "The Expatriate Academic and the African University," in *East Africa Journal* 7 (October 1970): 12–16.

Whitley, Steve. "English Language as a Tool of British Neo-Colonialism," in *East Africa Journal* 8 (December 1971): 4–6.

Whyte, William F. "The Role of the U.S. Professor in Developing Countries," in *American Sociologist* 4 (February 1969): 19–28.

Wolf, Eric, and Jorgensen, Joseph G. "Anthropology on the Warpath in Thailand," in *New York Review of Books* 15 (November 19, 1970): 26–35.

Young, K. "Special Role of American Advisors in Thailand—1902–1949," in *Asia* 14 (Spring 1969): 1–31.

About the Contributors

Philip G. Altbach is Professor of Higher Education and Foundations of Education at the State University of New York at Buffalo. He has been on the faculty at the University of Wisconsin and Harvard University and was visiting professor of sociology at the University of Bombay, India. He is author of a number of books, including *Publishing in India: An Analysis* (1976), *Student Politics in America* (1974), *Comparative Higher Education* (1973), and others. He has written for *Harvard Educational Review*, *Teachers College Record*, *Comparative Education Review*, and other journals. He is North American editor of *Higher Education*, an international quarterly.

Aparna Basu is Reader in History at the University of Delhi, India. She holds the Ph.D. from the University of Cambridge and is author of *Education and Political Development in India, 1898–1920* (1974). She is currently working on the history of education in India.

Remi Clignet is Professor of Sociology at Northwestern University. He has written extensively on education in the Third World and is author (with Philip Foster) of *The Fortunate Few: A Study of Secondary School Students in the Ivory Coast* (1966). He has also written *Liberty and Equality in the Educational Process* (1974) and has contributed to such journals as the *Comparative Education Review* and *Sociology of Education*, of which he is a former editor.

Douglas Foley is Assistant Professor of Education and of Anthropology at the University of Texas at Austin. Among his recent publications are *Philippine Rural Education: An Anthropological Perspective* and *North Town in Transition: Ethnic Relations in a South Texas Town, 1900–1975* (in press).

Bonnie Cook Freeman is Assistant Professor in the area of Cultural Foundations of Education, University of Texas at Austin. She has contributed to *Beyond Intellectual Sexism* (1976) and has written on women in American higher education as well as on labeling theory. Her speciality is the politics of education.

GENE GRABINER is Assistant Professor of Foundations of Education at the State University of New York at Buffalo. His speciality is the sociology of education, and he has written for *Crime and Social Justice, The Insurgent Sociologist, Contemporary Sociology,* and other publications.

KATHERINE IVERSON is a Ph.D. candidate in Educational Policy Studies at the University of Wisconsin–Madison. She has taught at Navajo Community College in Arizona and has worked extensively on the education of native Americans. Her dissertation concerns the acculturation process in the professional education of women.

CHARLES H. LYONS received his bachelor's and master's degrees at Harvard and his Ph.D. at Columbia. He has taught at Syracuse University, the University of Lagos, and Teachers College, Columbia. He is Director of the Overseas Liaison Committee of the American Council on Education. He is the author or co-author of four books: *Essays in the History of African Education* (1970), *Education for What? British Policy versus Local Initiative* (1973), *To Wash an Aethiop White: British Ideas about Black African Educability, 1530–1960* (1975), and *Africa and International Crises* (1976).

GAIL PARADISE KELLY is Assistant Professor of Foundations of Education at the State University of New York at Buffalo. She is author of *From Vietnam to America: A Chronicle of the Vietnamese Immigration to the U.S.* (1977) and has written on problems of minority groups in American education and on colonialism in Vietnam.

ALI A. MAZRUI is Professor of Political Science at the University of Michigan. His research interests include the study of Africa in world affairs, political culture, and social change. He is author of numerous articles and books, and his forthcoming works include *Who Are the Afro-Saxons? The Political Sociology of the English Language in Africa* (1975) and *A World Federation of Cultures: An African Perspective* (1975).

PIERRE L. VAN DEN BERGHE is Professor of Sociology at the University of Washington. He has been Visiting Rockefeller Professor in Kenya and Nigeria. He is author of *Power and Privilege in an African University* (1973), *Man in Society* (1975), *Race and Ethnicity* (1970), *Academic Gamesmanship* (1970), and other publications.

Index